jean-claude klotchkoff

burkina faso today

(2nd edition)

82 pages of colour photos
8 maps and plans

LES ÉDITIONS DU
JAGUAR

summary

panorama

Photo credits :
Pascal Maître/Saga images/Jaguar
except :
*Franck Verdier/Photo Luxe : pp. 2-3 -
p. 67 - p. 226
P.René Worms/JA : p. 51 - pp. 86-87 -
pp. 146-147 - p. 206
L. Giraudineau/JA : p. 158 - p. 187
F. Perri/Cosmos : p. 94-95
J.F. Castell : p. 219*

site by site

the journey

panorama

the land of the burkinabè

■ Geographers and cartographers certainly have cause to complain : in less than a century, Burkina Faso has changed names six times ! Originally called the "Mossi Kingdoms", after the age-old West African empire founded by the Mossi people, Burkina Faso came under French control at the end of the 19th century and in 1904, along with several other territories, became known as the "Colonie du Haut Sénégal-Niger" (Upper Senegal Niger). Fifteen years later, the Mossi kingdom split off from the other territories, becoming the "Colonie de Haute Volta" (Upper Volta). Further changes took place in 1932 when Upper Volta was carved up and integrated into the administrative territories of the neighbouring colonies. This explains why during the colonial period, the old earthen mosque in Bobo Dioulasso features on stamps from Côte d'Ivoire.

In 1947, Upper Volta regained both its traditional borders and the name it was to keep for another thirty-seven years. When independence was granted in 1960, neither the borders nor the name Upper Volta (referring to the upper courses of the Black Volta, Red Volta and White Volta, the main rivers running through the country) were changed. The country itself, on the other hand, entered a long period of political instability.

The "land of Honest People"

When the fiery Captain Thomas Sankara took over power at the beginning of the 1980s, his first and foremost aim was to put a stop to the rampant corruption affecting not only Upper Volta, but the whole of the African continent. He therefore instigated a series of vigorous measures and, to ensure that such practices once and for all became a thing of the past, renamed the country. In 1984, Upper Volta thereby officially became known as the "Land of Honest People" (Burkina Faso), and was declared a People's Republic.

Visitors will quickly appreciate that the "Land of Honest People" deserves an additional title : the "Land of Hospitality". One would be hard pushed to find a kinder group of people in Africa than the affable, smiling and extremely obliging people of Burkina Faso. In the towns and at all levels of the social hierarchy, relations between the Burkinabè and foreigners are most courteous and without affectation. In banks, restaurants, markets, and corridors of the ministries, visitors are warmly welcomed, even playfully so, if they show a genuine interest in this country of which the Burkinabè are so proud. Such pride is not misplaced considering that although Burkina Faso is frequently affected by the terrible droughts which ravage the whole Sahelian region bordering the Sahara, the people nonetheless manage to maintain their dignity and sense of solidarity during difficult times.

It is not easy, however, for a country of about sixty different ethnic groups, most of whom have their own language, to always get along and remain united under the same flag ! Always anxious to understand "others", the peaceful Burkinabè have proved they can live together without succumbing to demonic "tribal" wars, unlike other Third World and even European countries(for example in ex-Yugoslavia).

Village hospitality

This heart-felt hospitality is even more apparent and touching in "the bush". When visitors go to the villages or family compounds where the vast majority of this farming nation live, they will often be given an unforgettable reception. Once thoughtfully settled in the shade of a baobab or mango tree, visitors will be offered calabashes of *dolo* (millet beer) before being invited to eat *tô* just as if they were an old family friend. During the dry season, once the harvests are in, the villagers are even more accommodating and visitors will probably see one of the many traditional ceremonies which take place at that time of year : the younger generations' initiation ceremonies, purification of the villages and regeneration of the land, funerals, etc. In almost all parts of Burkina Faso, visitors may have the chance to watch stunning masquerade dances performed according to age-old rites and accompanied musically by drums and balafons.

A landlocked country

With a surface area of 274,200 km², Burkina Faso is a small country about half the size of France. Shaped like the blade of an axe, it is situated in the heart of West Africa. Whilst the Niger River itself does not flow through the country — the interior delta of the Niger skirts in an arc round the north and east of Burkina — several of the Niger's small tributaries, like the Sirba and the Tapoa, do rise up in Burkina Faso's high plateaux before flowing in an easterly direction.

Burkina Faso is a landlocked country situated in the heart of the Sahelian region, more than 500 km north of the Gulf of Guinea. As its economy depends largely on the import and export of transportable goods to and from Europe by boat, the Burkinabè are obliged to travel southwards to ports of neighbouring countries, like Abidjan in Côte d'Ivoire, Tema in Ghana, Lomé in Togo, and Cotonou in the Republic of Benin.

An economy based on transportation

Convoys of trucks set out from the Atlantic coast every day and head for Ouagadougou, the capital of Burkina Faso, and Bobo Dioulasso, the economic capital , heavily laden with hydrocarbons, cars, and other manufactured goods from the industrialised countries. En route they pass convoys from Burkina, laden with bales of cotton, fruit and vegetables (mangoes, French beans) or livestock. From time to time, the road intersects the small railway linking Burkina Faso's two major cities and Abidjan. Trains from both countries shuttle backwards and forwards carrying merchandise and people — particularly the many Burkinabè who have emigrated southwards to look for work on the coffee and cocoa plantations, or as "house boys", traders and taxi drivers in the towns.

An almost flat country

Sandwiched between the humid, southern countries (Côte d'Ivoire, Ghana, Togo and Benin) and the Sahelo-Saharan countries in the north (Niger, Mali), Burkina Faso is comprised of often very flat, sometimes monotonous savanna. As most of the country lacks in any real high grounds, Burkina Faso has always served as an easy passage between the region bordering the Niger River where the major empires like the Mali and Songhai empires developed, and the small southern kingdoms in the tropical forests or along the Atlantic coast, like the Ashanti kingdom in Ghana, the Dan-Hômé kingdom in Benin, and the Sanwi kingdom in Côte d'Ivoire.

Numerous migratory groups of all origins have thus passed through and sometimes even settled in Burkina Faso, for example the Mossi, originally from Ghana and perhaps before that from Lake Chad, the Mande (Marka, Samo, Bisa, Samoro, etc.) from Mali, and the Fulani and Tuaregs who, even today, continue their eternal nomadic migrations.

Some remarkable highlands

The plateaux (300 to 400 m on average) constituting most of Burkina Faso are not uniformly flat throughout the country. A few areas of high land dotted here and there fortunately embellish the landscape. The most remarkable are the "Falaise de Gobnangou" (Gobnangou Escarpment) — part of the foothills of the Atacora Massif in Benin — which extends into the national parks of eastern Burkina Faso, and the long "Falaise de Banfora" (Banfora Escarpment) in the west. The massif of which it is a part begins at Bobo Dioulasso, runs alongside Banfora and onto the Malian border where Burkina Faso's highest summit (Mount Ténakourou) is found culminating at 749 m. Although its height hardly rivals other taller mountains, Banfora Escarpment is nonetheless worth visiting as the sandstone has been eroded by water and wind into extraordinary natural curiosities like the Karfiguéla Falls, the Banfora "domes", and the rocks and peaks at Sindou, resembling ancient ruins. Other remarkable highlands are the green hills (green during the rainy season that is) in the Lobi region in south-western Burkina Faso, and several isolated highland areas like Naouri Peak (447 m) near Pô, south of Ouagadougou, in the Gourounsi region. Also worth a mention are the large, abrupt dunes at Oursi in the north of the country which give a foretaste of the vast Saharan regions in Mali (the Tanezrouft desert) and in Niger (the Ténéré desert).

Rivers and lakes

Several large rivers, lakes and dams provide the often overwhelmingly hot, arid savanna lands with a little freshness and humidity. The Mouhoun in western Burkina Faso (formerly known as the Black Volta) is the longest of these rivers, and the hairpin bends in its course has intrigued travellers for many years. From its source in the Banfora Escarpment, the Mouhoun flows northwards and should logically disappear into the Malian sands south of the Bandiagara Escarpment. Instead, however, it abruptly doubles back on itself north of Dédougou and flows straight down into Ghana. The explanation for this detour is simple : the northern tributary, the Sourou, has harnessed the Mouhoun and completely redirected its upper course. In Ghana, the Mouhoun merges with the Nakambé (formerly the White Volta) to forme the huge Lake Volta. Since the recent completion of the Akosombo dam near the Gulf of Guinea coast, the lake dominates a large part of region.

The Volta Rivers

The other Volta Rivers — the Red Volta (Nazinon) and the White Volta (Nakambé) — cross the central region of Burkina Faso from north to south, cutting across the Central Plateau, a Mossi preserve where clusters of family coumpounds (*zaka*) can be seen surrounded by farm land. At Kaya, Lakes Bam, Dem and Sian feed into the upper course of the Nakambé. Bam, Burkina Faso's largest natural lake, has permitted the considerable development of market gardening and the town of Kongoussi, which exports a lot of vegetables, is nicknamed the "French bean capital".

For many years, the areas surrounding these rivers and lakes were avoided by the Burkinabè as diseases like malaria and onchocerciasis were rampant there. Extensive cleaning and draining projects have since been successfully carried out, however, and the large areas of reclaimed arable land are now inhabited by whole families of Burkinabè farmers.

Lake Tengrela

The remarquable Lake Tengrela is situated near to Banfora. Surrounded by rice paddies and sugar cane plantations, it is also traditionally a prime fishing spot. The lake's beautiful bucolic landscape and the local "quivering" dancers who, according to custom, dance during the major celebrations after the harvests, are well-known to tourists. Lake Tengrela is linked to Comoé River which rises up in the Banfora Escarpment in western Burkina Faso, then cuts into Côte d'Ivoire where it zigzags through the landscape and flows into the Gulf of Guinea.

The numerous man-made dams dotted throughout Burkina Faso have become an integral part of the landscape of several large towns, notably the capital Ouaga-

*Although Burkina Faso's large herds of cattle
have been frequently decimated by the cyclical droughts
affecting the Sahelian regions,
they are now expanding, and embellish the northern
savanna lands once again.*

the people

dougou and Ouahigouya in the north. Providing running water to the towns, they meet both the inhabitants' needs and irrigate market gardening areas.

A bird sanctuary

Oursi Pool far to the north is another well known tourist spot near to Gorom Gorom, and is both a magnificent bird sanctuary and a meeting point for Fulani and Tuareg nomadic shepherds. Sabou Pool near to Koudougou is also well known and people come from all over Burkina Faso to see its sacred crocodiles.

Finally, Pendjari River in the southeast — a natural border between Benin and Burkina Faso — attracts wildlife safari-goers visiting the country's large parks and reserves. Visitors can see lions drinking from the Pendjari and hippopotami frolicking in its waters all day long…

■ Compared with other West African countries, Burkina Faso is still a predominantly rural country. With 27% of the population living in the towns, and 73% in "the bush" (the country), Burkina has a very different look to that of Côte d'Ivoire where 41% live in the towns and 56% in the country, Benin (31% and 69% respectively), Ghana (36% and 64%) and Togo (30.8% and 69.2%) — all situated to the south of the country and bordering the Gulf of Guinea. Even the northern Sahelian countries, Mali and Niger, are becoming increasingly urbanised in comparison to Burkina Faso (over a third of the population now live in the towns), as more and more people abandon work in the countryside.

Rural Africa

In Burkina Faso, "traditional African villages" with their mud huts surrounded by farming land and their traditional festivities are still common, unlike in so many other African countries where, as megalopolises mushroom and more and

THE DAYS OF IRON HORSES

■ *For centuries, the powerful Mossi empires—especially the Yatenga empire—owed their supremacy on the battlefields to their fearsome cavalry. During the course of time, however, the rigours of the often blazing climate, and epizootic diseases unfortunately got the better of "man's greatest conquest" in Africa.*

Nowadays, the Burkinabè's love of horses manifests itself in their interest in the "Pari Mutuel Urbain" (people in Burkina Faso enjoy betting on the Parisian horse races, broadcast on television since 1990) and in their love of "two wheelers": the bicycles, mopeds and motorbikes, baptized "iron horses" (koutouwefo, in Moré). This modern means of locomotion has had an unprecedented impact in Burkina where "two wheelers" are as common place in the bush as in the towns. Some mopeds are even used as taxis. This passion is understandable given the low cost of running these machines imported or manufactured on site (at SIFA in Bobo Dioulasso), the facility with which one can travel in this "flat country", and also the fact that it is possible to carry over 200 kg of goods on a "two wheeler".

Given the success of the "little queen" (the bicycle), it is no surprise that the country periodically organises a highly popular sporting competition: the "Tour du Faso", in which both European and African cyclists compete.

more people leave the countryside and its arduous farming work, such traditions are becoming increasingly rare.

Unequal distribution

With ten million inhabitants living in a country half the size of France (274,000 km²), that is an average of 38 inhabitants per km², Burkina Faso can hardly be described as over-populated. Whilst this ratio is less than half that of neighbouring Ghana (73 inhabitants per km²), and Togo (74 inhabitants per km²), it is much greater than Burkina's northern neighbours Mali and Niger, which have population densities of 7 to 9 inhabitants per km², owing to the fact that whole regions of these two countries are desert land.

Population distribution is highly unequal in Burkina Faso, however. The Mossi region on the Central Plateau around the capital Ouagadougou resembles a kind of Milky Way, with the region's many villages scattered like star dust around a few major constellations. Kadiogo, the province where Ouagadougou is located, has the highest population density with nearly 400 inhabitants per km². The Kouritenga region further to the east (around Koupela) is also highly populated, with 122 inhabitants per km².

The rest of the population is concentrated — albeit less densely than in the centre of the country — around Bobo Dioulasso, another major centre in western Burkina Faso. On the other hand, the large regions around the edges of the country are virtually uninhabited. In the north-east, where extreme climatic conditions prevent the development of agriculture, the sun-burnt steppes are frequented by scattered groups of Fulani and Tuareg nomadic pastors alone. Scarcely inhabited nowadays, the savanna regions in the south-east of the country have become huge natural parks for the country's large wildlife — lions, antelopes, elephants, monkeys and hippopotami.

Reclaimed land

In spite of their abundant supplies of water and good arable lands, Burkina Faso's forested river valleys were avoided by man for many years and understandably so given the rifeness of terrible diseases like malaria and onchocerciasis, which can cause blindness and sometimes even be fatal. Fortunately, over the last twenty years, the World Health Organisation has brought expert entomologists, doctors and engineers together from all over the world to fight such diseases throughout the whole of West Africa. In 1973, therefore, experts began studying the habits of the fly responsible for transmitting "river blindness" (onchocerciasis) in the basin of Burkina Faso's three major rivers, then began a programme to systematically destroy this fly. Today, more than 47,000 km² of land have been reclaimed in the Burkinabè valleys and families of farmers have begun to settle there.

Ethnic groups

Although united under the same flag, the Burkinabè, far from being a homogeneous group, are divided into over sixty different ethnic groups.

The Mossi, the largest group, comprises of four and a half to five million people, some of whom have emigrated to neighbouring countries, particularly Côte d'Ivoire. The Mossi are in fact one of the largest ethnic groups in the whole of West Africa. According to oral traditions, the Mossi originally came from the Lake Chad region in the east. Severe droughts or conflicts with other central African peoples are likely to have caused them to emigrate to the west, where they appear to have initially settled at Gambaga, now in northern Ghana. It is here that the legendary meeting took place between the hunter Riaré and Princess Yenenga, the Gambaga king's daughter. Their child, Ouedraogo, founded the first Mossi kingdom at Tenkodogo. Descendants of the first kingdom later moved further northwards into modern day Burkina Faso, establishing the Mossi kingdoms of Ouagadougou and Yatenga (Ouahigouya).

Thanks to the strength of their army, especially their cavalry, and to the highly sophisticated organisation of their kingdoms, the Mossi were able to resist the attacks of warriors from the larger West African empires like the Songhai empire, and to perpetrate their traditions and dynasties right up to modern times. In fact, the *Moro Naba*, the Mossi emperor, still lives in Ouagadougou surrounded by pages, ministers and courtesans. Although he still has considerable moral authority and is highly respected in Burkina Faso, his influence and other privileges were greatly redu-

ETHNIC GROUPS

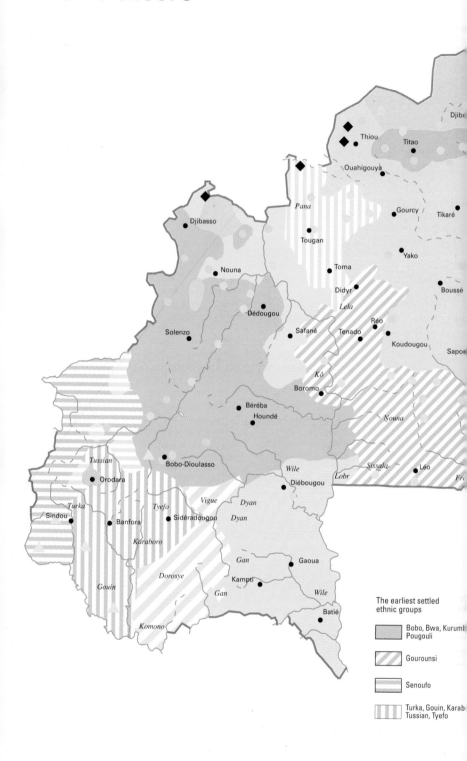

Djib

Thiou

Titao

Ouahigouya

Pana

Gourcy

Tikaré

Djibasso

Tougan

Yako

Nouna

Toma

Didyr

Boussé

Lela

Dédougou

Réo

Solenzo

Safané

Tenado

Koudougou

Sapo

Kô

Boromo

Béréba

Houndé

Nouna

Tussian

Bobo-Dioulasso

Wile

Sissala

Léo

Orodara

Diébougou

Lobr

Fr

Turka

Tyefo

Vigue

Dyan

Sindou

Banfora

Sidéradougou

Dyan

Karaboro

Gan

Gaoua

Dorosye

Kampti

Gouin

Gan

Wile

Komono

Batié

The earliest settled
ethnic groups

Bobo, Bwa, Kuruml
Pougouli

Gourounsi

Senoufo

Turka, Gouin, Karab
Tussian, Tyefo

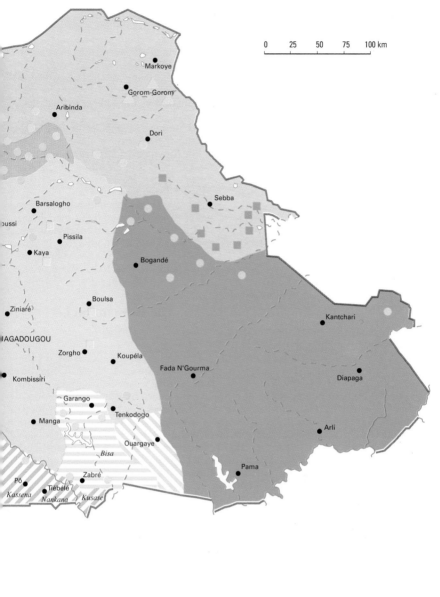

Markoye

Gorom-Gorom

Aribinda

Dori

0   25   50   75   100 km

Barsalogho

Sebba

oussi

Pissila

Kaya

Bogandé

Ziniaré

Boulsa

Kantchari

AGADOUGOU

Zorgho

Koupéla

Kombissiri

Fada N'Gourma

Diapaga

Garango

Tenkodogo

Manga

Arli

Ouargaye

Bisa

Pama

Zabré

Pó

Tiébélé

Kassena   Nankana   Kusase

thnic groups originally from he left bank of the Mouhoun	Neo-Sudanese ethnic groups	Mande ethnic groups	Sahelian ethnic groups
Lobi, Dagara, Birifor	Mossi	Marka	Peul-Rimaïbe Touareg-Bella
Gan, Dorosye, Komono, Vigue	Gourmantché	Samo	
	Yansé	Samogho, Bisa, Sembla, Bolon	Ethnic groups of uncertain origin
	Songhai	Yarsé	Dogon
		Dioula	Syemou

ced during the French colonial period (from the end of the 19ᵗʰ century until Independence in 1960), when modern institutions were set up and a President was designated. The Moro Naba no longer has the right, for example, to collect taxes, judge murders, nor recruit armies. The framework of the empire and its vassal kingdoms still exists, however. Although the village, district and provincial chiefs have also lost most of their prerogatives, they too still have moral and political influence. The Moro Naba disposes of a complete government in Ouagadougou, even if their ministerial responsibilities are now only honorary.

The "False Departure" Ceremony

Received at the Moro Naba's court for over a century now, European travellers are always most impressed by the ceremonies which still take place according to age-old rituals. Whenever the emperor presides over receptions and public ceremonies, events are always most majestic. He can be seen surrounded by swarms of pages (*sorhoné*) ready to execute his every whim, and by high ranking dignitaries, or ministers, like the *Baloum Naba*, head intendant of the palace, the *Larallé Naba,* guardian of the dynasty's ancestral tombs, the *Kamsaogo Naba,* head of the eunuches, and the *Tansoba Naba,* head of the armies, accompanied by the *Ouidi Naba,* head of the cavalry, the *Gounga Naba,* head of the infantry, and the *Soré Naba,* guardian of the war drum.

Whenever the Moro Naba leaves his palace, he is accompanied by a group of dignitaries, cavaliers and griots who sing his praises and celebrate the great achievements of his ancestors.

Love or duty ?

One of the most charming ceremonies — the "False Departure" Ceremony — takes place every Friday. The Moro Naba leaves his palace at sunrise and makes for a groomed and adorned horse held by a waiting page. As he is about to mount, a wave of lamentations arises from the different groups of dignitaries prostrated on the esplanade. The Mossi chief changes his mind, returns to the palace and comes back out dressed in white, applauded by his subjects. The ceremony commemorates an event that once took place: when the wife of one of the Mossi emperors left him and returned to her family, the then Moro Naba decided to go to look for her. Just as he had mounted his horse, news came that his territory was being invaded by a hostile army. The question that hung on everyone's lips was would he choose love or duty ? Finally he dismounted, reassured his entourage, and personally took command of the events in hand. Acting as a great leader should, he put duty before love !

For the most part resistant to Islam, more than 70 % of the Mossi are still animistic. In the larger towns, however, a Mossi Muslim minority exists.

The Mossi are predominantly a farming people and live throughout the central region of Burkina Faso in either the towns — Ouagadougou, Koudougou, Ouahigouya — or scattered in "the bush" in *zaka* (family compounds) which sometimes form small villages.

The Gourmantché people

The Gourmantché, "cousins" of the Mossi, also appear to descend from the semi-legendary ancestor Ouedraogo. Even less influenced by Islam than the Mossi, more than 90 % are animists. Predominantly farmers and hunters, the Gourmantché, whose "capital" town is Fada N'Gourma, live in eastern Burkina Faso near the large "W" national park and Arli Reserve.

Fulani eternal wanderings

Fulani and Tuareg nomads live mainly in the more desert-like steppes to the north-east of the country. The origins of the Fulani pastors are not well known, but it is clear that they differ from the origins of the other ethnic groups in the region. They may have originally come from Ethiopia or even Yemen a thousand or so years ago. Some archaeologists claim to recognise Fulani in the rupestrian paintings discovered in the Algerian Tassili in the heart of the Sahara. Dating from several thousand years before the Christian era when this desert was still green, the paintings show pastors herding their cattle across huge pastures.

The timeless Fulani migrations from east to west still continue today. In the past, some groups settled, converted to Islam and founded powerful empires, like the Sokoto empire in Nigeria, the sultanates in northern Cameroon, the Macina empire in Mali, the Fouta Toro kingdom in Senegal and the Fouta Djalon kingdoms in Guinea. Ardent converts to Islam, these Fulani frequently declared "holy wars" (*jihad*) on animist peoples and on other half-hearted Muslims.

The Fulani doctrine

Most nomadic Fulani tend not to have converted to Islam, however, but have remained faithful to the Fulani "doctrine". This philosophy of life encourages the Fulani to exalt the beauty of the open spaces where they lead their cattle in search of new pastures and to continue their nomadic life. Fulani men and women appreciate the beauty of the human body, and thus adorn themselves with necklaces, bracelets and earrings. One of their finest festivities is the *gerewol,* which could be described as a male beauty contest. Adolescents on the verge of manhood paint and decorate their faces with jewellery and ostrich feathers before a dance where they are lined up and judged by young women in their age group. The most hand-some are chosen according to the shininess of their teeth and whites of their eyes which they show off as they skilfully pull faces.

Fulani encampments can be seen around the towns of Dori, Gorom Gorom, Djibo and Aribinda where Fulani come to buy or sell cows at the cattle fairs on market days.

With the "Blue Men"

The Fulani share the vast areas in northern Burkina Faso with another nomadic group: the Tuaregs. The Tuaregs are a Berber people and, like the Fulani, differ from the other ethnic groups in Burkina Faso. Originally from North Africa, the Tuaregs gradually migrated southwards across the Sahara, initiating "the camel revolution". As the Sahara became increasingly arid, horses, which are vulnerable to heat and thirst, were replaced by dromedaries brought from Arabia.

The arrival of these "desert vessels" encouraged the development of a whole economy based on trans-Saharan cara-

THE LEGEND OF THE "DOUBLE"

■ *Dabiré, ancestor of the Dagari, realised one day that there was something mobile and distinct from his body within him. When travelling, he realised that he was extremely hungry. Armed with his hatchet and his bow, he came to an area rich in game: ambushing and killing a bounding gazelle with his poisoned arrows, skinning, cutting up and choosing a succulent piece to roast took no more than a few minutes. As he did not have the ingredients to make an accompanying millet mush, it came into his head to knead a few balls of clay, which before his very eyes, turned into freshly baked cakes. What a feast, God only knows!...*
He was about to finish off the last mouthful when the first rays of sunlight and the crowing of the cock filtered into the small recess where he has spent the night. He woke up to find his stomach as empty as the night before! His quiver was still hanging from the wall, and not one arrow was missing! He then understood that he had not moved... that he had dreamed the whole thing!
Whilst his body stayed where it was, his "double" had escaped from within without warning, travelled, hunted, feasted then come back to find him in the same place and as hungry as before. What a relief when your "double" comes back from its voyage and finds you in the same place... What if it forgot to come back, or could not find you anymore? What a disaster! That would certainly mean death.

MARCEL PATERNOT
"Lumière sur la Volta"

*About sixty different ethnic groups
live together harmoniously in Burkina Faso,
thereby constituting the country's particularly
rich cultural and traditional heritage.*

vans which linked the major kingdoms in sub-Saharan Africa to the Mediterranean countries. The Tuaregs specialised in caravan transportation, bringing gold, slaves and wild beasts to the north, and manufactured goods and salt to southern countries like Ghana, Mali, Songhai, etc. From the 8th to the 10th centuries, Islam penetrated deep into the Sudan via the same caravan trails.

The Tuareg desert lords

The camel trails came to an end with the introduction of modern day air, sea and road travel, however, bringing about the ruin of the Tuareg "desert lords", who now live from cattle rearing alone. This too is threatened, however, by the successive waves of droughts which have recently struck the Sahelian regions, wiping out whole herds. Many Tuaregs have thus left the desert and bush and headed for the towns where they often find it difficult to get used to settled and usually inferior jobs as "house boys", caretakers, miners, chauffeurs and truck drivers.

In the past, the Tuaregs, who are not strict Muslims, lived in rigidly hierarchical, autonomous tribal groups structured according to a strict caste system, rather than in kingdoms. Noblemen and marabouts were at the top of the hierarchy. The former were highly skilled warriors who never hesitated in fighting powerful Sudanese kingdoms like the Songhai and, later on, the Saharan military companies created by the French colonial power to wipe out Tuareg and Moore "dissidence" in the Sahara. The marabouts were well-read Muslims connected to aristocratic Tuareg families. Next came the *Imraden* (vassals), the *Itagan* (Tuaregs captured in raids, but who were nonetheless free) the *Inaden* (artisans, particularly blacksmiths) and finally, slaves and the *Bellah,* their settled servants.

PREPARING SHEA BUTTER

During his stay in Timbuktu at the end of the 1820s, the French explorer René Caillié noticed a tree whose fruit was greatly sought after by villagers in West Africa. This was the famous "shea tree" as the karite is called nowadays, which Caillié describes in the following passage:
"The shea tree or cé is very widespread in the Timé area (now Guinea); it grows wild, is as tall as a pear tree and has the same bearing capacity. When the tree is young, its leaves are six inches long, grow in clumps, have a very short petiole and rounded ends. When the tree has reached a certain age, the leaves become smaller, resembling those of a St John pear tree. Its very small flowers bloom in clusters at the tips of the branches supported by a very short pedicel. They have white petals and many stamen that are barely visible to the naked eye. The ripe fruit is a large as a guinea fowl egg, almost oval and of equal size at both ends, and is covered in a film. The pulp is a quarter of an inch thick, greenish, floury and tastes very good: the Blacks like it a lot and I ate it with pleasure. Under the pulp is a second very fine film that looks like the white skin inside an egg shell. This covers the kernel, which is a light, white coffee colour. Once the two films

flora and fauna

■ Situated in the Sahelian zone, Burkina Faso, unlike the humid countries in equatorial and tropical Africa, does not have an exceptionally luxuriant flora. Nature has endowed the region with "providential trees", however, which compensate for the inconveniences of its somewhat arid climate. Baobabs, karites, mango trees, gum trees and even the odd palm are found growing throughout most of the country and their leaves, fruit, wood, roots and bark seem to have been specially put at man's service!

"Providential trees"

As bulbous and wrinkled as an elephant, the baobab — from the Arabic name *bu hibab*, meaning "fruit of many seeds" — is especially common in the north of the country. Nicknamed "monkey bread", its huge, club-shaped fruit which hangs from a kind of cord, and has edible seeds and pulp, is greatly appreciated by children in Africa. Scientists confirm that the children's choice is a good one as the baobab fruit is rich in vitamins C and B1, phosphorus, protein and lipides. Baobab leaves are collected by the women and used in the sauces accompanying the *tô*, the national dish. The flour extracted from the leaves contains mucilage — which facilitates digestion — calcium and vitamin A. The medicinal virtues of the herbal tea made from baobab leaves and roots, which acts both as a fortifier and as a tonic against diarrhea, are also undisputed. Other parts of this tree are also used for day-to-day purposes. Highly resistant fibres are extracted from the bark, for example, and used to make rope, baskets or hammocks.

Common in the dry regions, the gum tree *(Acacia senegalensis)* is another "providential tree". For years, it was one of the major natural resources exported from the Sahelian countries (Senegal, Mauritania, Mali, Burkina Faso) to all parts of Europe. It was used to make the liquid glue so common in classrooms and offices before gum arabic was replaced by synthetic products. Nowadays its gum is still used for pharmaceutical purposes (packaging and capsules), in confectionery (gumdrops, chewing gum, powdered drinks), in stationary (glue on envelopes,

and pulp have been removed, the fruit is covered in a shell as thin as an egg shell. The kernel alone is as large as a pigeon's egg. The fruit is left to dry in the sun for a few days, then crushed in a mortar. Once ground into flour, it becomes the colour of wheat bran. The flour is placed in a large calabash, and kneaded by hand whilst adding lukewarm water until it has the consistency of a paste. More warm water is added to find out whether it has been kneaded enough: if the oily particles separate from the bran and rise to the surface, more warm water is added until the butter separates from the bran floats. It is then scooped off with a wooden spoon, put in a calabash and heated over a large fire. It is then skimmed to make sure that any remaining bran is removed. When it is well cooked, it is poured into a calabash with a little water in the bottom to facilitate removal. Thus prepared, it is wrapped in the tree leaves where it will keep for two years without going off. The butter is an ash white colour and has the same consistency as tallow. The Blacks sell it, eat it, rub it on their bodies, burn it for lighting, and assure me that it sooths pains and wounds, and is used like a cerate (ointment)."

packages, stamps), etc. In Africa, the gum sold in the market is also used to thicken various sauces like *gombo*.

The jujube, whose sugary berries are much appreciated by nomadic pastors, is one of the prickly shrubs (gum trees, acacias, etc.) found growing along with solitary clusters of baobabs and dry, short grass in the steppe regions of northern Burkina Faso.

Different types of vegetation

Further southwards, the vegetation becomes denser. The sandy steppes give way to savanna and scattered forests. The sight of large herds of cattle moving across huge, flat spaces in search of new pastures becomes rarer, and by the Central Plateau north of Ouagadougou, villages and their farming lands become part of the landscape. Eastern Burkina Faso, on the other hand, is also sparsely populated and its huge open spaces have been designated national reserves (the Arli and "W" parks) for the savanna wildlife.

These regions also have their "providential trees": karites, or "butter trees", whose butter-like fat is used in cooking, for glazing the roughcast on huts, or for making skin and hair cosmetics. The pulp and seeds are also used to make a dietetic flour or used in sauces. Tamarind and mango trees — often planted in the centre of the village to provide shade ideal for the elders' meetings or a siesta —bear large quantities of succulent fruit. Tamarind fruit is used to make a tasty fruit juice and the delicious Burkinabè grafted mangoes, cultivated in large plantations in the west of the country, are enjoyed all over Europe.

The more humid climate in the south and south-west of Burkina Faso gives rise to more lush savanna and pockets of dense forests, particularly gallery forests along the rivers. One of the best examples is the "Baignade du Kou", a small river near to Bobo Dioulasso where an open-air café perfect for Sunday picnicking has been set up in the shade of huge trees.

Vast natural parks

According to zoologists, no place in the world offers large herbivores such a wide range and abundance of edible plants as the Sudanese savanna in Africa. Elephants, giraffes, antelopes and rhinoceri roaming in these vast open spaces can

The whole of the country is involved in the fight against both desertification and above all deforestation, a problem that affects all countries in Africa's Sahelian regions. Trees are consequently being replanted wherever possible.

effectively find ideal feeding grounds with adequate supplies of buds, leaves, roots, tubers and all sorts of berries and fruit — fortunately, as most of these herbivores are particularly voracious. An elephant, for example, eats 180 to 270 kg of fodder a day !

The West African savanna, although not as rich as the central, eastern and southern savanna lands, is nonetheless home to a particularly wide range of wild animals. There are about a hundred species of large mammals compared to barely fifteen species in tropical Asia and about ten in South America. The African savanna is a kind of paradise on earth frequented by giants—elephants, hippopotami, lions, giraffes and a great variety of large antelopes (sable antelopes, impalas, bubals, kobs, etc.). Sadly, many of these large mammals are threatened by poachers, especially the elephants which are massacred for their much sought-after ivory. Their habitat is also disappearing due to deforestration and the expansion of farm land.

Protected zones

Although Burkina Faso's savanna boasts abundant wildlife, it too is susceptible to such problems and the Burkinabè have therefore created several vast natural parks and reserves to protect the country's animals. Burkina Faso's remaining large forests were also classed as conservation zones by the colonial administration, and the Burkinabè government has tried to protect them more in order to stop them from being completely decimated by villagers in search of firewood. Most of these forests are found in the south of the country and generally form gallery forests along the rivers ; for example the protected Deux Balé forest near Boromo and the series of forests and reserves which run along the upper course of the river Mouhoun (formerly known as the Black Volta).

The most noteworthy national parks open to the public are the Arli national park (76,000 ha), and the "W" park (230,000 ha) in the far east of the country, and the Kaboré Tembi national park (150,500 ha) south of Ouagadougou.

The lions' domain

The arboraceous savanna in the east is a popular roaming ground for lions, an animal which is still found in quite large numbers even though it is not a protected species. Lions are considered choice game by hunters who, between 15 December and 15 March, come from all over the world to take part in organised safaris.

In the past, lion hunting was the predilection of Gourmantché villagers in the Pama and Fada N'Gourma regions who, protected by magic potions, hunted with bows and arrows alone. Nowadays they are only allowed to kill the king of the animals if it attacks the village and kills someone. In this case, villagers will be invited by officials in charge of the rivers and forests to a specially organised hunt for the "man-eating" lion.

As lions like large, open spaces with some kind of shade to sleep in, they live in the arboraceous savanna rather than in the forests, steppes or desert. Naturally lazy and sociable, lions spend much of the day in groups, asleep under trees and bushes. The lion is a carnivore and generally attacks herbivores, especially antelopes. When lions hunt in groups, they may also ambush larger mammals like buffaloes or giraffes. Rather than chasing their prey, like leopards, lionesses are more likely to wait by water points and leap on the backs of unsuspecting, passing prey. Although lions have a highly developed sense of smell, they usually rely on their eyesight and hearing, when hunting. Lions do not need to hunt every day: zoologists have calculated that on average, one lion consumes a mere twenty-odd antelopes per year.

Nomadic rather than settled, lions apparently have no boundaries and will sometimes wander distances of up to thirty kilometres in one go. Adult at three years old, they rarely live beyond thirty years old. Lions are polygamous, living with several lionesses who, more than once a year, may give birth to litters of two to six lion cubs after a three and a half month gestation period.

The largest land mammal

Along with the lions, Burkina Faso's elephants are becoming more and more of an attraction on wildlife safaris in the reserves. They can be seen in their largest numbers in the Deux Balé forest west of Ouagadougou and in the Nazinga Game Ranch. Larger than its Asian cousin, the African elephant is the world's largest land mammal. There are two kinds of *Loxodonta africana* elephant: the savanna elephant and the forest elephant. The former, substantially larger than the latter, may reach up to 4 metres tall. Both kinds of elephant have more or less the same lifestyle and can often be found living together in overlapping regions.

Savanna elephants often retreat into wooded areas when threatened by poachers, and forest elephants leave their natural habitat during the rainy season in order to find fresh grass in the savanna. Elephants generally eat fruit, leaves and colza rather than grass and, unlike giraffes and antelopes who store unchewed grass in their paunches which they regurgitate later, elephants are not ruminants. Both greedier and more gourmet than certain other animals, due to their size and weight (around 3 to 7 metric tons), elephants drink large quantities of water (80 to 100 litres) and eat huge amounts of fodder (180 to 270 kg) every day. This does not stop them from being selective, however, and they will often destroy the lower branches of a tree in order to reach the youngest, and often highest leaves. With their trunks they will often pick this fruit rather than that and use their tusks to unearth tubers.

Elephant tusks

Ironically, elephants do not often use the ivory tusks which get so many of them killed by poachers. Their main purpose is to serve as weapons during friendly jousts between young males or the occasionally more bloody combats between rival adults. Elephants sometimes use their tusks as picks or chisels to break bark off trees—a delicacy of which elephants are particularly fond—or to extract earth from the salt marshes. Tusks often grow crookedly, becoming a nuisance to the elephant. Exceptionally, their tusks, or upper incisors, multiply and some elephants have up to eight or nine tusks.

Weighing from 50 to over 100 kg, the male elephant's tusks are usually larger than those of the female (rarely over 10 kg). Invisible at birth, the "milk tusks" begin to show at three months and continue to grow slowly, weighing only 2 to 3 kg when the elephant reaches puberty at around 10 years old. It is not until the elephant is about 40 to 50 years old—if it has been spared that long by hunters—that it enters "full manhood" bearing really impressive tusks. The trunk—a large, muscular mass tipped with two little pointed lips—is more frequently used by the elephant as a hand, a bugle, a hose pipe or a truncheon! The elephant's sense of smell and feeling are located in the trunk, senses which, along with hearing, are particularly well developed. Elephants' eyesight is much weaker, however, as their eyes, which are badly placed on the side of the head, do not enable the elephant to see in front.

African elephants, especially the savanna elephants, have particularly well developed ears that may reach up to 1 metre wide and 1.80 metres long, and have several functions.

As well as permitting the elephant to hear, its ears also act as coolers (elephants are particularly vulnerable to heat) and are used to communicate emotion (when an angry elephant is about to charge, it spreads its ears).

The "matriarch", chief of the elephants

Elephants are highly evolved animals disposing of a language of sound signals — ranging from trumpeting and rumblings to infrasonic sounds — and gestures made using the trunk, head, ears and eyes. Unlike most other large mammals, elephants do not mark out an exclusive "territory" for themselves. They live alongside numerous other species in unlimited areas were there is access to water, pastures and salt marshes. Large groups of elephants may come together to form huge herds, especially when they feel threatened by hunters. When not threatened, however, elephants tend to split up into small groups of three to four, sometimes even ten elephants.

One distinctive feature of these microsocieties is the separation between the sexes. On the one hand there are groups comprised uniquely of young male adults and others where a mature adult is surrounded by younger "pages". Females and their very young to pre-pubescent offspring are usually grouped around an elderly female, or matriarch. When the young male elephants reach puberty at around 10 to 12 years old, they are chased away from the group and go to join the nearby young adults. The "rules" prevalent in the female group are quite remarkable and constitute a highly evolved society: the elephants never fight and always display a great sense of solidarity. The group will always wait for the slowest and aid the wounded. Such behaviour is unique in the animal world where the weak and infirm are usually mercilessly abandoned to predators.

Adult males only join the female group during the rutting period. The gestation period (21 to 23 months) is one of the

A lion rests in the scrubland.
A male Buffon kob grazes on once fire-blazed land.
An elephant that frequents both the forest and savanna.
Warthogs on their way to a pool (photos G. Sournia).

longest amongst mammals. At birth—which often takes place at night in thickets—baby elephants already weigh a good hundred kilos. For the first four to five months they feed on their mother 's milk alone (more than 10 litres a day) then gradually supplement their diet with plants. Closely guarded by their mothers and other females in the group, baby elephants show vague signs of independence very early on. Up until the age of about 7 to 8 years old, however, young elephants may still fall prey to lions and crocodiles, not to mention poachers who, in killing mothers for their ivory, sentence orphaned elephants to death as they will rarely find an adoptive mother.

Natural pharmacies

Elephants are constantly on the move, especially in the cool of the night when they usually look for food and water. They often cover distances of 30 to 50 km in one go — sometimes even 100 km — particularly when looking for water during the dry season or new pastures in the rainy season. As farming lands are expanded, however, elephants can no longer wander at free will and are condemned to live cut off in protected places, which are often too cramped to allow them to increase their population.

Sensitive animals

During the day elephants spend much time sleeping leant against trees or occasionally lying down with their heads resting on banks of earth. If they come across a stream or creek, they will spend hours bathing as their skin is highly sensitive to heat and does little to protect them from the sun, and also to escape the many insects and parasites that bother them. Once out of the water, they dust themselves down with earth in the same way that humans use talcum powder. Elephants occasionally visit their "pharmacies", the natural salt marshes where they eat soil rich in kaolin (which is good for their stomachs) and other trace elements like calcium, iron, phosphorus, cobalt and sodium and potassium salts.

FOREST OR SAVANNA ELEPHANTS?

"...On paper and in the museums, the distinction beween the savanna and forest species is easy. On site, however, it is a different story. Of course, if an elephant from the coastal forests in Côte d'Ivoire or Gabon and another from the Kenyan savanna are placed side by side, no confusion is possible. Each one reveals pronounced characteristics of their race.
The first is significantly smaller, with a well-padded form, lower forequarters, a markedly receding forehead, smaller, rounded ears (hence the name "cyclotis"), almost straight tusks growing downwards, and usually darker, almost black skin. The second is of a taller stature, the front of the body at almost the same level as the back part, a straighter forehead, huge, triangular ears, and tusks that curve upwards, a generally more emaciated form, and greyish skin. In short, when looking at two specimens from the extreme end of the region the species is found in, there is no problem, but in the intermediate zones, or in the mixed forest-savanna zones, it is far from being as simple. In the areas that were still forested in the Fifties between Gagnoa and Sinfra in Côte d'Ivoire, I saw "savanna" elephants alongside elephants that were unmistakably the forest kind.

Over the last few decades, Africa's elephants were subjected to relentless assault by poachers and, had it not been for strict regulations like those stipulated in the Washington Convention which forbids all trade in ivory, these elephants could have become totally extinct.

Some dispensations were granted at the June 1997 Harare conference which may well threaten the elephant's status again.

The savanna, and especially the national parks in eastern Burkina Faso, is also home to the buffalo. Of the three main types found in Africa, the subspecies of the Cape buffalo found in West Africa is the lightest (if it can be called light!) weighing from 200 to 450 kg, compared with its cousins from central and southern Africa (the Cape and African buffaloes) which weigh from 500 to over 1000 kg. Buffaloes are generally considered to be very bad natured and are feared by hunters and villagers alike. They are in fact peaceful animals which like to live in family groups of a similar structure to those of the elephant. Buffalo herds are also led by an elderly female whilst the adult males live alone or in small, separate groups. Like elephants, buffaloes love wallowing in creeks and rivers…

So why, one may ask, do they have such a bad reputation? It is in fact the fault of bad hunters: when a buffalo is wounded, it becomes enraged and mercilessly charges its aggressor. The aggressor — if he lives to tell the tale! — will no doubt recount his shock in discovering that this clumsy and sluggish-looking animal is in fact remarkably agile and vivacious. Another of the short-sighted buffalo's surprising characteristics is its relationship with its rather unlikely companion, the oxpecker bird, a kind of starling which stays perched on the buffalo's back feasting on its parasites. As soon as an intruder appears, the oxpecker raises the alarm by screeching shrilly, thereby warning the buffalo of the potential aggressor's presence.

A voracious herbivore

Although buffaloes do sometimes live in the forests, they too prefer open spaces and are perfectly at home in the vast Sahelian savanna. During the day time they hide from hunters in the bushes, sleeping

In the heart of the savanna in northern Togo, I saw specimens that any museum specialist would have classed as the forest species, and again, recently, in the south of Burkina Faso near to Ghana, groups of chubby, smallish elephants with rounded ears cohabited without actually mixing with other families of noticeably larger, more slender elephants with incontestably triangular auricula. A real headache! One must therefore not become obsessed with perfectly divided races, but admit that with elephants and certain other living species including our own, it is better to avoid all schematisation as several factors come into play.
As botanists, travellers and hunters have confirmed for a long time now, there is a progressive variation (scientists call this "clinal") in size, tusk length and colour for a whole range of African animals as one moves from west to east across the continent.

PIERRE PFEFFER
Vie et Mort d'un Géant, l'Éléphant d'Afrique
(L'Odyssée/Flammarion)

and waiting for dusk before going in search of food. A particularly voracious herbivore, the buffalo consumes large amounts of fodder, apparently worrying more about the quantity than the quality. Having found food, the buffalo then heads back into the bushes to ruminate slowly in peace. Buffaloes never move too far away from water as they drink a lot and often.

Lions and man are the buffalo's main predators. Since big game hunting took off in Burkina Faso a few years ago, buffaloes and certain types of large antelopes have become the prime targets during the big safaris organised in the eastern reserves.

The giant sable antelope

After the kob and koodoo found in other parts of Africa, the sable antelope is the queen of the thirty or so different species of antelopes living in the Burkinabè savanna. Nicknamed the "horse antelope" due to its resemblance in size and speed to man's greatest conquest, it measures between 1.25 and 1.60 m, weighs over 250 kg, and when under threat, gallops like a thorough-bred at the race course. Considered a mythical animal in the savanna and Sahelian regions, it often features in Bambara and Sénoufo carvings. It is not by chance that the multi-national company "Air Afrique" (in which eleven of the African States hold shares) chose the sable antelope as its emblem.

A quarrelsome animal

Like the buffalo, sable antelopes like large open spaces and tend to live near to water in groups of 20 to 50 antelopes. Adult males prefer being alone and only come back to the herd during the rutting period. Having found a mate, the pair move away from the group to mate and continue to live together during the gestation period. Once the female has given birth, she rejoins the herd.

Essentially herbivorous, the sable antelope rarely eats leaves and fruit. It is a quarrelsome animal and begins fighting with its fellows at a very young age. If the sable antelope manages to find adequate supplies of food and water and is not bothered by its predators (man and lions) it will remain settled for long periods. If it does not, it will travel long distances until it does find a satisfactory resting place.

Many other sorts of antelopes can also be found in Burkina Faso's national parks. Amongst the larger species are the waterbuck (160 to 270 kg), nicknamed the "unctuous kob" due to the oily secretion that protects its thick hide; the bubal (125 to 200 kg) whose elongated, narrow forehead gives it a somewhat gormless look; and the impala (90 to 135 kg), cousin of the bubal, which makes long migrations during the rainy season.

Several medium sized antelopes live in the Arli park: the shy, mainly nocturnal bushbuck (32 to 77 kg); the Kobus kob (70 to 90 kg) which, less timid than the bushbuck, can be seen in groups of 20 to 40 in the open savanna; and the smaller royal antelopes, which live alone or in pairs near to rivers and creeks.

Other species of small antelopes — all of them slight and lithe — hide away in the bushes of the savanna, for example the red-flanked forest duiker (11 to 14 kg), the grey duiker, or *sylvicapra grima* (10 to 14 kg) and the pretty golden reddish oribi (9 to 10 kg).

Baboons, organised monkeys

If it is often difficult to spot lions in Burkina Faso, it would be incredible not to bump into a group of baboons crossing roads and tracks both day and night. They are as numerous and well distributed throughout the Sahelian regions of West Africa as the anecdotes they have inspired.

These monkeys which look so much like dogs that one species is called cynoscephale or "dog's head" monkey, weigh around 30 kilos and have large fang-like canines. They have a bad reputation, particularly amongst truck and car drivers. If a vehicle kills or wounds a baboon and then stops or breaks down, woe betide the people in the car as they will be literally lynched by the baboon's stone-throwing, vicious, biting companions. Baboons live in highly organised groups of 20 to 30 members, always move around on the ground, and show great solidarity before their predators (lions, panthers and... man!). Together these large monkeys form real "military" societies with both officers and lower-ranking soldiers.

It is possible to see baboons as they file along Burkina Faso's roads and tracks or doze in bivouacs under the acacias in the national parks. Immediately, the males will form a circle around the females and babies and the young adults keep a slight distance, acting as guards.

*The Burkinabè are justifiably proud
of the country's large wild animals.
Large parks have been created to protect them,
notably those in the east of the country:
Arli park, "W", Kaboré Tembi, etc.*

When moving from place to place, the baboons' disciplined ranks evoke the Roman army! The cortege is headed by a group of adult males, followed by the females and babies. Next come the dominant males, who constitute the main body of the troops, then the young males who bring up the rear. Even when in the open, the baboons are therefore protected from potential enemies by this group of young adult males who are ready to attack at the first sign of trouble. When trouble comes, the baboons break into a chorus of angry barks which dissuades most aggressors. If the aggressor persists, however, he will find himself at the mercy of a pack of particularly fierce fighters capable of giving a lesson he will not forget! In order to eat and drink in peace, baboons have developed a sort of defence pact with antelopes who frequent the same feeding and drinking grounds as the baboons. Mixing together at these sites, each party is of service to the other. The baboons benefit from the antelopes excellent sense of smell and in return offer their powerful eyesight and their strength.

Submission to dominant males

Even though baboons have huge canines and are omnivorous, they are in fact mainly vegetarians, eating grass seeds, shoots and roots and a variety of pods, fruit, buds and flowers from the different trees and bushes growing in the savanna. Every now and then they supplement their diet with meat, eating the occasional grasshopper or termite or even fledglings, lizards, rodents and young antelopes.

Although the baboon's society is rigidly hierarchical and revolves around a handful of dominant males who always stick together, both the role of the female and sexual behavioural patterns are quite different from those in all other groups of mammals. The female may mate with both dominant and lower-ranking males with whom she will have a fleeting liaison rather than forming a stable relationship. She will not become part of a harem nor be the pivotal point in a family. Fertile on a monthly basis, females give birth to only one baby at a time after a gestation period of 5 to 6 months.

The young baboon, initially totally dependent on its mother who carries it around on her back, will quickly try to assert its independence and at the age of two to three months, will go to play with other youngsters. Although the youngsters already consider themselves independent at this point, all the adults will be quietly watching their movements from afar, intervening with a growl if a youngster oversteps the mark.

Early learning

As the zoologist Pierre Pfeffer has noted: "It is through this accumulation of happy or unhappy experiences, that youngsters progressively learn to know their place in this perfectly organised society. Little by little, caresses or rebuffs will teach them the rank of each other individual. This rank may vary for females, but is rigorously established amongst adult males who uphold strict rules of domination and subordination.

"The males highest up in the hierarchy are those most frequently groomed by the others, a very important act in social relations between all monkeys and both a sign of respect and affection on the part of the monkey carrying out the grooming.

"These dominant males also occupy the best resting places and have first choice of the food. When a dominant individual majestically passes a subordinate, the latter moves respectfully out of the way, showing its behind in a sign of submission. If he inadvertently fails to show his respect quickly enough, a swift clout will soon remind him of his duty. Furthermore, when arguments break out between lower ranking baboons over a comfortable place in a tree or over an enticing female, a commanding growl from a dominant male will put an immediate stop to the disturbance."

Red and green monkeys

The much smaller patas monkey, or "red guenon" (10 kg) and the " green monkey" (5 kg) are a real headache for farmers in these regions as their often large groups destroy the village plantations. They can be seen more or less all over Burkina Faso either in the bush or in the reserves. More timid than the green monkeys, the patas monkeys are constantly on the look out for prowling panthers. To avoid falling prey, they post sentinels in the trees whilst the youngster and females, grouped together in a harem under a dominant male, sleep or eat together. At the slightest sign of trouble, the whole group will bolt very rapidly. Moving at nearly 50 km/h, patas monkeys are the fastest of all primates.

The panther, a formidable predator

Even though the panther (called the leopard by the British) preys on crop-destroying monkeys, it is not an animal the Africans appreciate. Much more formidable than the lion, this feline will not hesitate to approach villages at night in order to attack the domestic animals — sheep, goats, calves and dogs — and sometimes going as far as attacking a man. Man, on the other hand, also hunts leopards for their hides which are sold to make expensive fur coats popular in some industrialised countries.

The panther is a solitary animal and an extraordinary hunter, literally gliding through the savanna grasses without the slightest sound, or perching up in the branches of a tree waiting to drop down on its prey, breaking the victim's spine. The panther's diet is more varied than most, ranging from fish and antelopes to birds and turtles.

During the mating season, the panther temporarily gives up its solitary life to mate. After a three month gestation period, females give birth to two or three cubs which are raised in seclusion, hidden away in rocks, caves and bushes.

Other large predators live in the Burkinabè savanna, notably the doglike carnivores—jackals, lycaons and hyenas—which prey mainly on antelopes and sometimes on domestic animals. Jackals and hyenas also eat carcasses and often follow after lions in the hope of scavenging any left-overs. Africans tend to despise these animals and their role as bush "dustmen", and hyenas often feature as the devious, unpleasant characters in many traditional tales.

In the oral traditions, the hare—an intelligent and cunning character—is often associated with the hyena, the underdog personifying all negative characteristics, especially stupidity and unkindness. Hyenas are mainly nocturnal and live alone or in pairs. They hunt for carcasses which can usually be located wherever vultures are present. When hyenas leave their lairs to go hunting, they howl sinisterly and may also "laugh" when they find food or during the rutting period. Zoologists have noticed that at this time, hyenas group together for strange, moonlit meetings:

BURKINABÈ PROVERBS

■ *If a horse has ten grooms, he will be thirsty.*
Man has two feet, but cannot follow two paths at a time.
Today's underpants are better than tomorrow's trousers.
Sitting doing nothing will not remove the thorn from the foot.
If a scorpion stings a stone, it wastes its venom.
The stranger likes to be told "you are welcome", but above all prefers to be told "take that".
If you do not have enough water to bathe in, wash your face.
Grasshopper by grasshopper, the calabash is filled.
When the antelope runs, its little one does not lag behind.
The house abandoned by the squirrel is a palace for the hedgehog.
If the shade does not stretch as far as the antelope, the antelope will go to the shade.
The worm that lives in the cailcedra does not know that other trees also have good qualities.

"The noise they make is indescribably horrible and mating is preceded by complete pandemonium".

In the company of "river horses"

Burkina Faso's rivers and creeks may attract most of the large bush animals, from monkeys and lions to elephants and antelopes, but none of them spend as much time bathing and basking in the waters as the hippopotami (whose name means "river horse"). Lighter than an elephant, this animal still weighs over three metric tons, but is nonetheless capable of moving gracefully and briskly, especially when walking in the water. Hippos spend most of the day sleeping and bathing with their companions.

The hippopotamus is a sociable animal and lives in Burkina Faso's larger pools in groups of 15 to 30 individuals, sometimes many more. Visitors should try to make the traditional Sunday excursion to the "hippo pool" near Bobo Dioulasso, where it is possible to approach the twenty or so large amphibious animals in a boat (designated a "biosphere reserve" by UNESCO a few years ago). Hippos can also be seen in the eastern wildlife parks and in the Pendjari River at the border with Benin. Hippopotami are voracious animals, eating over 60 kg of aquatic grasses and other kinds of plants a day. They usually wait until nightfall before leaving the pools to go and look for plants in the bush. Sometimes they may move more than 10 km away from their aquatic retreats.

Fierce fights between hippos

Hippopotami have long knife-like canines, but these are used for fighting rather than eating. Their society is organised around the dominant males' fiercely defended harems, and rivals intrude strictly at their own risk! Fierce fights will take place in the water and the rival hippos often end up with terrible wounds that leave semi-permanent scars. Excellent swimmers, hippos have found a natural refuge in the water and can stay underwater for 2 to 6 minutes. Their attraction to water is easy to understand given their sensitivity to the sun and insect bites and the risk of their skin drying out: the water is their natural refuge from the heat, horseflies and mosquitoes.

*Worshipped by villagers and sought after
by tourists, crocodiles are often found living in pools
whose waters are also used for
agricultural purposes.*

Hippopotami only present a danger to man if man bothers the hippos by bumping into them in a canoe or by inadvertently catching a baby hippo in fishing nets. Such cases have occurred, resulting in several fatal accidents. Generally, however, hippos have a harmonious relationship with fishermen who keep a respectful distance. In fact fishermen welcome the presence of hippos in the pools. As these large animals digest in the water, their excrement acts as a natural fertilizer and thereby greatly multiplies the number of fish in the pools.

"Sacred cayman pools"

Another large amphibian animal is also found hiding away in the waters of Burkina Faso. The crocodile, a large reptile wrongly called the "cayman" in Africa, is highly revered by villagers, who associate it with the soothsayers, and is also becoming more and more of a tourist attraction. Several "sacred cayman" pools can be visited in Burkina Faso, notably the Sabou pool near to Koudougou, west of Ouagadougou.

For the price of a chicken or two, youngsters will lure large, tamed saurians out of the water and climb on their backs to be photographed.

The monitor, a reptile similar to the crocodile, is also found living in Burkina Faso. It is an enormous, carnivorous lizard which feeds on small prey like squirrels and tree shrews.

Although there are fewer aquatic birds on Burkina Faso's rivers and lakes than on the upper delta of the Niger north of the country, at any moment one may observe the seemingly laborious flight of the heron, cormorant or snake bird, or that of the rapid kingfisher. Wherever one finds buffaloes, hippos or elephants frolicking in a pool, the magnificent, immaculate white buffalo weaver (*Bubilcus*) or the oxpecker (*Buphagus africanus*) which is the same size as a starling, will also invariably be seen perched on their backs eating insects and parasites.

The heart of the savanna is a paradise for the various birds of prey. The savanna offers them limitless hunting grounds, where some hunt for small rodents and birds, others for snakes and others for the carcasses of large mammals which they

THE KING OF THE ANIMALS

■ *Lions are very sociable animals. Rarely found alone, they tend to live in family groups of one or more adult males, several females and a majority of adolescents and youngsters. Each pack frequents large areas, moving around freely. They are not territorial, and in one night, may travel over 30 km. Although lions mainly hunt at night, they are in fact more diurnal than any other feline, unless they are disturbed. They spend the hot part of the day sleeping in the bushes and under trees. Herbivorous mammals habitually preyed upon by lions seem to sense when the lions are sated, and continue to graze peacefully, sometimes only a short distance away. Lions have a highly developed sense of smell, and their sense of hearing and eyesight are excellent. Their "voice" is the well known roaring sound, which can be heard for distances of up to 8 km. The lions' diet consists of herbivorous mammals, from little antelopes and impalas to young hippos and elephants, zebras, bubals, gnus and even crocodiles and snakes. When lions hunt in groups, they can kill a giraffe or an adult buffalo, and can even drive warthogs out of their burrows. Whilst lions mainly hunt large prey, old or infirm lions feed on small mammals, birds and even rats. Cattle and even man are sometimes attacked, making some lions "man eaters". Their choice of prey is not only influenced by the relative abundance of the different species, as lions prefer hunting certain animals rather than others when given the choice. Lions hunt using their eyesight and hearing rather than their sense of smell. They usually track down their prey near to*

find near town slaughter-houses or by following packs of lions.

It is fascinating to watch these admirable birds in flight, as they use shafts of rising warm air to glide majestically upwards before effortlessly swooping down on their prey.

Acrobatic champions

Some of these birds of prey are true air acrobatic champions, particularly the bateleur eagle which is capable of breathtaking loops, rolls and dives. They are also formidable predators, using their long, knife-like pointed claws to rip their prey to pieces. The martial eagle, whose 2.50 m wingspan makes it the largest eagle in Africa, has fearsome claws enabling it to prey on animals of its own weight, like kids, monkeys or young jackals. It usually feeds on birds like guinea-fowl, bustards and francolins, however.

Some birds of prey are able to catch their prey in mid flight, for example falcons and especially the "chicquera" which is partial to turtle doves and bats. By clearing the bush and towns of carcasses, most of these predators carry out a useful but despised service for man. It is often possible to see swarms of Egyptian vultures swooping down on the rubbish heaps near markets, and in the bush, kites and white-headed vultures battle with hyenas and jackals for the lions' left-overs.

Other kinds of birds of prey are more selective, even specialised, in their choice of food than the "bird dustmen". The magnificent fishing eagle feeds almost exclusively on fish for example, whereas secretary birds, serpent eagles, buzzards and harriers eat snakes. Falconets and pygmy falcons eat insects, especially grasshoppers.

watering holes. Crawling flat along the ground, they get very close, then jump on their victim's back, breaking its neck with their powerful front paws, or strangling it. Although lions will sometimes hunt alone, they more commonly hunt together, using group tactics: a few lions will stay down wind and follow the victim, driving it into an ambush situation where one of the members of the group is hidden, usually a female as it is more often the lioness that kills. Lions do not hunt every day. Their annual average consumption is sometimes quite low—no more than 20 animals per lion. Once they have eaten, lions drink abundantly.

Lions are polygamous, and lionesses are fertile every few weeks throughout the whole year. The average gestation period is 105 days. The lion cubs are born in a hideaway in the dry grasses or rocks. Weighing about one pound when born, they are carefully raised by their mothers. They are very playful, are weaned at 10 weeks and begin to be independent at one year old, although they usually stay close to their mothers until they are 18 months old. The mortality rate is quite high until about two years old, especially for male cubs. They are not completely adult until they are three years old, and may live for up to thirty years.

JEAN DORST AND PIERRE DANDELOT
"Guide des grands mammifères d'Afrique"
(Delachaux et Niestlé).

All the protecting deities—buffaloes, elephants,
snakes, antelopes, owls, etc.—
descend into the streets of the villages during
the traditional festivities organised
by the Bobo at the end of the dry season.

prehistory and history

■ Thanks to the discovery that our extremely ancient ancestors the *Australopithecus* lived in Ethiopia, Kenya and Tanzania, approximately two to three million years ago, we now know that Africa was most probably "the birthplace of humanity". It is likely that these "hominids" set out from this departure point in East Africa and little by little settled throughout the African continent and the rest of the world. Their descendants developed and adapted, eventually evolving into modern man: the *Homo sapiens.*

For the moment, no traces of the *Australopithecus'* migration to West Africa have been found. The increasingly numerous scientists studying the African continent hope, however, to discover the migratory itineraries followed by our forefathers.

Vestiges of Prehistory

In Burkina Faso, it is necessary to make a great leap forward in time before finding any vestiges of Prehistory. Most go only as far back as the polished Stone Age in the Neolithic era (approximately 10,000 years BC), the period when man began to settle, discover agriculture, religion, pottery, basket making and cattle rearing. The country's most important deposits of lithic matter have been discovered in the south-west of Burkina Faso in the region of Bobo Dioulasso, Banfora, Sindou and Gaoua, and, above all, include axes of all shapes and sizes, coins, polishing utensils, adzes and divers pieces which probably served as farming tools.

Large megalithic monuments have also been discovered near Dori in the north of the country. According to some historians, they may have been used as necropolises, like in Western Europe. Caves and stone shelters have been searched in both northern and western Burkina Faso. The rupestral drawings found in some caves, like those in Aribinda, portray animals and cavaliers and probably date from several thousand years ago. Finally, pieces of pottery including funeral vases and bronze statuettes have been found in various places all over the country.

Imposing ruins

There are also hundreds of ruined habitations and villages in Burkina Faso which really intrigue scientists. These vestiges, which cannot yet be dated precisely, are mainly located in the Lobi regions in the south-west of Burkina Faso. The most important were discovered at Loropeni, west of Gaoua. Their origin is highly controversial. According to the most fantastic hypotheses, these houses are said to have been built by the Egyptians or even the Phoenicians! It is now almost certain, however, that these two ancient peoples never made the major maritime voyages around Africa as was once thought. The houses were perhaps built by Burkina Faso's first inhabitants, the Gan and the Koulango. They may also be much more recent, built by Arabic or European slave traders as slave depots in the 15th and 16th centuries…

From Lake Chad to northern Ghana

These ruins are not the only Burkinabè mystery: in fact entire chunks of Burkina Faso's history are elusive. Practically nothing is known about what was going on in Burkina Faso during the several thousand years from the first few centuries of the Christian Era until the period corresponding with the European Middle Ages.

In the neighbouring regions of Mali and Niger, on the other hand, we know that major empires formed and fell. The Ghana empire, for example, fell under attack from the Almoravides during the 11th century and the Mali empire was supplanted by the Songhai at the end of the 15th century.

What was happening in Burkina Faso during the same period? Who lived there? What relationships did they have with the other empires? Were they forced to surrender after fierce battles or were they spared by conquering armies? Were these vast savanna regions deserted? It is impossible to answer these questions until tangible evidence is found.

The griots, African bards

There are "oral traditions", but specialists treat such sources with great caution as for centuries, these semi-legendary historic tales and genealogies have been passed from generation to generation by griots, the African bards. Everybody knows that the griots, just like any other story tellers, are public entertainers, great flatterers — especially when they belong to an important chief's court — and incorrigible liars.

According to these sources, the Mossi — who were later to form powerful empires in the region of the Niger loop — are said to have come to the region in approximately the 11th century. It would seem that they were originally from the Lake Chad region, but were chased away by a Saharan people, possibly Berbers.

The Mossi people

Their long trek appears to have brought them to Ghana first of all. Nowadays, the little town of Gambaga right in the north of Ghana is considered the first point of dispersion of the Dagomba, Mamproussi and Nankana peoples, who were the forefathers of the future Mossi and Gourmantché dynasties. During either the 12th or the 14th century, the powerful king Nedega reigned over these people in northern Ghana from the capital Gambaga.

According to the semi-legendary tales passed on by the griots, Yenenga, King Nedega's daughter, liked to go horse riding outside Gambaga, and lost her way in the forest one day. It was there that she met the great elephant hunter Riaré and they fell in love immediately.

Ouedraogo, "the stallion"

Once married, they had a son, Ouedraogo ("the stallion") named in memory of his mother's famous horse ride. When he reached adulthood, Ouedraogo left Gambaga and went to settle further north at Tenkodogo, "the old earth", where he founded a new dynasty. This little Mossi town south-east of Ouagadougou is still venerated as the birthplace of the powerful Mossi empire, which was so well organised and had such a strong army (especially its cavalry) that it managed to dominate this part of West Africa and to survive right up to the modern day.

In Tenkodogo, Yenenga and Riaré's son fathered many children. Historians do not agree on the date when Ouedraogo came to Tenkodogo, nor on the chronology of the first few generations to come after this first Mossi king. Some claim that the foundation of the Mossi empire dates back to the 12th century, others to the begin-

THE LEGENDARY ORIGINS OF THE MOSSI EMPIRE

■ *Here is the French historian, Robert Cornevin's account of the legendary origins of the Mossi and the foundation of Tenkodogo, birthplace of the empire:*
"...In the 18th century, a powerful Nedega chief, whose capital was situated at Gambaga (in the north of modern day Ghana), ruled over the Dagomba, the Mamproussi and the Nankana.
His daughter Poko (Yenenga) was distinguished by her Amazonian qualities.
One day her horse carried her too far into the woods, where she was taken in by an elephant hunter called Riaré, who was probably Boussansé and traditionally of royal descent. He gained Yenenga's hand in marriage and took her to live in the forest near to Bouti.
As the Gambaga region was overpopulated at that time, Yenenga's son, who was called Ouidiraogo (stallion) after the motive of his parents' meeting, easily got the young people to leave with him. He then founded Tenkodogo, contraction of Tenga Kodogo (old land), where he had many children..."

ning of the 15ᵗʰ century. As it is impossible to be sure, the date remains a mystery. The most noteworthy of Ouedraogo's children are Zoungrana, the successor to the Tenkodogo throne and Rawa, who headed northwards and founded the Zandoma kingdom (which would later become part of Yatenga). It is not known whether Diaba Lompo — who the griots say moved round on a flying horse — was Ouedraogo's eldest son or cousin. History — or legend — does tell us, however, that he settled at Pama, west of Tenkodogo, where he founded the Gourma kingdom.

Ouagadougou and the Oubri kingdom

Like his uncle Rawa, Oubri had itchy feet. Not wishing to stay in Tenkodogo as his father Zoungrana and his grandfather Ouedraogo had done, Oubri set off to conquer the west with a complete army. He was soon to find that these territories — later known as the Oubritenga, or "Oubri Lands" — were already inhabited by the Nyonyosé and the Gourounsi, who appear to have been the first peoples to have settled in Burkina Faso. The Nyonyosé's little capital Kombemtinga ("The Land of Warriors") fell after violent battles. In order to make sure that these courageous warriors really were subordinate, Oubri decided to completely integrate the Nyonyosé into the new Mossi kingdom and culture. He also changed the name of their capital to "Wogdgo" ("Come and honour me!"), which indicates how determined the new king was to obtain total allegiance from his vassals. Later on, "Wogdgo" was changed to "Ouagadougou", and Burkina Faso's future capital definitively came under the control of the Mossi.

A centralised empire

During the 15ᵗʰ century, the foundations of the first Gourmantché and Mossi kingdoms of Tenkodogo, Ouagadougou and Oubritenga were thus laid. Very soon, they were to adopt a particularly efficient and solid organisation which would enable them to resist all efforts to dismantle them, whether in the form of outside attacks or disputes within the Mossi community itself. At the top of the hierarchy was the emperor, the Moro Naba, who was venerated like a god as he symbolised the sun, and who was elected by the court's top dignitaries. He was chosen from the descendants of Oubri, as the kingdom of Oubritenga immediately asserted its preeminence over the other Mossi kingdoms. As head of the army, supreme judge, and collector of all taxes and levies, the emperor was all powerful. The empire was made up of kingdoms divided into provinces, which were subdivided into fiefs made up of several villages.

In this highly centralised system, all contact between the top and bottom passed via the different rungs of the hierarchy (like in modern day armies). As the French historian Tauxier wrote at the beginning of the century: "The Mossi empire was centralised. The internecine fighting which often took place amongst other Black peoples from village to village, quarter to quarter, and even *soukala* to *soukala*, did not affect the Mossi. Hence, internal peace and security reigned. Furthermore, not only did this centralised power prevent anarchy, but also stopped the kingdom from being devastated by conquerors. Thus, whereas the Djermabé plundered the Gourounsi kingdom of independent villages and small districts and by fire and sword founded a kingdom, they did not dare attack their neighbours the Mossi for fear of the Mogho Naba's ten thousand cavalrymen. Internal and external tranquility were assured (…) On entering the Mossi kingdom, one was struck by the absolute security in which the inhabitants lived, whilst everywhere else wars and slave traders despoiled the villages. People enviously referred to the Mossi farmers who went to their fields alone, pick axes slung over their shoulders, whereas everywhere else, the head of the family had to have his weapons in easy reach both day and night…"

Yatenga, a powerful Mossi empire

As the first Mossi kingdoms Tenkodogo and Oubritenga were enjoying a peaceful existence at the beginning of the 16ᵗʰ century, a surprisingly powerful sister kingdom was being founded in northern Burkina Faso, namely the Yatenga kingdom, the "Land of Yadega". Yadega was possibly Koumdoumyé's twin brother. Their father was Nassébiri, son of Oubri, both of whom were Oubritenga kings.

Having ousted his brother Yadega from the throne, Koumdoumyé became the Moro Naba of Oubritenga, thereby leaving Yadega no choice but to go and look for a kingdom elsewhere. This is precisely what he did, accompanied by his sister Pabré who first stole the royal Oubri dynasty's insignia from Koumdoumyé. They headed northwards to join Yadega's tutor, the war lord Swida, and settled at Gourcy (nowadays between Yako and Ouahigouya). From this northern base, Yadega launched numerous military attacks to conquer the neighbouring Samo villages. His successors continued in the same way, gradually increasing their territories. Once they had beaten the Mossi commandants already settled in the region along with the native Samo, Dogon and Kurumba, the Yatenga kingdom was born.

Naba Kango

The greatest figure in Yatenga history was Naba Kango (1757-1787), a particularly formidable chief whose story has always provided perfect griot material.

He first came to power in 1754, but was then usurped. Making the most of this disgrace, he travelled around Africa, met well-read people and learnt how to use fire arms. As the historian Michel Izard wrote: "After three years in exile, he returned to Yatenga heading a troop of Bambara, Bwa and Samo mercenaries, overthrew his rival and resumed his position on the throne. For thirty years, Naaba Kângo was to rule the Yatenga with undivided authority, fighting against the kingdom's ever turbulent aristocracy, against brigands who had profited from years of anarchy, and against idle mercenaries who threatened the security of the country. He waged wars against the Ségou Bambara and the Yako Mossi kingdom, went out to capture Dogons and Kouroumbas, and tried to expand his royal territory. Finally, and above all, he transformed the appearance of Yatenga by creating a new capital, and by increasing the role of royal captives in the State apparatus."

Kango left the former capital Gourcy and had an impenetrable fortress constructed at Ouahigouya, further to the north. He invited all the Yatenga chiefs to the inauguration in order that they solemnly swear allegiance to him. During the ceremony he found a name for his new capital: "Ouahigouya", meaning "Come and prostrate yourselves before me".

The Yendabri offensive

Other than the odd operation to set recalcitrant vassals back on the right path, few major events took place in the Tenkodogo and Oubritenga Mossi kingdoms during the period when the Yatenga kingdom was being established.

Some hundred years after the creation of the Oubritenga kingdom, however, Ouagadougou was designated the capital of the empire, and around 1795, due to the influence of the Moro Naba Dulugu who had recently converted to the Prophet's religion, Islam began to spread in the formerly animist Mossi kingdom.

Meanwhile, the Gourmanché — cousins of the Mossi settled in the south-east of Burkina Faso and descendants of Diaba Lompo, Tidarpo, Ountani, Banydoba, Labidiébo, Tantiari and Lissoangui — clung on to their territory, fighting to protect it from the onslaught of invading peoples like the Hausa and Fulani from Niger, the Bariba from Northern Benin and the Tomba from northern Togo. At the same time, they organised the administration of their kingdom by dividing it into provinces led by chiefs pledged to the Gourma king. As the first capital, Pama, was too close to the southern borders, it was attacked on numerous occasions by the Tomba who rased it to the ground at the end of the 17th century. When Yendabri (1709-1736), the greatest Gourmantché king, came to power, a vigorous offensive was launched southwards as far as Bassar in Togo, where he defeated the Tomba in a bloody battle. When he returned from this military campaign, King Yendabri transferred his headquarters from Pama to Fada N'Gourma (Noungou) for greater safety, and this was to remain the capital of the Gourmantché kingdom for ever more.

Gouïriko and Kénédougou rivalry

The Mossi and Gourmantché kingdoms in central Burkina Faso are not the only places of interest to historians. In the 18th century, the Gouïriko kingdom was also founded in the west of the country (around 1714) by the Dioula prince Famara Ouattara from the Kong kingdom (in the north of modern day Côte d'Ivoire). For over a century, the Ouattara, who made Bobo Dioulasso their capital, reigned over the region and attempted to subjugate the various native peoples (the Bobo, Bwa, Tyefo, Bolon, Sembla, Vigyé, amongst others). They managed this only with varying degrees of success, as the different ethnic groups often fought back in order to preserve their independence. The Lobi, for example, fiercely resisted the army led by Famara Ouattara's brother Bakari and forced him to retreat.

In the course of the next century, the Gouïriko Ouattara fought against a rival Dioula kingdom: the Kénédougou kingdom founded by the Traoré at Sikasso (south-west of today's Mali). These Dioula princes from Mandé first imposed their law on the Sénoufo and then attempted to dominate the whole of western Burkina Faso. Inevitably, they came up against the Ouattara from Bobo Dioulasso. In an attempt to capture some of their rivals' land, the Kénédougou kings helped the Bobo Dioula and their chief Molo Sanou, to revolt against the king of the Gouïriko, Diori Ouattara. The Kénédougou were not to enjoy the fruit of their intrigues for long, however, as, during the 1840s, they were well and truly defeated by Prince Baco-Morou, Diori Ouattara's brother.

These incessant wars weakened the Gouïriko, however, and their kingdom fell into decline during the second half of the 19th century. When the French colonial forces came to impose their authority at the end of the 19th century, they had no difficulty in getting Pintiéba to sign a treaty making his weak and drained State a French protectorate in 1897.

Mamadou Karantao

During Baco-Morou Ouattara's reign (1839-1851) another little dynasty founded itself a kingdom in western Burkina Faso between the Mossi and the Gouïriko kingdoms. The Muslim marabout Mamadou Karantao, from Djenné in Mali, settled at Boromo (between Ouagadougou and Bobo Dioulasso), giving himself a base from which to launch offensives throughout the region. Once he had subjugated the Ko (Gourounsi) from Boromo, he expanded his territory in the region of the former Black Volta loop, defeating the Gouïriko Bwaba vassals. In about 1850, he moved his capital from Boromo to the town Ouahabou he had just founded, after which he named his kingdom.

Karamokho Moktar

His son Karamokho Moktar later tried to expand the Ouahabou kingdom southwards towards the Lobi region, where he was to fight the Dagari, the Dyan and the Wilé. After defeat at Djindermé in 1887, he retreated however. The following year, Karamokho Moktar received a visit from the French explorer Gustave Binger and in 1897, signed a treaty of alliance with the French people.

Explorers and colonisers

In the 19th century, this territory in the heart of West Africa also began to interest Europeans who until then only knew the African coastline where they had set up trading posts. Early in the century, this interest appeared to be purely scientific. Geographers and cartographers were anxious that explorers be sent to complete navigators' innumerable coastal maps and planispheres on which all these inland regions had been left blank. In 1806, the Scottish explorer Mungo Park explored parts of the Mossi kingdom on behalf of the African Society in London. In 1828, the French explorer René Caillié made his famous journey to Timbuktu in Mali. Although he approached modern-day Burkina Faso, he did not actually cross the border. The German Heinrich Barth later explored the Mossi region in about 1853. Finally in 1887-88, Lieutenant Louis-Gustave Binger was the first Frenchman to explore Burkina Faso. Times had changed, however. The Berlin Congress had just taken place in 1884-85 and the Europeans were dividing up Africa between them. It was no longer a matter of innocently drawing up maps of Africa, but of founding colonial empires and plundering Africa of all its riches.

In the course of their voyages in Africa, these early European explorers were to witness its tormented history. During the 19th century, many conflicts broke out, especially in modern-day Burkina Faso. Mention has already been made of the rivalries between the Gouïriko, the Kénédougou and those in the little kingdom of Ouahabou. Devastating incusions were also carried out by the Kong warriors in the Lobi region, by the Djermabé from Niger in the Gourounsi region and by the Samory in the region of Bobo Dioulasso.

In 1815, Bakary Ouattara, descendant of Sékou, king of the Kong (from the north of modern-day Côte d'Ivoire), began to make murderous attacks on the Wilé people from north of the Lobi region, and burnt the villages of Dissin, Pirkwon and Poura. These forays temporarily came to an end when Bakary was killed by a poisoned arrow, but unfortunately, in 1850 his son Karakara launched a new offensive and once again devastated the Lobi region (siege of the town Karangasso), then the Wilé, Pwa and Dagara regions. These forays were not over yet. Dabila, Kara-kara's grandson, came to the region later, under the pretext of helping the Wilé and the Pya, and in fact attacked the Wilé whom he temporarily defeated at Babemba, Memer and Saala. He did not succeed in subjugating the Birifor in the period from 1885-1892.

Djermabé attacks on the Gourounsi

The Gourounsi region directly south of the Mossi lands did not share the same formidable reputation its powerful neighbour had earnt. Badly armed and badly organised, the Gourounsi were easy prey for the Djermabé invaders from Niger in the east. It was in fact they who originally called on the Djerma to arbitrate their internecine disputes in 1860 and in 1872, but when the Djerma settled at Sati, near to Léo in 1883, they turned against the Gourounsi who they held to ransom and raided, led by their chief Kazaré. When the latter was killed by an arrow, he was replaced by Babato who invaded the Bobo region, where he was defeated in 1885 by a coalition of several native peoples, then in 1893 by the Samo near Tougan. The following year, something unexpected happened. Hamaria, one of Babato's lieutenants, changed camps and helped the Gourounsi fight his former chief. In 1886, as fighting once again broke out between the Gourounsi and the Djermabé, Sarantyé Mori, son of the great Malinké chief, the Almamy Samory Touré, intervened to reconcile the two chiefs. In fact, he was secretly nursing the idea of taking over the Gourounsi region. The plot was discovered by Hamaria, who went to the French troops under Lieutenant Voulet and signed a treaty of alliance at Sati in September 1896. The French thus intervened two ways. On the one hand, they made it known to Samory that they had become the Gourounsi's ally, thereby forcing him to withdraw his troops. On the other hand, they fought with the Djermabé from Babato who they defeated first at Gandiaga, then at Léo at the beginning of 1897.

Tiéba and Babemba's offensives

The Kénédougou Sikasso kingdom, already marked by rivalry with the Gouïriko in the first half of the 19th century, came back into the limelight at the end of the century when ruled by King Tiéba Traoré. Having emerged unscathed from the long siege carried out in vain by the Almamy Samory from 1887-88, Tiéba decided to take advantage of the Gouïriko's weakness and capture lands in the south-west of the Gouïriko Bobo Dioulasso kingdom. Tiéba thus set up headquarters in the Turka village of Wolonkoto, west of Banfora and Tengrela, once he had defeated the Diomo Samoro (near to Orodara). He then attacked the Kéta and Sidi in the Toussian region (north of Orodara) and, at the beginning of 1892, massacred all those who he could not take to Sikasso as slaves. By the end of the same year, Tiéba had reached the outskirts of Bobo Dioulasso having already taken Péni and Noumoudara. All the Gouïriko and their vassals mobilised in order to defend themselves against the Sikasso king. The day before the battle which was to have taken place at Bama, north of Bobo Dioulasso, Tiéba was poisoned by spies sent by Niandané Ouattara, king of the Gouïriko.

The Kénédougou armies withdrew for a while, but were to invade again in 1893 under the command of Tiéba's brother, Babemba. He came back to the Toussian region with his troops in 1896 in order to fight the Turka near to Banfora. He came up against a coalition of native people from south-western Burkina Faso, however, and was forced to retreat. When he reached Sikasso, he came face to face with the French. The town was taken, Babemba killed himself (May 1898) and the Kénédougou kingdom dissolved.

Samory on the outskirts of Bobo Dioulasso

Another even more powerful conqueror — the Almamy Samory Touré — also coveted Burkina Faso. Having extended his hold on northern Côte d'Ivoire and southern Mali, and having tried in vain to take Sikasso (the 1887-88 siege), he then marched on the Gouïriko. Three columns of Samory's *sofas* (soldiers) converged on Bobo Dioulasso in 1896. They were fought off by the British based in Ghana, however. The column led by Samory's son, Sarantyé Mori, raided Dokita instead where he successfully fought with the Birifor (Lobi) and their British allies in March 1897, then headed northwards. Samory captured the Kong kingdom in May 1897, then joined his lieutenant, Ngolo, and Sarantyé Mori at Dar-Salamy on the outskirts of Bobo Dioulasso. Just as they were about to attack the Gouïriko capital, Samory's troops were attacked by the Tyefo Amoro's troops from Noumoudara. Samory doubled back and rased Noumoudara to the ground, killing all the inhabitants. As British and French troops were advancing, however, (the latter were about to take Sikasso, thereby dissolving the Kénédougou kingdom in May 1898) the Almamy was forced to retreat to Côte d'Ivoire where he was captured at Guélémou in September 1898, and deported to Gabon.

The French treaties

Initially just bystanders, by the end of the century, the French had taken a leading role in the dramas being played out in Burkina Faso. Whilst waiting for Samory to withdraw, the French in the west successively signed Protectorate treaties with Dédougou, the Ouahabou kingdom and with Diébougou in the Lobi region (April-May 1897). The following month, Commander Caudrelier occupied Ouarkoyé, then signed a treaty with the Gouïriko at Bobo Dioulasso in September 1897. During the following year, the French soldiers subjugated the whole Banfora region when, by capturing Sikasso, they brought the Kénédougou kingdom to its knees.

From Yatenga to the Ouagadougou kingdom

It was not long before the plan elaborated by French staff in Mali to bring all of Burkina Faso under French control came to fruition as eventually even the Mossi kingdoms, once reputed for their solid political organisation, came under French supervision. In fact the French met with very little opposition, as civil wars and internal rivalries had completely weakened the Mossi kingdoms. In 1895, Captain Destenave, who had come from Bandiagara in Mali, reached Yatenga where the Naba Baogo was caught up in a struggle with his nephew Bagaré. By glorifying the virtues of French military support, Destenave got the Naba Baogo to sign a Protectorate treaty with France on 18 May 1895. He quickly abandoned the sovereign to his destiny, however, preferring to keep a safe distance during the ensuing battle between Bagaré and Baogo. The latter was killed by an arrow, and Bagaré, now the Naba Bulli, became the new Yatenga chief in June 1895. The French immediately switched allegiances, and supported the new Naba as he fought

*Like Animism and Islam, Christianity is now
deeply rooted in Burkina Faso, thanks to missions first established
by the "Pères Blancs" at the beginning of the century.
Ouagadougou, the head of the parish, was endowed with a cathedral
in the Thirties when Mgr Thévenoud was still around.*

against the former Naba Baogo's partisans. Their resistance, which developed into real guerrilla warfare, was to last long after the Naba Bulli's reign (he died in 1899), and calm was only momentarily restored in 1912, after two other Naba (Ligidi and Kobga) had been at the head of Yatenga. The most tense moment came in 1899 when bad harvests brought famine to the whole kingdom.

The Moro Naba Wogbo

Bokary-Koutou, who in 1890 forced the dignitaries to elect him Moro Naba Wogbo ("the elephant") in succession to his brother, the Moro Naba Sanom, initially remained passive when the French invaded Yatenga. In 1897, however, once the Naba Bulli was firmly installed at Ouahigouya and the French had no more wars to wage in Yatenga, they turned to the capital of the Mossi empire, Ouagadougou. The Moro Naba Wogbo refused to receive them and did not hide his long-standing hostility to the French treaties as he knew full well that they would only lead to the loss of his rights and supremacy. He wrote Captain Destenave in no uncertain terms, when he entered Ouagadougou at the beginning of 1897: "I have consulted the spirits for a long time and they always replied that if I ever saw a White man, I would die. I know that the Whites want to kill me and take over my lands and moreover, you claim that they are going to help me organise my lands. I happen to like my lands just as they are. I do not need them at all. I know what I need and what I want. I have my goods. Think yourself lucky that I do not have your head chopped off. Leave and, above all, never come back".

The colonial period

The French army maintained steady pressure, however, and in order to avoid a blood bath, the Moro Naba Wogbo fled to Ghana. Stripped of all his rights, he was replaced by the Moro Naba Sigri who signed the Protectorate treaty with France. In February 1897, Lieutenant Voulet went to Tenkodogo, birthplace of the Mossi

THE OUAGADOUGOU APPEAL

■ *In May 1980, Pope Jean-Paul II made his first visit to Africa. Amongst other countries, he visited Zaire, Ghana, Upper Volta (now Burkina Faso), and Côte d'Ivoire. On 10 May he came to Ouagadougou, where he made a memorable appeal to the whole world and especially the major powers, on behalf of all deprived Africans.*
"I, John-Paul II, Archbishop of Rome and successor to Peter, raise my beseeching voice because I cannot remain silent when my brothers and sisters are threatened. I am the voice of all those who have no voice, the voice of the innocent who are dead because they had no water or bread, the voice of fathers and mothers who have watched their children die, without understanding, or who will always see the consequences of the hunger they have endured in their children, the voice of generations to come, who should no longer have to live with this terrible menace hanging over their lives. I appeal to every one! Let us not wait for the droughts to come back. Let us not wait for the sand to bring death again. Let us not permit that the future of these people always remains threatened. The scale and effectiveness of yesterday's solidarity has shown that it is possible to listen to the voice of justice and charity alone, not the voice of individual and collective selfishness. Hear my appeal!"

empire, not only to gain the allegiance of the Naba, but also to stop the rapid advance of British troops led by Captain Donald Stewart, who were also intending to take possession of the Mossi lands. After peaceful talks, the British withdrew without opposing French possession of the Mossi territories.

The eastern and northern parts of modern day Burkina Faso (Gourma, Liptako, the Dori region) submitted to Captain Destenave at the same time.

On the eve of the 20th century, the first Christian missionaries began to set up in these regions. After founding a mission at Fada N'Gourma in 1899, the "Pères Blancs" led by Mgr Hacquard settled at Koupela and Ouagadougou in 1900 and 1901. Three years later, the Mossi regions were incorporated into the colony Upper Senegal-Niger.

From the First to the Second World War

On the eve of the First World War (1941-18), calm appeared to reign throughout the whole of the French colonial empire. Soon, however, the massive forced conscription of Africans who were sent off to fight in Europe, and the introduction of forced labour for those who stayed behind provoked a generalised revolt during the period from 1915 to 1917, especially in some regions of Burkina Faso. After the war, Upper Volta split off from Upper Senegal-Niger and became a separate colony for thirteen years. In 1932, the French colonial powers redrew the map of the empire and did away with the colony Upper Volta which was partitioned between Côte d'Ivoire, the Sudan (now Mali) and Niger.

Building the railway

Two years later, the railway being built from Abidjan to northern Côte d'Ivoire reached Bobo Dioulasso. The last stretch to Ouagadougou was not completed, however, as work was stopped when World War II broke out (1939-45). Once again, the Africans made a major contribution to this new conflict, and many soldiers from what is now Burkina Faso joined the "Tirailleurs Sénégalais" (Senegalese infantrymen) sent to fight in Italy and Germany.

The Moro Naba Koom II, who had succeeded his father Sigri in 1905, died during the war. He was replaced by the Moro Naba Sagha who reigned in Ouagadougou from 1942 to 1957.

The run-up to Independence

Upper Volta's former borders were reconstituted after the war and in 1947, along with all the French colonies, Upper Volta became an Overseas Territory (Territoire d'Outre-Mer) as stipulated in the new 1946 French Constitution. The Constitution guaranteed to give the new territories in the AOF ("Afrique Occidentale Française", or "French West Africa") a certain degree of autonomy. Africans were thus allowed to participate in the new "Conseils Généraux" (Governing Councils) which worked closely with the French Governors (notably voting on the budget and taxation) and in the "Grand Conseil" which worked alongside the Governor General of the AOF.

In 1946, a meeting of all African MPs was held in Bamako. Amongst those present were Felix Houphouët-Boigny from Côte d'Ivoire and Ouezzin Coulibaly from Upper Volta. The RDA ("Rassemblement Démocratique Africain") was born out of this conference, and was allied with the French Communist Party until the Communists left the government in 1950.

The traditional chiefs and the colonial authorities in Upper Volta were hostile to this new party, reproaching its obedience to the communists and the disproportionate role of the Ivoirians (Houphouët-Boigny was the president of the RDA). They welcomed the more moderate "Union Voltaïque", on the other hand, which sided with the "Indépendants d'Outre-mer" party (the IOM) from Senghor (Senegal). In 1953, the IOM congress was held at Bobo Dioulasso and the party asked the French government for greater autonomy in the former colonies and greater rights and power for the Africans.

After the RDA won elections in Africa, Houphouët-Boigny, now Minister of State in France, worked with the Socialist Minister Gaston Defferre on the 1956 "Loi-Cadre" law which, without actually changing the 1946 Constitution, put French West Africa on the path to federalism. The "Loi-Cadre" came into effect in 1957, establishing a Governmental Council in each of the Overseas Territories. The Council's ministers were elected by the Territorial Assembly, which was elected by universal suffrage. The French Governors still presided over these Councils, albeit with increasingly less authority.

In Upper Volta, the RDA won the elections and in 1957, its leader Ouezzin Coulibaly became the Vice President of the "Conseil de Gouvernment".

Independent Upper Volta

When the British granted independence to Ghana in March 1957, the Algerian war broke out, and in 1958 General de Gaulle came to power in France, the move towards independence in Sub-Saharan Africa was accelerated. Favouring the concept of federalism, General de Gaulle decided to give more autonomy to the future African Republics, which were nonetheless still part of the "Communauté Française" (based on the concept of the British Commonwealth). Apart from Guinea which, led by Sékou Touré, called for immediate independence and complete separation from France, all the other African territories overwhelmingly voted "yes" to the referendum de Gaulle organised on 28 September 1958. Following the death of Ouezzin Coulibaly, Upper Volta's RDA found itself with the leader, Lieutenant Maurice Yaméogo. On 11 Décember 1958, the Republic of Upper Volta was declared a Member State of the French Community.

A few months later, on 11 July 1960, Upper Volta declared its Independence (which was later celebrated on 5 August). Its new constitution instigated a presidential regime and Maurice Yaméogo was elected as the first President. At around the same time, the new State also became a member of the United Nations.

The Land of "Honest People"

Five years later in 1965, new elections were held and President Yaméogo was reelected. On 3 January 1966, however he was overthrown by the Army led by Lieutenant Colonel Sangoulé Lamizana, who took over power and soon became a General. Called to vote in a referendum, the people of Upper Volta approved the 1977 Constitution destined to restore a civilian regime and instigate a three-party Government. In 1980, however, General Lamizana was in turn overthrown by the Army, and Colonel Saye Zerbo took over power. During the same year, Pope John Paul II made his first visit to Africa, and at Ouagadougou, made an appeal to the whole world on behalf of all deprived peoples.

Two years later, the Commandant Jean-Baptiste Ouedraogo overthrew Saye Zerbo. He was not Head of State for long, however, as in 1983, he was replaced by Captain Sankara who established the supreme ruling body, the "Conseil National de la Révolution". The following year Upper Volta changed its name to Burkina Faso (the "Land of Honest People").

Burkina Faso today

In 1987, Captain Sankara was overthrown and killed and the new President Blaise Compaoré began the "Mouvement de Rectification". The "Conseil National de la République" was dissolved and replaced by the "Front Populaire". In order to bring an end to the economic crisis that was ravaging Burkina Faso, President Compaoré launched the Structural Adjustment Programme in 1990. The Programme came into effect in 1991. In December of the same year, President Compaoré was reelected to office, having gained more than 86 % of the votes in the elections. In May 1992, President Blaise Compaoré's party, the OPD-MT, won a majority (78 of the 107 seats) in Burkina Faso's parliamentary body. In recent years, there has been a series of significant economic events in Burkina Faso, notably the introduction of a privatisation programme of State-owned companies in 1992, the inauguration of the Tambao manganese mine in May 1993, and, above all, the devaluation of the CFA Franc in January 1994 which significantly boosted export products.

At the end of 1996, the 19th Franco-African summit was held in Ouagadougou, and in May 1997 President Compaoré's party won a new majority in Burkina Faso's parliamentary elections.

*Having inherited the legacy of the revolution launched
at the beginning of the 1980s, Captain Blaise Compaoré—who was
elected President of Faso in 1991—is now involved
in the hard task of democratising the country,
whilst simultaneously developing and freeing the economy.*

religion and traditions

Based on animist rites, the traditional African religions have remained a mystery or been frowned upon for a long time. In "educated" circles where the major revealed religions prevail (Christianity and Islam), traditional religions are often considered "primitive" and the veneration of "fetishes" treated as superstitious and barbaric idolatry. It is common knowledge that, carried away by their proselytic ardour, many of the Christian missionaries who came to convert the Africans, organised spectacular autos-da-fé during which masks and statues used in animist rituals were burnt. This was a terrible loss of cultural heritage for people all over the world, and today, exhibitions and uprecedented auctions reveal the importance now attached to these humble objects carved deep in the bush.

Thanks to the work of ethnologists, people are now more familiar with these animist religions and can begin to appreciate their profound spirituality, complex rituals and their highly symbolic value, all of which emanate great poetry.

In Burkina Faso, where 70 % of the population still practise animism, over sixty ethnic groups still make sacrifices to the spirits, ancestors and other protective deities that dwell in the bush. Even though the rituals and representations of the deities (masks, statuettes) vary enormously from one ethnic group to another, the animist religions do have a lot of points in common.

Mainly monotheists

Contrary to what most people think, the majority of animists are monotheistic. They believe in one god, the maker of the universe: Wouro, for example, is the supreme god of the Bobo, Thagba the god of the Lobi, and Koulo Tiolo the god of the Sénoufo, an ethnic group in western Burkina Faso. For reasons which vary according to the different ethnic groups, this supreme god withdrew deep into the universe after having created the earth, stars, men, animals and the elements. The gods' withdrawal accounts for the apparition of a pantheon of innumerable "secondary" gods and occult powers — like dead ancestors — who liaise and act as intermediaries between man and his Creator.

DEATH AND ILLNESS AMONGST THE MOSSI

Death is of great importance for the Mossi and illness, especially wounds and accidents, are attributed to evil spirits. Healers and bone setters practise their medicine using plants, tree leaves and bark. Priests often resort to sacrifices and exorcism rites.

Any Mossi person who dies of an illness lives on in the person of the Kourita *until the day of the* Kouré *(which is a kind of official burial carried out by the whole community after a first shrouding). This very ancient custom is of a solemn nature. The* Kourita *is generally represented by a woman from the deceased's family who dresses and behaves like the deceased, taking on his/her place until the community definitevely buries the body. The* Kourita *carefully shaves her head the day of the* Kouré, *thus showing that she has fulfilled her duties and that her role is over. The ritual is more complicated when the* Moro Naba *dies: on the day of the* Kouré, *a young boy in the family will be chosen to represent the deceased for the rest of his existence. He will also hold the title of* Kourita *and, in this capacity, can accede to the honours and homage paid by the people. The* Kouré *always takes place on a Sunday and is the occasion for festivities, sacrifices and dancing.*

Incarnated in the earth, trees, water, stone or animals, these deities behave somewhat like man: they are capricious, sensitive, even irascible and, when angry, never hesitate in inflicting all kinds of calamity on the villages. It is they who are responsible for bringing diseases that kill men and beasts, for causing women to be sterile, for bringing droughts which destroy crops, etc. At any given time therefore, African animists must always be aware of what precautions to take and be ready to interpret esoteric signs, carry out rituals, formulate requests to occult powers and make sacrifices to them.

Sacrifice and libation

When African farmers want to clear a field, for example, they must ask permission from the owner — a protecting spirit — to whom they will sacrifice poultry or offer libation. As they begin to plant, they know their hoes or ploughs are scratching the nourishing Mother's belly and might risk wounding her. They must therefore carry out a number of rituals and sacrifices before ploughing the first furrow. Similarly, before going hunting, the hunter will first consult the soothsayer, prepare poisons which will harden his arrows and pronounce secret formulae to ensure that the arrows reach their target without indisposing any spirits in the bush (this is particularly common amongst the Gourmantché in south-eastern Burkina Faso).

Animist beliefs

From a very early age, Africans learn the rudiments of these animist beliefs from the tales and legends that their parents and grandparents tell them. These tales familiarise the youngsters with such beliefs without indoctrinating them as, at that age, they are still too young to understand their full significance. The real revelation takes place at the end of adolescence during the different stages of initiation. The young people are taken from their families and villages into the bush where they are instructed by the elders in charge of their initiation. The

On the Thursday, the Mossi, who are very sociable people, go to the market to thank the deceased's friends who helped and supported them. Every year, the day of the dead is celebrated. The eldest son is naturally the deceased's heir and therefore becomes chief of the hut and redistributes the inheritance amongst the family. The deceased's eldest daughter or a younger son can also be his heir.

HISTOIRE GÉNÉRALE DE L'AFRIQUE
(under the direction of Ibrahima Baba Kaké and Elika M'Bokolo)

elders will explain the creation of the universe to them, teach them about the different deities, taboos, rituals and the codes of conduct which regulate village life.

The "poro" initiation

Some initiations last almost a lifetime, as is the case with the *poro* initiation practised by the Sénoufo, an ethnic group living in western Burkina Faso and northern Côte d'Ivoire. As the ethnologist Bohumil Holas explains: "With the exception of privileged individuals who are designated guardians of customary law and all things sacred, the normal cycle of the Sénoufo *poro* lasts twenty-one years, divided into three seven year periods. The last period, the most important, involves relatively harsh moral and physical trials which, by the end of his reclusion, make the *tiolo* a socially valid, perfect man, apt to carry out all duties that the family or society may ask of him during his lifetime".

Leaf masks

One or two examples help illustrate the great beauty and poetry of these beliefs. The Bobo in western Burkina Faso believe that their supreme god originally established harmonious order in the world he created. On earth he divided human beings and things into two groups: on the one hand those in the bush — domain of unfettered, violent and wild life — ruled by the god Soxo, and the other hand, those in the village — a place of peace and order — where man and domestic animals lived under the protection of Dwo. The perfect equilibrium which reigned before Wouro withdrew into the depths of the universe was soon compromised by man, however, and has remained threatened ever since. Man constantly encroaches upon the bush by clearing the land and chasing away the wildlife. In the villages, he does not obey the rules and at all times risks incurring the wrath of the deities.

Luckily for man, Wouro hurriedly sent the very good-natured deity Dwo to help man mend his ways and reestablish order and equilibrium on earth.

Dwo's intervention in the villages is celebrated by stunning festivities. As the ethnologist Guy Le Moal wrote: "Every year in each Bobo village, masks made of leaves come out of the bush where they have been made in great secrecy. Once welcomed by the priests, they enter the village which they purify as they run about in all directions. As they brush past the villagers and their homes, they collect up the harmful effluvia that have accumulated from day to day as a result of the inhabitants' wrong doings". The masks carry all the festering disorder away into the bush, leaving the human community cleansed behind them. Dwo is also incarnated in other masks whose power is equally beneficial to man. Made of large, fibre tunics surmounted by carved, wooden animal heads — owls, fish, buceros, snakes, buffaloes, antelopes — these masks which represent the village's protecting spirits, intervene at the end of the dry season in order to call the rains and to fecundate the earth.

A failed creation

Sénoufo cosmogony is equally imaginative and ingenious, which is hardly surprising from a people whose artistic talent has produced some of the most beautiful pieces of statuary in Africa.

According to the Sénoufo, who come from western Burkina Faso, the supreme god Koulo Tiolo created the universe and the earth where he made the rivers flow, vegetation grow and created man and animals in ten days. His creation was not a success, however, so he withdrew leaving an imperfect world that was hostile and wild. When man was abandoned by Koulo Tiolo, he was no more than the bare outline of a creature living very close to the animal world. At this point, however, a kind deity — Kâ Tiéléo — who the Sénoufo affectionately call "Mother of the village", intervened to complete Koulo Tiolo's failed work.

"Mother of the village"

Protected by the Mother of the village, the first men split off from the rest of the world and, once they had acquired a language and began to learn certain techniques (agriculture, rearing, house building, pottery, clothes, etc.) reached the top of the hierarchy of living creatures. These advantages had to be earnt, however, and man pays back the deities by making sacrifices to them. Like that of other animist peoples, the Sénoufo universe is inhabited by many minor deities and spirits and the Sénoufo also devote a cult to deceased ancestors. They have to

*The Lobi from south-western Burkina Faso
erect earthen ritual statues
in front of their traditional huts
to protect themselves from hostile forces.*

be familiar with the spirits' habits and failings, and this takes all the learning acquired during initiation (the *poro* mentioned earlier).

Lobi cults

The Lobi, who live in the Gaoua region near the Mouhoun River (south-western Burkina Faso), also have a single, supreme god — Thagba — who is surrounded by a whole pantheon of secondary deities. As Piet Meyer, a Swiss ethnologist who recently studied the Lobi religious system, explains: "Right at the top is the "creator of all things", Thagba-y vv. He created the various Lobi spirit worlds which, although superposed, are dependent on one another; he also created the animals, humans and other creatures that live there, before withdrawing to the sky. Nowadays, it is extremely unusual for him to intervene directly in human life. This is left up to a multitude of invisible beings, the *thila*, who live on earth, occupying second place in the Lobi religious system. Different categories of beings who live in the bush beyond the villages and who, for the most part, are invisible, occupy the third (and bottom) place. They are responsible for passing on things of cultural value that the creator gave them to the Lobi, like millet, different remedies, divination, and even European arms".

Thagba (the sky), who is of masculine gender, has a wife (the earth). He sends rain to fecundate the earth which in turn produces crops. The whole earth is considered sacred, and man must therefore be careful not to sully her, otherwise she cannot be fecundated. This is the case when murder is committed or when coupling takes place out of the village, on the ground itself.

White river spirits

As the French ethnologist Madeleine Père, who lives in Garoua, has shown, the Lobi cult of the earth involves an innumerable number of beings and things which are related to her: caves and the animals that live in them, certain trees

---

LOBI FUNERAL RITES

In the 1950s, André Vila was staying in the Lobi region when one of the villagers died.

"When the old women have finished washing the body, a strip of new cloth specially put aside for the occasion is used to gird the deceased's loins. The customary plaited fibre belt is broken. Then, the body is sat up against the soukhala (hut) wall to await the beginning of the immanent first public funeral ceremony, the questioning of the deceased. It is essential, for both the family's and the deceased's future tranquility to known whether the latter was the victim of evil doings. If this is the case, and if vengeance is not carried out, the deceased's soul cannot rest in peace and will come back to haunt the near ones, usually at night, which is very unpleasant. Wrapped in a mat, the body is rested on the head of two bearers. The crowd awaits in silence. The relatives ask the following questions:
—"Why did you leave us?"
—"Did anyone inflict illness upon you?"
The body leans to the left (the bearer too) which means: "no".
—"Did anyone put poison in your food?"
The body leans to the left: "no".
—"Did anyone hit you"? Left again: "no".
In the event of an affirmative answer, the bearers would be irresistibly drawn to the guilty party, thus revealing his identity in front of everyone. This no doubt corresponds to our burial certificate.*

and stones, and waterways — especially the Mouhoun (formerly the Black Volta), as this is the river the Lobi's ancestors crossed when they came from the east and settled on the right bank of the river. Its waters are of course inhabited by supernatural beings which look like white-skinned humans. Consequently, when the first Europeans came to the land of the Lobi, they were taken for river spirits! All animals which live or used to live in the Mouhoun — some, like the hippos, disappeared a long time ago — are considered sacred and are the object of a cult.

This is because during times of war in the past, hippopotami were sometimes used as mounts by the more "sporty" Lobi warriors as they crossed the river to escape from their enemies. Ceremonies regularly take place on the banks of the Mouhoun and other rivers in the Lobi region. Finally, ancestral cults are highly developed amongst the Lobi and are the object of numerous rituals.

Protecting amulets

As Jacques Anquetil notes in his book on arts and crafts in Burkina Faso:"Highly superstitious, the Lobi wear numerous protecting amulets (ram horns, cowrie shell necklaces, etc.) consecrated during magic rites. Hence witches, soothsayers and rain-makers are considered very important in the Lobi region".

"In front of their *soukala*, the Lobi erect altars made out of earth or wood representing almost shapeless human figures or animals in order to appease the vital forces of slain animals and chopped-down trees. These altars and their large carvings are becoming increasingly rare".

The land of the ancestors

Along with initiation rituals and rain-making ceremonies, funerals are also the occasion for numerous festivities throughout Burkina Faso.

For the Africans, and especially for animists, death does not have the same tragic connotations as in the West, as the dead do not completely disappear from the land of the living. Whereas the buried body turns into dust, its "double" leaves the body and, although now invisible, stays in close contact with the whole family. The dead thus appear in dreams or, during sacrifices, manifest themselves in the sacrificial animal's final posture. When in the land of the ancestors — who themselves have become deities — the dead can foresee the future and may inform mortals of what is going to happen, just as they can appeal to the deities to stop catastrophes from befalling a village.

Funeral rites

The entry of the deceased into the land of the ancestors depends on the funeral rites carried out by the living members of the family. If the rites are not carried out properly or do not respect the traditions, the deceased cannot enter the land beyond and is condemned to roam the village like a lost soul, aggressing the living and spreading disaster. This explains the importance Africans attach to funerals, which take place with great pomp and necessitate serious financial sacrifices.

The whole village goes to inform the relatives, even those who have "gone up" to the town, inviting them to attend the expensive celebrations where millet beer flows freely and large cattle are killed for feasts which sometimes last a good ten days.

Right at the beginning of the ceremony, the body of the deceased is usually carried through the village on a stretcher in order to encourage it not to come back to torment the inhabitants. To be sure that the deceased will not seek vengeance, the remains are questioned to find out whether the deceased was poisoned by a friend or a relative. If this is the case, the guilty party must be found and punished as quickly as possible, otherwise the deceased will not rest in peace.

The protecting ancestors

After the festivities during which masks come out and traditional musicians play drums, balafons, flutes, etc., the deceased is buried. A few months later, if the living have respected the customs, and, when questioned by the soothsayer, the deceased declares him/herself satisfied and confirms that he/she has entered the land of the ancestors, ceremonies take place to mark the end of the mourning period. Similar to the Roman household gods, the deceased becomes one of the village's protecting powers for ever more, and thus becomes the object of a cult to whom domestic altars are erected.

For some peoples in Burkina Faso, the state of being dead is not definitive. The

*The Naba, descendant of
the great Yatenga Mossi dynasties,
still lives in the Ouahigouya palace
surrounded by his court officials.*

Bobo, for example, believe that the dead remain in *Laara* (the underground beyond) for variable periods of time before being reincarnated as children. It is then up to the newborn's parents and the soothsayer to determine which ancestor has taken refuge in their child's body.

In the Diébougou region in south-western Burkina Faso (home of the Lobi, Birifor and Dagara), religious celebrations are held to honour Daguéo, the spirit who protects grave diggers. These ceremonies usually take place at the beginning of the year, three months after the harvests. As one specialist has noted: "The god Daguéo is represented by a dried branch hung with the sacred calabashes used in burials. When a hunter is buried, the ceremony is most spectacular, more like a theatrical play than a funeral as the main events in the deceased's life are acted out."

The Muslim minority

In a country where traditional beliefs are still widespread, the main revealed religions, like Islam and Christianity, have not had a major impact. Islam — which is predominant throughout North Africa from Morocco to Egypt, and is the main religion in all the Sahelian countries from Senegal to Somalia, including Mali, Niger and Chad — seems to have avoided most of Burkina Faso. On a map, Burkina Faso looks like an island surrounded on all sides by followers of the Prophet's religion. Burkina Faso's northern neighbours, Mali and Niger, are mainly Muslim. The southern neighbours — Côte d'Ivoire, Ghana, Togo and Benin — have also been partly converted to Islam, especially the northern regions bordering on Burkina Faso, where the greater part of their Muslim communities are concentrated. This anomaly can be explained by the country's history: for centuries, Burkina Faso was ruled by powerful Mossi aristocrats whose chiefs — the *Naba* — either rarely converted to Islam, or converted very much later on — as is the case of the *Moro Naba* of Ouagadougou at the end of the 18th century. Converting to Islam was hardly in these monarches' interest, as their semi-divine power was essentially based on their traditional religions. Later, when the French colonised Burkina Faso, Christianity was encouraged instead of Islam, and hence the new masters of French West Africa were responsible for slowing the spread of Islam.

Several Muslim settlements do exist in Burkina Faso today, however, both in the east and west. The western regions converted to Islam when they were ruled by the Dioula sovereigns from Kong. The eastern regions are partly inhabited by Muslim Fulani and Tuaregs. In total, a third of Burkina Faso's population are Muslim.

The arrival of the "White Fathers"

At the end of the 19th century, not long after the French started colonising Burkina Faso, the first missionaries settled in the country and began converting the people to Christianity. The "Pères Blancs" (White Fathers), the famous religious order created by the French cardinal Charles Lavigerie in 1868, first of all tried to convert the Sahelian regions of Africa in stages, beginning with Algeria. A Sahara-Sudan "apostolic prefecture" was set up, as were a certain number of parishes in the Saharan stations of Laghouat, Biskra and Ouargla. On two occasions (1875 and 1881), the missionaries tried to penetrate the French Sudan, as it was then known, via the old trans-Saharan camel routes, but both times were massacred by the Tuaregs. In the light of this failure, the Pères Blancs decided to skirt round the Sahara via Senegal. In 1895, they set up a mission at Ségou in Mali, then at Timbuktu. Four years later, Mgr Hacquard, apostolic vicar of the Sahara-Sudan, explored the Mossi kingdoms and founded a mission at Fada N'Gourma. In 1900, the Pères Blancs set up another mission in Koupéla, then, the next year, in Ouagadougou as the Mossi capital was designated the headquarters of the new apostolic curacy in the French Sudan. Later, several missions sprung up over Burkina Faso: in Réo (1912), in the Gourounsi region, at Bondoukoui in Bobo country and in Toma in the Samo region (1912), in Pabré (1926), Koudougou (1931), etc.

The missionaries' work

As Christian missions spread throughout the former French Sudan, new administrative divisions were created in 1921, when the curacy of the French Sudan was divided into the Bamako curacy and the Ouagadougou curacy, and in 1927 when the Bobo Dioulasso apostolic prefecture was founded.

As well as trying to convert the Sahelian regions of Africa, the missionaries also formed a solid base in Burkina Faso by setting up numerous institutions, notably the Pabré and Koumi seminaries, the Ouagadougou and later the Gilongou catechism schools, dispensaries and the order of the Black Sisters of the Immaculate Conception.

Ouagadougou's oldest White man

Although Christianity was originally perceived in Africa as the colonial or "White man's religion", the extreme devotion with which these Pères Blancs worked can hardly go unmentioned. In Burkina Faso as in other countries, they established the country's first real hospital infrastructures and promoted high quality technical and general education in schools scattered throughout Burkina Faso. This wide range of activities was coordinated from above by one of the best known French missionaries in Africa, Mgr Joanny Thévenoud (1878-1949).

Originally from the Savoy region in France, Thévenoud, who had just been ordained a priest, was only 24 years old when he came to Upper Volta in 1902. He was one of the rare Europeans to live amongst the Africans and, later on, was known as "Ouagadougou's oldest White man" for a long time.

During his first 18-year stay, he devoted considerable energy to developing missions in the Mossi region. When in charge of education, he set up schools in Pabré and Manga and also founded a carpet-weaving workshop in Ouagadougou. He went back to Europe for a short period, then returned to Africa in 1921 as he was nominated apostolic vicar of Ouagadougou — which meant that he was Upper Volta's first bishop. During the same year, he reopened the Réo mission and, the following year, founded the order of the Black Sisters. In 1923, he set up the Bam mission, then in 1925, the "Petit Séminaire" (seminary) in Pabré. In 1930, Thévenoud transferred the Ouagadougou catechist school to the recently created Gilongou mission. He went on to set up missions in Koudougou, Kaya, La Toden and Garongo, and the "Grand Séminaire" in Pabré (later transferred to Koumi). In 1934, he ordered that construction work on the unfinished Ouagadougou cathedral be completed. As the bust and plaque on the cathedral's esplanade confirm, Mgr Joanny Thévenoud is considered the "founder of the Burkina Faso Church and a pioneer of social works".

The other well-known figure in the Burkinabè Church is his Eminence, the recently retired Cardinal Paul Zoungrana, one of the first African vicars nominated by the Vatican. As his Eminence pointed out when he inaugurated the new Notre Dame des Apôtres Church at Patte d'oie, Ouagadougou, in August 1992, the occasion coincided with the 50th anniversary of Mgr Thévenoud's ordainment of the first three Burkinabè priests in 1942: "1942 was an important year for our Church. It marks the beginning of when the sons of this country took charge of their own evangelisation…" During his homily, Cardinal Zoungrana also pointed out that fifty years later, his clergy comprised of over three hundred Burkinabè priests.

Christianity, today the religion of 15 to 20 % of the population, has nonetheless not supplanted either animism, which remains predominant in the country, nor Islam (20 to 30 % of the population).

Amongst the important events which have marked Burkina Faso's Christian world, were Pope John Paul II's two recent visits to Africa. The Supreme Pontiff's first major voyage to Africa in May 1980 was the most memorable. It was during this voyage that John Paul II made his famous "Ouagadougou Appeal" (see insert), that had such great repercussions throughout the Third World.

Other churches

Besides the Catholic Church, other churches have been established in Burkina Faso, notably the Protestant Church which has missions in Bobo Dioulasso, Fada N'Gourma, Diapaga, Kaya, Batié, Ouarkoye, etc. Elsewhere, other smaller churches or sects have been set up, for example: the Baptists, the Assemblies of God, the Pentecostal Church, the Apostolic Church, the Evangelical Church, the Bible Life Church, the Christian Alliance...

arts and culture

■ Along with the Baoulé from Côte d'Ivoire, the Dogon from Mali and the Fang from Gabon, most of the ethnic groups in Burkina Faso are amongst Africa's greatest sculptors and their work is collected by major museums all over the world.

Beautiful masks

The large wooden strip masks carved by Bobo sculptors in the Bobo Dioulasso region are particularly beautiful. The largest, which are sometimes up to three metres tall, represent the snake, the village's protecting spirit. Other smaller, highly stylized masks are also zoomorphic, representing diverse protective spirits like the owl, for example, whose round eyes are made from concentric circles and whose hooked beak is formed by a disc and a lath. The geometric designs decorating the beak are one of the village clans' "coat of arms". Other examples are the butterfly, whose form resembles a large aeroplane propeller, the buffalo with its curved horns, the warthog, the cockerel and the fish. This carved bestiary was much admired by European cubist artists at the beginning of the century — Picasso, Braque, Derain, and Juan Gris, amongst others — whose interest then aroused the curiosity of collectors from all over the world.

It is worth mentioning that for the Africans, these sculptures do not have a purely aesthetic function, but are part of the often highly complex animist rites (see section on "Traditions"). The Bobo masks, for example, are used during the annual village purification ceremony which takes place before work is resumed in the fields in order to ensure abundant harvests.

Sénoufo poro carvings

The Sénoufo from south-western Burkina Faso, Mali and Côte d'Ivoire (around Korhogo), are also great sculptors. Working in wood, the carvers make the statuettes and masks used in the *poro* society's secret initiation rites (see section on "Traditions"). Amongst their best known works are the large and highly stylized, almost abstract sculptures representing sacred birds like buceros (the same protecting bird also features in the bas relief on hut doors or on the imposing Sénoufo decorated helmets).

Equally renowned are the Waniougo "fire breathing" masks whose formidable

*Burkinabè traditions are well conserved
in the Manéga museum near to Ouagadougou,
where displays include several masterpieces
of African statuary, like these strip masks.*

jaws evoke the hyena or other carnivores. These sometimes double-faced masks are renowned for their irascible character. They are prone to spreading diseases, causing women to be sterile, or even inciting murder. Much more hieratic, the small anthropomorphic *Kpélié* masks are sculpted in series. Decoration around the face or surmounting the forehead — geometric patterns, figurines representing women, buceros or chameleons — may vary, however. These masks are classics of African art, but those many of the traders sell to tourists are usually imitations. One unusual feature is the two small pieces of wood protruding from the cheeks of the mask. These are not moustaches nor whiskers, but little legs that symbolically link the mask to the earth.

Ritual objects

Other stunning Sénoufo ritual objects are : the canes carried by *poro* initiates which have carved knobs representing female figurines : the large *Déblé* statues representing mythical ancestors (especially the first grandmother); and finally, the extraordinary decorated helmets surmounted by a kind of wooden grill carved with highly stylised figurines. Whilst the meaning of such carvings is a mystery to the layman, initiates will recognise and understand the schema of the cosmos as created by the divine architect Koulotiolo in the carvings.

Abstract sacred art

As the Africanist B. Holas writes: "Sénoufo sacred art manifests a definite predilection for large subject matter and, at the same time, cultivates a schematic foreshortening which borders on abstraction. It thus reflects the rules of a philosophical language which imposes rigorous economy of means of expression.

"Theoretically, a simple allusion should suffice for initiates of the same degree to understand the whole idea. In other words, symbols replace the spoken word which is considered improper because it lacks the subtlety required and demanded by a deeper understanding of things. It is thus

ART, MYTHS AND COSMOGONIES

■ *Here it is time to talk about Black art, which according to legend, made its apparition when death appeared amongst immortal men. As long as the forms embodying life were eternal, there was no need to reproduce them nor to express the laws of the world in these reproductions. As soon as things and beings became transitory, on the other hand, it became necessary for man to provide life with artificially created successive relays. The concern went even further, however. Not content to sculpt suitable forms in materials that if not actually imperishable, were at least renewable, the Blacks attempted to make objects that not only represented the forces, but also acted as milestones marking the laws and principals presiding over the movements of these forces. As the expressions of these principals and these laws saturated the ritual needs, the expression took the form of ordinary utensils and day-to-day objects. Thus certain ornaments carved in wood placed together in a certain order, tell the "story" of the major events in the creation. Elsewhere, a collection of clogs would have the same effect. Amongst other things, art is therefore a projection of myths and cosmogonies in a ritual or common material.*

MARCEL GRIAULE
Originalité des cultures (UNESCO)

that the member of the *poro* will understand the meaning of the more or less esoteric signs carved on the decorated helmets that novices of the society wear during the public ceremonies marking the end of their first trial in the *sinzanga* enclosure".

Flourishing arts and crafts

In this predominantly agricultural country, where industry has not yet developed to the point of manufacturing household objects, arts and crafts still reign. Craft work is not simply thriving but, in spite of pressure from imported objects, is apparently expanding. Enamelled bowls from Nigeria and plastic goods "made in Hong Kong" have not yet replaced the traditional terracotta *canaris* skilfully made by Burkina Faso's innumerable potters. Some of the humble items ranging from furniture, musical instruments and kitchen utensils to agricultural tools, are made with such care and skill that they could be classed as art works.

In south-western Burkina Faso, for example, the Lobi elders make beautiful three-legged stools carved with anthropomorphic heads for the young initiates. Needless to say, these objects are now much sought after by museums all over the world.

Basket work

Basket work is especially fine in Burkina Faso where the Bissa, for example, weave elegant, geometrically patterned baskets using millet stalks. The rims are covered with leather and sometimes decorated with cowrie shells. The Gouin from Banfora weave remarkable stacking baskets for weddings by plaiting palm leaves. The rims are also covered with leather and there are sometimes as many as twelve baskets stacked together.

Burkinabè pottery

Burkinabè pottery is equally remarkable and can be found on sale in specialised markets like the one in Bobo Dioulasso or in the smaller towns and villages like Ziniaré and Guilongou. Such pottery can also be admired in the homes of the Lobi in the south-west, or the Kasséna (Gourounsi) south of Ouagadougou.

In the women's huts inside the *soukala,* pottery of all shapes and sizes is heaped onto dressers that line entire walls. Some Burkinabè pottery is black and glazed, some red and white. Great attention is paid to the usually geometric designs. The Kurumba pots from the north of the country have raised patterns, whereas the Mossi and Gourmantché pots have engraved or painted designs.

Lost wax bronzes

Traditional weaving and dying is another craft speciality in Burkina Faso and the geometric or checked covers woven in the north, especially in Dori, are particularly beautiful. Metal work is also highly reputed in the north where Fulani and Tuareg jewellers make heavy silver bracelets, ankle bracelets and numerous engraved pendants. The Fulani also use gold to make the huge earrings Fulani women wear.

Family workshops specializing in the increasingly common "lost wax bronze" technique have flourished in the Mossi region in the centre of the country and in the Bobo and Dioula regions in the west. Innumerable bronze bracelets, rings, necklaces and statuettes like those once ordered by traditional Mossi chiefs and by the emperor, the Moro Naba, are made in the Niogsin quarter of Ouagadougou.

Leatherwork also became extremely popular when the northern nomadic peoples developed cattle raising (cows and goats). The nomadic groups either tan the hides themselves or send them to specialised tanneries set up in Ouagadougou and Kaya. Having dyed the raw material, the Fulani and Tuareg artisans then make leather sandals and a whole range of bags, sabretaches, purses, wallets, poufs and cushions of all sizes. Many of these articles have hand-painted geometric patterns or are decorated with different coloured, plaited strips of leather.

Burkina Faso's artisans are also highly skilled musical instrument makers and specialise in traditional instruments like drums, flutes, xylophones and lutes.

The arts and crafts show

The Burkinabè authorities have taken several remarkable initiatives to encourage these thriving craft activities. In 1969, for example, the "Centre National de L'Artisanat d'Art" was set up to train young artists and craftsmen in all kinds of modern and traditional disciplines, ranging from sculpture and basketwork to batik-making.

Furthermore, the decision was taken to expand arts and crafts exhibits in the Ouagadougou National Museum (currently under renovation) where in the past, only traditional masks and statuettes were exhibited. Finally, the biennial SIAO (the "Salon International d'Artisanat de Ouagadougou"), a major Pan-African show that brings together hundreds of artisans from all over Africa — was set up a few years ago and has become a great success attracting a wide and enthusiastic public.

Tales, adages, proverbs and riddles

Oral traditions are still more prevalent in Africa than written literature. Even though many of the elders do not know how to read or write, it is they who are considered the most knowledgeable. Tales, epic poems, adages, proverbs and riddles have been memorized since time immemorial and transmitted from generation to generation by word of mouth. It would be disastrous if an elder died without passing on this heritage! As the traditional Malian writer Ahmadou Hampaté Bâ put it so well: "When an elder dies, a library burns". Although in all the young African nations, education and literacy rates have improved enormously since Independence was attained in the Sixties, this has mainly involved the younger generations, and most elders still live amidst the oral traditions.

Burkina Faso's oral traditions are particularly rich due to the diversity of its ethnic groups (there are more than sixty of them) and the durability of its traditional social structures. It is the elders, therefore, who still hold power and ancestral knowledge.

The role of elders and griots

From a very early age, all children in Burkina Faso learn to perceive the world through the tales their grandparents tell them in the evening.

Just like in tales told all over the world, these stories conjure up princes and princesses, heroes, animals and spirits as well as also passing on certain moral values. Of the animals, the hare is noted for its smartness, the hyena for its spinelessness and

the spider for its wisdom. Similarly, when adults launch into interminable afternoon discussions as they chew on cola nuts or drink millet beer, proverbs and adages enliven, punctuate, advance or conclude their long speeches. Nursery rhymes and riddles are most popular amongst the little children. Occasionally a griot — a kind of African bard — will come to perform in the centre of the village or in the court yards of family compounds. Griots are all-round performers who dance, sing, play musical instruments and above all, mime and act as they tell their stories. Generally, griots do not entirely fabricate these tales, but elaborate events from African history, weaving rich, epic tapestries embellished with thousands of anecdotes about the great achievements of powerful Mossi chiefs and their brushes with bellicose neighbours from Macina or Songhai. Although these mimed and sung tales are based on true events, the minor characters and narrative details are pure inventions. It is this ability to improvise a whole story from a few sparse truths that determines the griot's artistic ability. They are not just actors, but also authors whose ephemeral works disappear with the passage of time — unless, of course, a passing ethnologist happens to record and transcribe the narratives onto paper, which was how the country's first written works emerged.

Oral traditions and written works

After Independence, written literature began to develop alongside Burkina Faso's ever-thriving oral traditions. Such literature is strongly marked by the oral traditions as, after being cut off from their roots during the long colonial years, many African writers began by delving into their past and early traditions in order to rediscover their own identities. In the Sixties, therefore, numerous works devoted to African history and studies on traditional African societies flourished. In Crépuscule des Temps anciens, for example, Nazi Boni chronicles the history and traditions of the Bwaba people. Similarly, Professor Joseph Ki-Zerbo devoted a good part of his life to compiling a monumental general history of Africa, which has been translated into nine languages. Other traditionalist authors include A.S. Balima, Gomboukoudougou V. Kaboré and Dim Delobson.

During the same period, the sociologist Yamba Tiendrebeogo, a dignitary in the Moro Naba's court, delved into the

*The Gourounsi are true self-taught
architects and artists,
and have developed a stunning art of building
and decorating their houses
with painted murals.*

vast heritage of the oral traditions to write his *Contes du Larhallé,* a collection of tales, proverbs and mottoes that are integral to Mossi culture.

Griot-inspired poetry

Amongst the most talented poets are Samba Armand Balima, Jacques Guégané and above all, the lawyer Frédéric Pacéré Titinga, winner of the "Grand Prix Littéraire d'Afrique Noire" in 1982. Titinga is a particularly prolific author, and the broken verses and syncopated rhythms of his poetry are greatly inspired by the griots' diction. The content of his works ranges from traditional life in the Mossi villages (*La Poésie des Griots,* Editions Silex, 1982) to the defence of wider causes, like his *Poèmes pour l'Angola.* As the critic Sanogo Bakary so rightly said: "This is the place to recall that the author (Pacéré Titinga) is part of the oral trend in African poetry which delves into tradition and adds its personal re-creation. One can feel through the very typography that the poem is destined to be declaimed and not trapped in writing. The work is the reflection of the African word which is rich in images and symbols".

Two short extracts from the anthology *Du Lait pour une Tombe* (Editions Silex, 1984) illustrate this well:

"There exist/ There will again exist/ On the earth/ Some/ Connoisseurs/ Who struggle/ In silence/ Who cry/ In silence/ Forbidding/ To shed/ Tears".

"One must/ Let/ The/ Power/ Destroy/ Itself./ I mean/ The centre./ Men/ Are not afraid/ Of/ The future./ One must/ Let/ Tomorrow Come/ Itself".

A living theatre

Burkina Faso's theatre has proved its vitality with companies like "Yenenga" (which has put on the plays of Moussa Savadogo, among others) and the "Théâtre de la Fraternité" run by Jean-Pierre Guingané, whose most successful productions were *Coups de Piston* collectively written by the company, *Tu ne m'entendras plus* by Simone Simporé, *Parents de Délinquants* by M. Goungounga and

A WHISTLE LANGUAGE

■ *The very musical Gourounsi people who do not already play in a traditional orchestra, like to play a flute like a kind of long wooden whistle when they go off into the bush. Virtuosos on this wind instrument, they have invented a real whistle language, called* lyelé, *which enables them to communicate with other Gourounsi without alerting strangers. The shepherds — who often wear several whistles around their necks — are experts in long-distance communication with other pastors. They signal the presence of danger to each other but also tease each other in this strange language, or launch challenges.*

The shepherds do not have the monopoly of lyelé, *however, and it is also used by the villagers, as Father François Nicolas, a Catholic missionary in Réo, remarked in the 1930s. When teaching Bible classes to the young people, he noticed that his pupils were constantly disturbed by their whistling friends who were tired of waiting for them outside:*

"They take revenge by whistling the names of my students: a polite way to get them to hurry up (...). Along with his normal name, each of our boys effectively has a nickname or a "combat name", a sort of motto or proverbial phrase, that each one tries to keep untarnished from all defeat or shame.

The impatient whistling meant my people were hurried to be done with the class: "Tain-tain... The sun is up, let's go into the bush". My good Christians do not move, the invitations are still too

works by playwrights from Côte d'Ivoire (Bernard Zadi), Chad (Baba Moustapha) and Senegal (Marouba Fall).

Music in the Sahelian regions

As explained above, the griot — a kind of African troubadour — both composes and performs traditional music in Burkina Faso. When not wandering from village to village alone, the griots often join together to form traditional orchestras at the court of Mossi Chiefs (Naba) or at the Moro Naba's court itself. The musical ensemble usually comprises of percussion instruments which accompany a solo singer. Instruments include *luinssé* drums, which are tucked under the arm, and little *bendéré* drums. Together these drums seem to transcribe the griot's declamations into rythms and sounds. Singing griots may recount their masters' great achievements and run through their very complicated genealogy for hours.

The *balafon*, a large traditional xylophone which, although found throughout West Africa, is particularly prevalent in Burkina Faso, is an integral feature in all celebrations. During the Bobo celebrations at the end of the dry season, for example, the balafon accompanies the dance of the masks — a magnificent spectacle incorporating all art forms from music and dance to painting and sculpture.

Musical traditions

During these large traditional celebrations, the balafon is often accompanied by drums and numerous wind instruments like whistles, flutes, clarinets and horns. The transverse flute is predominant amongst the Bisa, the Mossi, the Sénoufo and the nomadic peoples like the Fulani. The Lobi in the south-west of Burkina Faso (the Gaoua region) are very musical and during long walks in the bush, often improvise very nostalgic melodies on a wooden carved whistle worn around the neck. The Gourounsi (south of Ouagadougou) have invented a complete whistle language (see inset). Virtuosos on the *bobal* clarinet, the Bisa from south of the

vague, but soon become more specific...
"Train-train... One cannot caress a thorn bush". That is the "combat name" of Paul on my left. He scowls a little, and continues to listen to my lesson on angels.
"Fi...tifi. One cannot carry a newborn elephant in a pouch". Large Hilarion knows he is being called; his neighbours glance at him briefly... Angels are pure spirits; it is difficult to explain, in spite of the very clear notes dictated by a teacher freshly awarded his angelical diploma!
"Train...fi...fi...tain...", they whistle outside: "Even the hand of the blind man finds his mouth" — "Tin...tin... It is not possible to assemble the stone of the mill with an egg" — "Fi...tain...fi...fi. An ember in the hand weighs more than a beam".
My students become restless. I explain the angels' Rebellion. They are not listening to me anymore, however, but are getting impatient: they are being summoned. Their "combat names" and additional cheers get louder, more urgent...
All of a sudden the class bursts out laughing... It must be because of the whistles outside which speak a language I do not understand. I ask the reason: "Father", someone answers, "the low whistle (the double bass, as it were) does not know Jean-Marie's "combat name" and he is whistling: "Marie, Marie, Marie" as if calling a woman". There was nothing left to do but end the class..."

Throughout Africa, dance and
traditional music are inseparable.
Drums of all shapes and sizes
are the predominant feature of the music.

Mossi region also play another wind instrument peculiar to their ethnic group: the *boumpa*.

Unusual instruments

The "mouth bow" is both a wind and string instrument and has a single string which the player holds between his lips and hits with a stick. The sound is modified according to how far the player's mouth is open or closed.

Another remarkable instrument is the *sanza* or "thumb piano", a small portable "piano" with metal strips for keys.

A large range of string instruments are also found in Burkina Faso where techniques differ greatly from classical Western instrument making. The most common are the *doudouga*, an old instrument with one string, and the two stringed *kondé* lute. The latter is a magnificent, beautifully-shaped, long instrument which is either played on its own or accompagnies singers for hours. In Burkina Faso, singing is also renowned for its vitality and originality. Traditional Bisa singers, for example, nearly always use a five-note scale and are fond of tremolo and vibrato.

The spread of Christianity in Burkina Faso has breathed life back into religious music. In many churches, the congregation joins in as the choir sings mass. Generally, the liturgy is in Moré (the most widespread language in Burkina Faso) and is accompanied by singers and musicians playing traditional African instruments, notably drums. Several Burkinabè priests have composed typically African masses, for example, the priest Robert Ouedraogo who recorded a *Messe des Savanes*, with the help of the choir from the Pabré seminary near Ouagadougou. Another priest, Georges Yaogho, also worked with the Pabré seminary choir to record the beautiful *Psaumes du Mossi* and the *Chants sacrés Mossi*.

Popular music

Even if Burkinabè popular music is not yet as internationally well-known as Senegalese, Ivoirian and Zaïrian music, it is nonetheless thriving. Most groups play in clubs in Ouagadougou or Bobo Dioulasso, or during Pan-African music festivals and the "Semaine nationale de la Culture" (national cultural week).

Of the many, sometimes ephemeral bands formed, the best known are "Super Volta", "Volta Jazz", "Bozambo", "la Famille Bassavet" and "Vampires". The most popular band appears to be "Desi et les Sympathics". Such bands have brought very good musicians to the public attention. Those musicians (often singers and guitarists) are making records and embarking on international careers—for instance Moustapha Tiombano, Seydou Zombra, Cissé Abdoulaye, Toé Niongui and Jean Tapsoba. Some have even won highly esteemed awards (i.e.: RFI's "Maracas d'Or").

Cultural weeks

In 1983, the Burkinabè authorities began organising a national cultural week in order to breathe life back into its culture and stimulate artistic creation in the country. Every year, the event takes place in a different location, whether a major centre like Ouagadougou or Bobo Dioulasso or a small town like Gaoua. During the cultural week, the country's dance companies and traditional bands get together to perform, arts and crafts exhibitions are organised and literary contests are held. A jury picks out the best performers in each category, the aim being to encourage the various artists to take advantage of Burkina Faso's particularly rich traditional cultural heritage. During the festival, other fringe events take place, including fashion shows, cookery competitions, conferences and debates on cultural matters.

Sahelian architecture

Round huts with pointed, thatched roofs are found throughout sub-Saharan Africa. They are so widespread that they have become emblematic to the point where they tend to eclipse other styles of wonderful traditional African architecture. In Burkina Faso, not all homes resemble the round huts and granaries characteristic of the Mossi *zaka* (family compounds), even if this style is found throughout the country. In the old quarters of large towns like Bobo Dioulasso and in little villages tucked away in the bush, other less common architectural styles reveal the African artisans/masons' extraordinary creativity. Usually using earth as their building material, they have developed the superb "Sudanese" style evocative of

cubist sculpture which is found throughout the Sahelian regions (for example, the Mopti and Djenné mosques in Mali and the old town of Zinder in Niger). Unlike hewn stone, parpens, aluminium sheets or glass, earth is malleable and can be easily shaped to suit the builder's every whim. It could be said that the builders are in fact more like sculptors or potters modeling clay forms. Moreover, earth has the added advantage of being free and is also an excellent insulator against noise and heat.

The old quarters

In Burkina Faso it is worth visiting the old quarters of Bobo Dioulasso where mud houses with roof terraces encircle the very old earthen mosque. With its many towers, cylindrical minarets and bristling posts (used as ladders by masons and as perches by birds), the mosque evokes the "ideal palace" of Facteur Cheval, a French naive artist.

Labyrinth houses

Lobi and Gourounsi habitations are the finest examples of this earthy architecture. Throughout history, the Lobi, a particularly resistant people, often did battle with their bellicose Kong neighbours and the Samory *sofas* (warriors) without ever being defeated. Settled near the border with Côte d'Ivoire in the southwest of Burkina Faso, they used to take refuge in these earthen fortress houses where they could protect themselves from all external attacks.

Protective fortresses

Like medieval European fortified castles, the Lobi habitations are huge with almost no openings. In the past, there were no entrances in the external walls and the only access to the houses inside was via ladders made from notched tree trunks which led onto the roof terraces. As soon as the alarm was given, the ladders were removed and the Lobi awaited their enemy safely hidden on the roof terraces armed with poisoned arrows. As Lobi compounds usually have a well in the courtyard and immense millet granaries and stables for the cattle inside, they were also equipped to withstand a siege.

Now that the Lobi are no longer threatened by such ferocious enemies, their compounds have one or two entrances leading into a hall. The layout of the compound's rooms is still the same, however. The various rooms are often lit simply by a single trap door in the roof, and are linked together by narrow, closed corridors. The rooms and corridors form a very dark labyrinth and one would not be surprised if the minotaur were to emerge from the shadows! In spite of their rather sombre appearance, the Lobi compounds can be quite elegant as the facade and walls of the interior rooms are sometimes decorated with geometric designs in relief.

Organic architecture

South of Ouagadougou near the Ghanaian border, the Gourounsi compounds are even more spectacular. When approaching such a compound, the eye is immediately drawn to the large frescoes decorating the walls of the huts outside and inside. The Gourounsi women trace sumptuous checked, diamond-shaped, hatching or herringbone geometric patterns on the walls in black paint. Sometimes designs include complete bestiaries with skilfully painted stylised lizards, snakes, antelopes, lions, etc., or traditional portraits of man hunting with bows and arrows or farming, or more up to date, men travelling in bush taxis or on bicycles.

Unlike Lobi compounds which are very compact, the Gourounsi round huts with flat roofs are spread out over large areas and surrounded by high exterior walls. Low walls form interior courtyards of various sizes, linking the huts together. According to specialists, Gourounsi town planning is typically "organic". Just like live cells which split and multiply and form aggregates, the compound initially comprises of only the husband and his wives' huts. As their children reach adulthood and marry, the parents' compound is expanded to include the children's huts. After several generations, the compound becomes a mini galaxy of a hundred or so huts with their interior courtyards and granaries forming a series of concentric circles around the original core, the first family's compound.

A real maze

The function of the various sections becomes clear as one walks through the maze of alleys and courtyards. Some courtyards serve as corrals for small animals like goats and poultry, others as open-air kitchen/dinning areas, and others as playgrounds for the children or meeting places for the elders. The huts have narrow entrances you have to crawl into and are both a refuge from potential aggressors or the heat, and a bedroom for the numerous wives in the Gourounsi community.

There are also indoor kitchens which are used mainly during the rainy season, huge earthenware jars used as grain silos, stables and even artisanal breweries where the women make millet beer.

The traditional huts contain very little furniture — a few little benches, an armchair and innumerable calabashes which are used as bowls, containers for keeping small personal items and money boxes for hiding the owner's savings.

The earth used to make these compounds is of a very different texture to that used by the Lobi. Whereas the texture of the Lobi compounds is raw and cracked, the Gourounsi mix shea oil into the laterite they use, making it smooth and shiny. Once dry, the talented Gourounsi women paint their magnificent frescoes on this perfectly smooth, glazed-looking roughcast.

The capital of African cinema

Apart from a few educational documentaries on farming and hygiene made first by the French colonialists and then, after Independence, by Burkinabè officials, nothing whatsoever suggested that Ouagadougou would become an international film centre.

Being a poor country, Burkina Faso certainly had no illusions in this domain, knowing that the seventh art is an industry that requires substantial financial means. Moreover after Independence, Upper Volta as it was then called, did not appear to be a secret breeding ground for future film directors, unlike Senegal, for example, where directors like Ousmane Sembène had already made promising debuts.

In 1963, Sembène achieved a certain degree of success at the Tours Festival in France with his short film *Borrom Sarret*. Three years later he did it again with his film *La Noire de...* ("Black Girl of..."), the first African feature film. In 1968 his film *Mandabi* ("The Money Order") won an award at the Venice Film Festival.

*The beauty of their forms
and of their decorative frescoes place
the Gourounsi huts in Burkina Faso
amongst the classics of Sudanese earthen architecture.*

The first
FESCAPO

At that time, the Burkinabè Minister of Information had to get French directors to come to shoot the ministry's educational documentary films as there were no directors in the country.

In February 1969, however, an important event was to take place, which dramatically changed the course of events, namely the creation of the first "Festival Panafricain du Cinéma de Ouagadougou" (FESPACO). Although the first festival was modest — there were only fifteen films from four African countries and a public of 10,000 enthusiasts — it was nonetheless a starting point. The results did not discourage the organisers, who went on to programme a festival for the following year, the year after and up until today when this now biennial festival shows about a hundred films from all over Africa, organises conferences and creates a market for African films.

The development of cinema

1970 was a turning point for Upper Volta's cinema, as the Burkinabè authorities decided to nationalise the country's film concerns (six cinemas in Ouagadougou and Bobo Dioulasso) which until then had been monopolised by the major French distribution companies, and set up the SONAVOCI ("Société Nationale Voltaïque du Cinéma") to run these cinemas. In ten years, the SONAVOCI tripled the number of cinemas in the country and, using the takings, created a fund used to finance films made by Burkinabè directors. For a while boycotted by the distributors, Upper Volta later came to a friendly agreement with them and was able to project both foreign films and run its own cinemas.

African creations

Upper Volta's victory had repercussions throughout Africa and roused the conscience of top officials in other countries who also wished to "decolonise Africa's screens". Over the following years, meetings took place between the governments of countries belonging to the OCAM and led to the creation of the CIDC ("Consortium Interafricain de Distribution Cinématographique") the aim of which was to take charge of the importa-

tion of films and of the distribution network in Africa. Moreover, a Pan-African production company (CIPROFILM) was envisaged to produce the films of African directors. Unsurprisingly, it was decided that the headquarters of these companies would be based in the Volta capital!

"Le Sang des Parias"

1970 was an effervescent year for African cinema and, with the creation of the FEPACI ("Fédération Panafricaine de Cinéastes") which, by bringing together 33 countries, aimed to protect the young African cinema, the film industry became more organised.

In Burkina Faso, these initiatives began to stimulate cinema-related jobs and in 1969 and 1970, Sékou Ouedraogo shot several educational documentaries. It was not until the 2nd FESPACO in 1973, however, that Volta's first fiction feature film appeared. In his melodrama Le Sang des Parias (16 mm, colour, 90 mn), teacher- director Djim Mamadou Kola attacked the caste system (the money used to make the film came from the famous SONAVOCI's fund alimented by the cinema takings).

Four years later in 1976, it was the turn of René-Bernard Yonly — librarian at the University of Ouagadougou and president of the town's "Ciné-club" — to direct the second feature film in the history of Upper Volta's cinema. His film, Sur le Chemin de la Réconciliation (16 mm, colour) denounced politics and the political parties' habit of stirring up ill-feeling in the villages.

Talented directors

After these first two films came the master's stroke! In 1982, the first feature film made by Gaston Kaboré, former teacher at the INAFEC ("Institut Africain d'Education Cinématographique"), the film school that opened in Ouagadougou in 1977, and the then head of the "Centre National du Cinéma", came out on Volta's screens. Wend Kuunid ("The Gift of God") is a particularly well-filmed tale that takes place in a village, with two remarkably directed children as the central characters. This little masterpiece aroused interest in Europe when it was distributed there and brought attention to the promising new Volta cinema. Two other feature films also made their mark on the country's film history that year:

Paweogo ("The Emigrant"), a moral comedy by Sanou Kollo — a director who had already come to light with several short films like *Beogho Naba* (1978) on unemployment and young people, and *Les Dodos* (1980), an African tale — and *Le Courage des Autres* by the Frenchman Christian Richard, who used an entirely Burkinabè crew to shoot an African episode of the slave trade.

The "short film school"

Five years later, another young Burkinabè director confirmed all these hopes and the take off of his country's cinema industry. In 1990, Idrissa Ouedraogo's film *Tilaï* won the highest award at the Cannes Film Festival: the "Grand Prix du Jury". Unlike his predecessors, Idrissa Ouedraogo had never been, or wanted to be involved in anything else but filmmaking. In 1977 when he was only 23 years old, he was one the first students at the INAFEC, the film school that had just opened in Ouagadougou. Already in 1978, he shot his first short film *Poko* (16 mm, 20 mn, colour) which portrays the Burkinabè farmers' harsh life. His talent as a director was already apparent in this short film and it won an award at the 7th FESPACO in 1981. As Idrissa Ouedraogo himself emphasizes: "As practice makes perfect and as one must not waste money, the cheaper short film is ideal for learning the job".

A picture of daily life

Having shot other short films (*Les Ecuelles* 11 mn, and *Issa le Tisserand,* 20 mn, colour) and having finished his course at the IDHEC in France ("Institut des Hautes Etudes Cinématographiques"). Idrissa Ouedraogo started working on his first feature film *Yam Daabo* ("The Choice"). Shot in rural settings in Boromo and Ouahigouya, the film used only amateur actors and was filmed in Moré (the Mossi language). Its message is that African traditions are not dogmas and that in cases of absolute necessity, they can be abandoned. As the film's director explains: "This film portrays farmers who are victims of drought and who are waiting for the international food aid they have become dependent upon. Paradoxically, it is one of the elders who reacts and leaves the now sterile ancestral lands, taking his whole family to find good agricultural land. Did you know that in Burkina Faso, we have nine million hectares of farming land, of which only three million are farmed... The worst! I therefore wanted to show in this film that traditions should not lead to poverty and death: the ancestral lands are very important, but people should not hesitate in leaving them if children's lives are in danger".

"Grand Prix" at Cannes...

Yam Daabo, which was distributed in both Africa and Europe and was much appreciated by well-informed cinema enthusiasts, won eight awards at the 10th FESPACO in 1987. This was just the beginning of the consecration. In 1989, Ouedraogo's second feature *Yaaba*—the story of an unusual friendship between a young boy and an old lady who is ostracised by the villagers — received the "Prix de la Critique Internationale" at the 42nd Cannes Film Festival. The supreme distinction, the "Grand Prix du Jury", was awarded to Idrissa Ouedraogo the next year at the 43rd Cannes Festival (1990) for his third film *Tilaï* ("The Law").

...the critic's approval

As the critic Jacques Siclier wrote in the magazine "Télérama": "One cannot overstress the importance of this director from Burkina Faso who, even though his films are financed by co-production agreements with European countries, does not try to imitate Western cinema and, unlike other African directors, is not content to make somewhat unpolished experimental films with social messages. He draws his subject matter and style from the depths of African culture. *Tilaï* questions patriarchal power and the code of honour in Burkina Faso, which is no longer compatible with modern life. A man and a woman prefer their love to ancestral law. They are condemned and their story implacably becomes a tragedy. Idrissa Ouedraogo avoids all picturesque details, all that to our Europen eyes could be seen as simply folkloric. Nature is wild, the earth hard, demanding. The characters would be in harmony with the setting if they were not under ancestral constraints. For the women, everything is forbidden. It is thus necessary to transgress the law, so that the idea of the couples' individual success, of their happiness, can finally see the light of day. A refined film. Superb".

*Ouagadougou, the capital of African cinema,
is one of the rare towns in the world
to have erected an imposing monument
to film right in the city centre.*

Idrissa Ouedraogo's most recent films include *Samba Traoré*, a film that denounces the corrupting influence of the town and which won the Silver Bear award at the 1993 Berlin Film Festival; *Le Cri du Coeur* (1995), Ouedraogo's first film set in France; and *Kini and Adams* (1997), a touching and amusing English-language film about friendship set in Zimbabwe, and which was selected in the Official Competition of the 1997 Cannes Film Festival.

A social critique

Amongst other young, promising directors are Pierre Yameogo and Drissa Touré, both of whom presented their films at the 44th Cannes Festival in 1991. In his feature film *Laafi* ("Everything's fine") Yameogo portrays the difficulties in continuing in higher education. In *Laada*, Touré films the story of two young people who return to their birthplace where one of them accepts the tradition and the other does not. After *Laada*, Drissa Touré went on to make *Haramuya*, a scathing portrait of African city life, with its crimes and various types of trafficking. *Haramuya* was first shown at the FESPACO, then selected in the "Un certain regard" section of the 1995 Cannes film festival.

Dany Kouyaté's masterful first film *Keita* launched Kouyaté as one of Burkina's promising new talents. The film, which tells the legendary tale of the great Mandingue emperor Soundiata Keita, won the best First Film prize at the 1995 FESPACO.

the economy

■ Agriculture continues to be Burkina Faso's major economic activity. More than 90% of Burkina's ten million inhabitants and over 70 % of the working population survive on or are involved in farming. Unlike other West African countries, Burkina Faso's farm land is mainly devoted to growing food crops as the country is trying to rapidly become completely self-suficient in foodstuff. Cereals are therefore grown on most of the country's farm lands : sorghum in the wetter regions, and millet in the drier regions with sandy soil. With yields of over 2 million metric tons a year, these two African cereals alone account for 73 % of Burkina Faso's cultivated lands. Millet is generally grown in the arid northern region, whereas elsewhere, where it is more humid, sorghum is more common. In the Mossi region, in central Burkina Faso, both cereals are grown so that if an untimely drought hits the country, there will still be a harvest of sorts.

An agricultural country

Amongst the other complementary food crops grown are corn (293,000 metric tons a year), cassava, yam, rice (147,000 metric tons a year) and groundnuts (203,000 metric tons). Like rice and yams, most of them, are grown in Burkina Faso's more humid regions, for example in the extreme south-west (the Turka, Goin, Sénoufo and Lobi regions), Burkina Faso also produces 340,000 metric tons of sugar cane a year which is processed into sugar by the Sosuco plant in Banfora (22,000 to 28,000 metric tons a year).

In spite of efforts to develop food production, the country is not yet self-sufficient in this domain and has to import over 120,000 metric tons of cereals of year.

Cotton, fruit and vegetables

Certain food crops like rice, karite kernels, sesame seeds and groundnuts are also exported. Mainly concentrated in the west (Bobo country) around Boromo, Dédougou, Houndé and Bobo Dioulasso, cotton farming is thriving. Whilst only 32,000 metric tons of cotton seeds were produced per year in the Seventies, production has now reached 206,000 metric tons a year. Some of the cotton is treated in Burkina Faso (ginning, spinning and weaving mainly take place at the Kou-dougou textile complex), and some is exported to the Far East and Europe.

Cotton exports, which overtook exports of produce from cattle rearing about ten years ago, are now the main factor stabilising Burkina Faso's balance of trade.

Fruit and vegetables are also sold locally and exported. Market gardening and fruit production, which are dry season activities, developed around towns largely in response to demand from the city dwellers (mainly top civil servants and European expatriates), but also for exportation. French beans and tomatoes from Kongoussi (north of Ouagadougou, in the Mossi region) and grafted mangoes from Banfora (south-west) are now the country's third export product after cotton and produce from cattle rearing.

Cattle raising and fishing

Burkina Faso's livestock has now completely recovered from the periodic droughts that destroyed the country's pastures in 1974 and 1984/85. Today 4.24 million cows, 5.5 million sheep and 7 million goats are reared by nomads in the north, by both nomads and settled farmers in most of the country, and by settled farmers in the south. Output is nonetheless hindered both by traditions (for the Fulani pastors, for example, the cows are part of their heritage and must not be slaughtered) and by the reduction of pastures caused by desertification (due both to drought and to over-exhaustion of pasture land). However, the 1994 devaluation gave a significant boost to this sector which in the past was undermined by fierce European competition.

Freshwater fishing is practised in the rivers and streams in Burkina Faso (the Mounhoun, Nakambé, Nazinon, Comoé, Sourou, etc.), the lakes (Bam and Dem), the creeks, and the man-made dams reservoirs (ie: the Kompienga dam in the Gourma region south-east of the capital).

Water and modern technology

In an effort to help the country's agriculture develop, the Burkinabè authorities have undertaken a series of long-term projects designed to alleviate the inconveniences of the arid climate and to get around the rural farmers' archaic traditions. Situated in the Sahelian region, Burkina Faso is too frequently a victim of either cyclical droughts which affect the whole region or of a capricious pluviometry whose too heavy rainfalls furrow the good arable lands. One of the key concepts in Burkina Faso is therefore "water control", which is achieved by digging numerous wells, constructing dams and large areas of irrigation. A large dam was recently constructed on the River Kompienga near to Pama in the east of the country, for example, and now provides water to the farming lands.

Furthermore, its reservoir offers a plentiful supply of fish, and freshwater fishing now provides the local inhabitants with many resources. Another dam is currently under construction at Bagré, also in the east of the country.

Increasing farmland

Another of the government projects has been to increase the amount of good arable land. Until recently, only one tenth of the land was used for farming. In Burkina Faso's river valleys, millions of hectares suitable for agriculture were completely avoided by the farmers. Although rich in alluvium, terrible diseases like onchocerciasis (when larvae laid in the eyes by flies cause blindness) were prevalent in these valleys. Thanks to a huge and thorough clearing programme launched by the ONAT ("Office National de l'Aménagement des Terroirs") more than 47,400 km² of new land have been reclaimed, notably in the Mouhoun, Bougouriba, Sourou and Kompienga valleys. All that remained was to get farmers to emigrate from the overpopulated regions which could no longer feed their inhabitants — like Kouritenga in the Koupéla region or Oubritenga (Ziniaré) in the centre of the country — to the new lands. Here the authorities were no longer fighting against natural factors like droughts, but against man's deeply rooted beliefs and traditions. As Idrissa Ouedraogo's film *Yam Daabo* ("The Choice") illustrates so well, the Burkinabè farmers' sacrosanct attachment to their ancestral lands sometimes causes them to starve to death in their drought-stricken villages rather than to seek their fortune elsewhere on better land. A sizeable colony has formed, however, settling mainly in the Diébougou region (southwestern Burkina Faso) and the Zabré region (south of the capital).

Another tradition the authorities are trying to change is the practice of burning the bush to clear farming land as it leaves the charred land vulnerable to wind and rain erosion and even reduces fertility by burning bacteria and worms. In the place of rudimentary tool, like the *daba* (traditional hoe), still frequently used by the women to carry out extremely arduous work in the fields, the authorities also want to develop the use of horse or ox - drawn ploughs. In the 1990s, only 14% of farms used this kind of farming equipment. Finally, Burkina Faso's agriculture also suffers from the farming land being too fragmented. Practically all farming is carried out on little family plots.

The Burkinabè authorities are also faced with the fact that Burkina Faso is a land-locked country over 800 km from the sea (Gulf of Guinea). All of the country's export products are thus disadvantaged by the hefty extra rail and road transportation coasts incurred when taking the goods to the ports. These products are therefore less competitive than those from neighbouring Côte d'Ivoire, Benin, Togo and Ghana which all have easy access to the sea.

Transportation developments

As already mentioned, the problem of transportation is a real headache for all landlocked countries — and explains their obsessive determination to develop communication infrastructures no matter what. Burkina Faso is one of the best examples : in the Fifties, the arrival of the Abidjan railway line in Bobo Dioulasso, then Ouagadougou stimulated the economy and triggered the growth of these two towns. In the Sixties, the country immediately contributed to the expansion of African air transport by becoming one of the original member States of the multinational air company "Air Afrique". Finally, in the Seventies, Burkina Faso considerably developed its road network, constructing modern major national networks of surfaced roads linked to the networks of neighouring countries.

Tambao manganese

Nowadays the problem of the transportation infrastructure — which has greatly encouraged to the development of trading on a national and regional level — is most acute with regards to the mining sector which remains unexploited. Burkina Faso' substratum is in fact rich in resources but it is difficult to exploit them as they are far from the roads and often pose insoluble drainage problems. At the moment, a little antimony is mined at Mafoulo, some gold at Poura near to Boromo, marble at Tiara and phosphates at Kodjari. In total, this mining production involves just 2 % of the working population, and represents about 2 % of the GNP. Things would be different if the country's deposits of manganese, limestone, bauxite, copper and zinc were exploited, but that would necessitate major investments in the roads or railways, water reserves and mining towns, which is not realistic given Burkina Faso's current budget. International funding backers have already been approached but it would take a great deal more to persuade them, however, as their recent policy is to favour smaller, low-risk projects.

Ambitious planning

The ambitious project to exploit the neighbouring deposits of manganese at Tambao and limestone at Tin-Hrassan discovered in the far north-east of Burkina Faso just before Independence (at the end of the Fifties), has thus been put on hold for a while. According to specialists, the ore content of the Tambao manganese is high (52.5 %) and there are large reserves of about 10 million tons which would permit the constant extraction of about 500,000 tons a year. As for Tin-Hrassan's limestone, it could meet both the needs of cement works and the domestic market. As these deposits are off the beaten track, however, major work on the railway would be necessary to extend the line over 300 km eastwards from Ouagadougou to Tambao. The projected route would go from the capital to Markoye, via Barsologho and Gorom Gorom. The water that would be needed by the works treating Tambao's manganese and Tin-Hrassan's limestone, would come from reservoirs supplied by the River Béli, one of the Niger's tributaries, which flows close to Tin-Hrassan and Tambao. There are also plans to exploit the Perkoa zinc deposits.

Prosperous arts and crafts

In both the towns and villages of Burkina Faso, arts and crafts are very well developed. The arts and crafts sector includes both utilitarian activities, like clothes making, basketry or pottery, and a wide range of artistic activities like

*Artisanal exploitations like the one here near to Yako
are springing up all over Burkina Faso, a country rich
in gold-bearing deposits. At Poura in the west of the country
on the other hand, individual gold prospectors
give way to SOREMIB's industrialised exploitations.*

embroidery, wood or bronze sculpting, leather work, painting and jewellery making. This sector currently represents about 4 % of the GNP and employs over half of the people working in the industrial sector.

International craft shows

The public powers have not ignored the vitality of the many arts and crafts activities, and over the last few years, they have taken several initiatives to organise and support this sector better. The creation of the "Salon International de l'Artisanat de Ouagadougou" (SIAO), for example, has proven to be most opportune, as it enables Burkina Faso's artisans to meet and exchange experiences with colleagues from other African countries whilst also having the opportunity to exhibit their products to a wider public, thereby considerably enlarging their market.

Heavily dependent on agriculture, Burkina Faso's still embryonic industry has mainly developed parallel to the food, agriculture and textile industries.

Such industries have grown up near the major road axes and railways, meaning that their products can be easily transported to neighbouring countries with access to the sea (Côte d'Ivoire, Ghana, Togo and Benin). Most of the country's industries are concentrated around the two main urban centres Ouagadougou and Bobo Dioulasso, which are very well connected to the roads and railways, and in the secondary industrial centres Banfora and Koudougou. 71 % of Burkina Faso's industrial enterprises are located in the capital alone. As already mentioned, Ouagadougou owes its position as the country's major town to the arrival of the railway in the 1950s and to the fact it was designated the capital of the new State of Upper Volta when the country gained Independence in 1960. This meant that both the administrative structures of the new government and many businesses set up in Ouagadougou rather than in Bobo Dioulasso, the country's original economic centre.

Nearly all the large industrial groups have a base in Ouagadougou which has several industrial zones comprising of textile factories, breweries, canning factories and mechanical workshops.

Although industrialised earlier than its rival Ouagadougou, there are less businesses based in Bobo Dioulasso. On the other hand, however, three of the country's six largest industrial groups are found there : the "Société des Fibres Textiles" (SOFITEX, formerly called SFT). The "Société des Huiles et Savons du Burkina" (SHSB) and the "Société Industrielle du Faso" (SIFA) which makes all the "two wheelers" in the country and their spare parts.

Along with these three major businesses, other factories like breweries and canning factories are also found in Bobo Dioulasso. The "Société Africaine de Pneumatiques", a chemical and rubber business, is also based there. In total, about 18 % of Burkina Faso's industries are based in Bobo Dioulasso.

Secondary industrial centres

A few other secondary centres have also developed in Burkina Faso, specialising in one industrial activity. In Koudougou, west of Ouagadougou, for example, the large company Faso-Fani specialises in treating cotton, from the ginning, spinning and weaving to the printing of the material and is even involved in making hosiery articles.

The little town of Banfora, west of Bobo Dioulasso, specialises in food and agriculture: its sugar cane plantations supply the SOSUCO complex ("Société Sucrière de la Comoé") which produces from 22,000 to 28,000 tons of sugar a year.

Also based in Banfora, the "Grands Moulins du Burkina" produce flour and other foodstuff from imported cereals — like wheat — or local cereals like corn and sorghum. Further more, a factory producing alcohol (pharmaceutical and otherwise) has recently been set up in Banfora.

The future of Burkina Faso's industries also depends on the ability to supply the plants with abundant and cheap energy. Thermal power stations have been built, but they have the major drawback of running on fuel that is imported at great expense due to the long transportation distances. The Burkinabè authorities have thus begun to construct hydro-electric dams over the last few years, which will gradually help make the country self-sufficient in energy and also have the advantage of helping both industry (by supplying electricity) and agriculture (by irrigating large agricultural areas). The first dam was built on the Kompienga River near to Pama in south-eastern Burkina Faso and another is currently under construction at Bagré. The authorities also envisage linking up Burkina Faso's electricity network with that of Côte d'Ivoire.

The tertiary sector (services) is not as vast as it is in many African countries, employing only 13 % of the working population, compared with 31 % in Côte d'Ivoire, 34 % in Ghana and 35 % in Benin. The authorities in Burkina Faso have not only made efforts to control corruption in the civil service, but also to avoid the development of a plethoric bureaucracy. Within the framework of the Structural Adjustment Programme introduced in 1991, they have significantly reduced the number of civil servants.

Also part of the services sector, traditional and modern commerces from town and village markets to boutiques and supermarkets are especially active in a country which acts as the crossroads of the whole region, particularly since Burkina Faso has equipped itself with a good road network that links up with those in neighbouring countries and since its railway to Abidjan in Côte d'Ivoire and the ports has been revitalized.

Burkina also has access to the sea via Togo's cargo port in Lomé. Indeed, since the introduction of the "Solidarity with the sea" scheme, convoys of lorries accompanied by motorbike police now shuttle backwards and forwards between Lomé and Ouagadougou without being stopped for police and customs controls, which considerably speeds up the transportation of goods arriving in and leaving Lomé.

Tourism, the industry of the future

Tourism, a highly promising tertiary activity, is still embryonic in Burkina Faso where there are 150,000 foreign visitors a year. The recent development of hotels and transport infrastructures, the beauty of a country steeped in traditions, the security that reigns in the country and the warmth of the inhabitants all suggest, however, that a real "leisure industry" will soon take off in Burkina Faso.

RIDDLES

■ *What are always found in water but never blossom nor bear fruit? (answer: teeth).*
What go visiting but never come back? (leaves).
What bursts in the sky, without anyone picking up the pieces? (the stars).
What flaps its wings without flying? (a sieve).
I looked over the cliff top, and heard whisperings in a secret language, what was it? ("dolo", or millet beer fermenting).
All my father's sons have pointed teeth, what am I? (rice).
The owner of the house cannot see the hall nor the rooms, what is it? (an ear).
I tie up my horse in the house, but its tail can be seen outside (smoke).
A little man with a big knife (corn).
I killed my cow and drew its blood out by the tail (a pipe).
Which large tree leaf is divided into three? (the sky, the earth and water).

site by site

ouagadougou

■ Binger, the French Captain who came to explore the Mossi kingdom at the end of the last century, would be in for a shock if he went back to Ouagadougou today!

Instead of an agglomeration of insalubrious villages and barely more than 5,000 inhabitants, he would find a fresh-looking agglomeration, now the capital of Burkina Faso with a population of nearly a million people. He would be even more surprised to find that the round huts and swampy shallows were nowhere in sight, having been replaced by large, shady avenues, innumerable modern, futurist buildings — large hotels, conference centres, airline companies, banks — and even a Burkinabè version of the Parisian Bois de Boulogne with lakes and dams! He would be equally dumbstruck at the sight of the attractive main roads, as wide as flooded rivers, abuzz at all hours with ten of thousands of whizzing "two-wheelers"!

"Come and honour me"

As far back as the griots' tales go in history, there always appears to have been a little village on the site of modern day Ouagadougou. Probably founded in the 11ᵗʰ century by the Nyonyosé—apparently the first settlers in Burkina Faso—long before the Mossi came to the region, it was not long before they were taken over, however. Oubri, whose grandfather Ouedraogo founded the first Mossi dynasty, set out from Tenkodogo, south-east of Ouagadougou, and headed westwards to conquer new lands. He defeated the famous Nyonyosé and took over their little capital Kombemtinga, the "Land of Warriors". In order to assert his position as the new leader and to be certain that the Kombemtinga Nyonyosé pledged their allegiance to him, Oubri changed the name of the town to "Wogdo", meaning "Come and honour me". Griots, historians, geographers and explorers all played their part in deforming this drum beat sounding name. Over time "Wogdo" became "Wogodogo", then "Waghadougou", before finally becoming Ouagadougou.

Designated the capital of the Mossi empire under the Moro Naba Niandéfo in 1441, Ouagadougou was later to become the capital of Upper Volta (between 1919 and 1932, then again between 1947

OUAGADOUGOU MARKET IN THE 19ᵀᴴ CENTURY

■ *Between 1887 and 1889, the French Captain Binger travelled throughout the whole of West Africa where he spent some time in the Mossi kingdoms. This is his description of the Ouagadougou market :*
"The market is held in Waghadougou every three days, as is the custom in the Mossi region; on the other days, there is a little market. The only difference with the main market is the greater number of visitors and the din that is made. Like in the Follona region, dolo *is sold and, furthermore, the market is the rendez-vous of all the griots in the region—and there are plenty of them. If they only make a few cowries, they have the satisfaction (?) of being drunk by the evening.*
It is impossible to hear oneself think around the dolo urns with all these musicians playing their lounga *(stringed drums),* doudéga *(a kind of violin with a bow),* gangang-o *(a drum made from a calabash) and* ouér'a *(flute). After the dolo, in order of importance, are the prepared foods: rice,* lakh-lalo*, niomies, bean cakes, etc., then the cereals, millet, sorghum, rice, beans, soap, shea butter, the condiments, a little salt, and cola nuts. One also finds small quantities of quack medicines for leprosy, ophthalmia, guinea worm, sleeping sickness and erotic potions, then hats, mats, baskets, meat, etc.*

Overleaf:
Ouagadougou's large boulevard running from
Place des Nations Unies to the Presidential residence,
has been jokingly nicknamed Ouaga's "Champs Élysées".
Most of the country's ministries are found there.

and 1960) when the country was a French colony, and remained the capital of the new State of Upper Volta after Independence in 1960 (it was rebaptised Burkina Faso in 1984).

Ouagadougou's layout

Before setting off to visit this spread out, somewhat sprawling town, it is useful to first go back in history in order to understand Ouagadougou's layout and where its key sites are located. Back in the days of the Mossi empire, the Moro Naba's palace (which still exists, but is not open to the public) was situated right at the centre of the little town. Other quarters gradually developed around this central point, according to the needs of the emperor and his top dignitaries. Although the town was recently reorganised into "sectors", people in Ouagadougou still use the old names indicating what the quarter's past function was: *Larlé,* for example, was the head of the royal tombs' quarter, *Ouidi* the head of the cavalry's quarter, *Dapoya* the freed captives' quarter, and *Paspanga* the quarter where allegiance ceremonies took place each time there was a new emperor.

Just like the sun he was said to symbolise, the Moro Naba was also situated at the centre of the universe, or at least, at the centre of the Mossi empire which, due to its strict hierarchical organisation, managed to survive for centuries whilst other African empires crumbled on all sides. The Moro Naba still lives in his palace today and, even though his power was greatly reduced by the colonial powers and then when the Republic formed after Independence in 1960, he is still respected by the Mossi community today.

The monarch can still be seen at official events or during audiences at the palace and on such occasions is accompanied by court officials, pages, musicians and guards, all of whom will be splendidly dressed in traditional costumes.

The average foreign visitor is unlikely to be fortunate enough to be received by the Mossi sovereign himself, but may discreetly watch as he performs the beautiful "False Departure" ceremony (already mentioned in the section "Panorama").

The thing that is especially common in the Mossi markets, however, is kalgou *made from néré or netté fruit. The néré or nétté,* Parkia biglobosa, *is a very beautiful mimosa; the tree grows to 10 to 15 metres tall in the Mossi region. When in bloom, the tree is quite a strange sight with its flowers like beautiful scarlet red pompons. Its fruit are slender pods about 20 to 40 centimetres long, that generally hang in clusters of five to six pods. Inside are seeds and a floury, yellow pulp used in food and drinks. The seeds are used to make a sauce called* soumbala *by the Mandé, or* kalgou *by the Mossi. The seeds are roasted, then split open and fermented in water. Once peeled, they are made into a paste and shaped into different sized balls.* Soumbala *keeps for a very long time. It can be found on sale everywhere in the markets. The women use it in nearly all their sauces.*
It can safely be said that soumbala *or* kalgou *is the basic ingredient in all sauces, and is known throughout the Sudan. Europeans do not take to it easily, but by the end of my stay, I would eat these sauces with pleasure."*

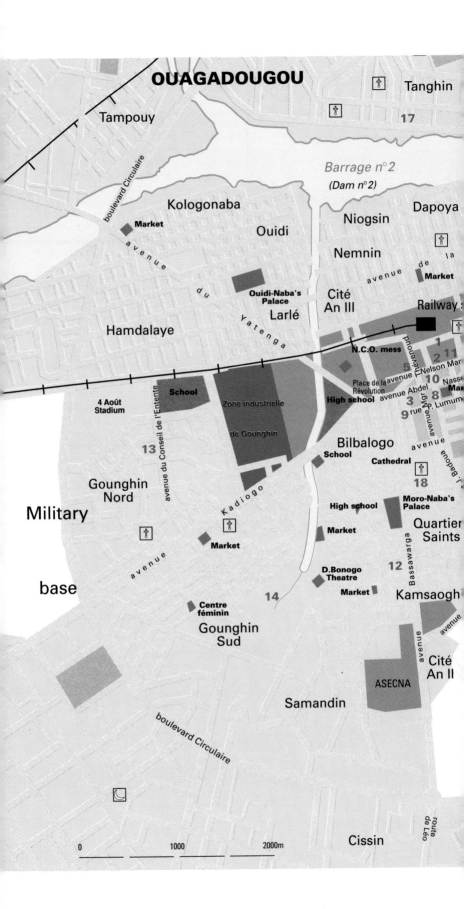

OUAGADOUGOU

Tampouy

Tanghin

17

boulevard Circulaire

Barrage n° 2
(Dam n° 2)

Kologonaba

Market

avenue

du

Ouidi

Niogsin

Dapoya

Nemnin

avenue   de   la

Market

Ouidi-Naba's
Palace

Cité
An III

Railway

Larlé

Yatenga

Hamdalaye

N.C.O. mess

1

2 11

5

T.Nelson Mar

10

Nass

School

Place de la avenue
Révolution

avenue Abdel

8

Ma

4 Août
Stadium

High school

3

P. Lumum

9   rue

avenue

Zone industrielle

13

de Gounghin

Bilbalogo

School

avenue

Cathedral

18

Kadiogo

Gounghin
Nord

Military

High school

Moro-Naba's
Palace

Quartier
Saints

Market

Market

avenue

12

Kamsaogh

base

D.Bonogo
Theatre

Bassawarga

Centre
féminin

14

Market

Gounghin
Sud

avenue

avenue

Cité
An II

ASECNA

Samandin

boulevard Circulaire

route
de Léo

0   1000   2000m

Cissin

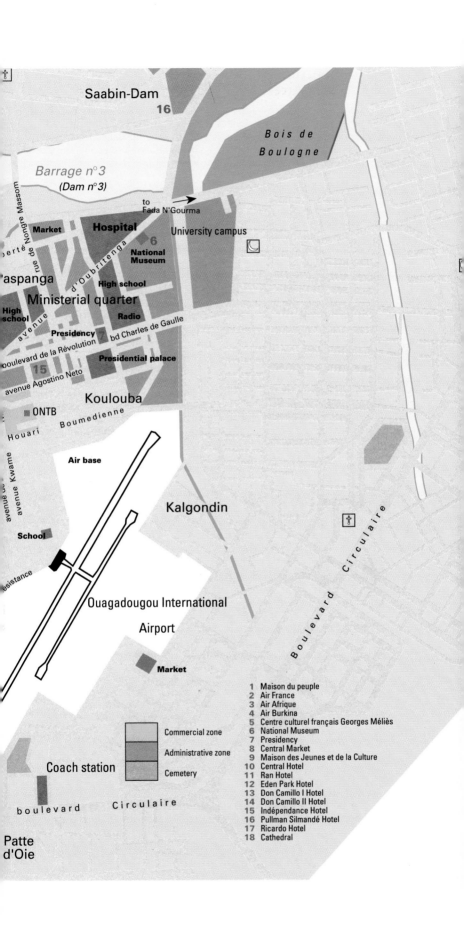

Saabin-Dam
16

Bois de Boulogne

Barrage n° 3
(Dam n° 3)

to
Fada N'Gourma

University campus

Market

Hospital

National Museum

6

aspanga

High school

Ministerial quarter

High school

Radio

Presidency

bd Charles de Gaulle

boulevard de la Révolution

avenue Agostino Neto

15

Presidential palace

Koulouba

ONTB

Houari Boumedienne

Air base

Kalgondin

School

Boulevard Circulaire

Ouagadougou International Airport

Market

1	Maison du peuple
2	Air France
3	Air Afrique
4	Air Burkina
5	Centre culturel français Georges Méliès
6	National Museum
7	Presidency
8	Central Market
9	Maison des Jeunes et de la Culture
10	Central Hotel
11	Ran Hotel
12	Eden Park Hotel
13	Don Camillo I Hotel
14	Don Camillo II Hotel
15	Indépendance Hotel
16	Pullman Silmandé Hotel
17	Ricardo Hotel
18	Cathedral

Commercial zone

Administrative zone

Cemetery

Coach station

boulevard Circulaire

Patte d'Oie

OUAGADOUGOU **91**

The Emperor's false departure

According to a ritual that has remained unchanged for centuries now, the Moro Naba leaves his palace every Friday morning and makes for his richly adorned horse that awaits him on the esplanade. As he goes to mount the horse, all the court officials and musicians waiting outside break into a frenzy of lamentations and drum rolls. The Moro Naba appears to change his mind, returns to the palace where he exchanges his travelling clothes for ceremonial dress before coming back out onto the esplanade where he is frenetically applauded by his faithful entourage. This beautiful ceremony commemorates the exemplary decision taken by one Mossi monarch, who, as he was about to go to find his loved one, received news that a rival army was approaching the town. The question that hung on everyone's lips was what would come first, duty or love? Aware of the great responsibility hanging over a man of his position, he acted on behalf of his people, preferring to lead his army and save the empire.

As already mentioned, when Captain Binger reached Ouagadougou at the end of the last century, he was disappointed with what he saw at that time. Waghadougou consisted of a few little villages with just over 5,000 inhabitants surrounded by an insalubrious creek. The size and structure of the town was not to change significantly until the railway reached the town in 1954.

Arrival of the railway

Although by then Ouagadougou was already the capital of Upper Volta and had a population of 30,000 inhabitants, it had nonetheless remained an extremely provincial agricultural market town. When the railway line linked it to the major sea port in Abidjan, however, Ouagadougou gradually began to catch up with the other major African agglomerations, becoming not just a nationally but internationally influential town. Further changes took place when the country gained Independence in 1960, as it was necessary to build new facilities to house the

OUAGADOUGOU IN THE 19ᵀᴴ CENTURY

On Friday 15 June 1888, the French Captain Binger reached Ouagadougou, natenga (capital) of the Mossi empire.
In his travel diary he wrote:
"Waghadougou or Ouor'odor'o is situated in a vast, arid plain which looks rather desolate at this time of the year. My groom has to go six kilometres eastwards to find fodder. The rains have only fallen three times this year, and it is apparently not until after a few violent storms, or veritable hurricanes occur at the end of June that the wet season rains stimulate the growth of greenery. Swampy shallows that do not dry up all year round separate the main village from the outermost huts to the west and north. The inhabitants dig holes along the swamps to get their water. Full of all kinds of organic matter, this water is inhabited by leeches that cause guinea worm. Men, women and children are affected by this illness.
I have seen people almost crippled with as many as five or six worms coming out of their knees, ankles and especially calves and thighs.
The area around these swamps is abounding in game. My table is always well supplied. Diawé even manages to provide my men

new political and administrative structures: office buildings for the new governmental bodies, housing for civil servants, and a whole string of social amenities (schools, hospitals, shops, etc.).

The population of Ouagadougou

As the capital's profile began to improve, more and more inhabitants were attracted to the city, notably farmers tired of working on drought stricken lands. In the period from the arrival of the railway in 1954 to Independence in 1960, the population of Ouagadougou doubled from 30,000 to over 60,000 inhabitants. From then on, the numbers regularly doubled every ten years, reached 110,000 in 1970, 250,000 in 1980, half a million at the beginning of the Nineties, and nearly a million today.

In order to accommodate all these new arrivals, the Mossi empire's little capital clearly had to undergo complete transformation. Main avenues were created radiating out from a new centre of gravity just north of the Moro Naba's palace and level with the Place de la Révolution.

All of them have changed names several times since they were built, but at present are now called: Avenue Kadiogo (the Bobo Dioulasso road), Avenue Yatenga (the Ouahigouya road), Avenue Nelson Mandela (the continuation of Boulevard de la Révolution and Avenue d'Oubritenga, heading in the direction of Fada N'Gourma) and Avenue Bassawarga (the Léo road).

A new town centre has developed around the central market, in the triangular zone between the railway station in the north, the President's residence in the east, and the Moro Naba's palace and the cathedral (built in 1934) in the south.

The green belt

Over the last forty to fifty years, huge works have been carried out to clean the creeks to the north and west of Ouagadougou. Set in the famous "Ceinture verte" (green belt) that forms an immense parabola around the city, the creeks and their system of dams provide the town with running water. French visitors, who

with meat, frequently bringing back seven or eight teals, a few partridges and two or three hares.
Waghadougou proper includes: the Naba's residence, the group of Muslim villages (which are of Mandé origin), the group called Zang-ana, inhabited by the Marenga (Songhai), the Zang-ouér'o or Zang-ouéto (Hausa), a few Tchilmigo (Fulani) and other groups of non-Muslim Mossi.
However, it is convenient to consider as part of Waghadoughou the seven surrounding villages called: Tampouï, Koudou-ouér'o, Pallemtenga, Kamsokho, Gongga, Lakhallé and Ouidi. Each one has its own Naba. I would say that the combined population of all these groups is under 5,000 inhabitants. The buildings are round, made of mud or matting called séko, depending on whether they are inhabited by Muslims or fetishists. One does see flat roofed, square buildings here and there, however, amongst which I cite: the Imam's house and the mosque (a wretched little construction), a storeyed hut inhabited by El Hadj (Isaka's friend) and five square huts that are part of the

(see p. 97)

*The many public fountains
add a touch of freshness
to a parched Sahelian town like Ouagadougou
and are the occasion to discover the work
of the Burkinabè bronze artists.*

probably spotted this huge green belt from the airplane when they flew into Ouagadougou, are always pleasantly surprised to learn that one of these forest areas (by the Hotel Silmandé and dam N° 3) is called the *Bois de Boulogne*.

The little airfield built to the south-east of Ouagadougou during the colonial period was developed into a major international airport after Independence and now caters for long haul flights operated by international airline companies like "Air France", "Air Afrique", "Aeroflot" and "Air Algérie".

A sprawling town

For a long time, the capital's original quarters—*Koulouba, Paspanga, Dapoya, Zone Commerciale, Bilbalogho, Saint Léon, Samandin, Niogsin*, etc.—all fitted neatly into the immense basin bordered by the green belt and the "Aviation" (the town's airport).

Gradually, however, this large area was no longer capable of containing the demographic explosion and new quarters of Ouagadougou began to develop far beyond the dams (*Tanghin, Saabin* and *Somgandé*) and the airport *(Kalgondin).*

Working-class areas quickly sprang up and, in turn, sprawled out beyond the city's new borders: the huge *Boulevard Circulaire* (Ring Road) that runs right around Ouagadougou. In the 1980s, large modern suburbs like the *Cité de l'Avenir, Cités Sicogib,* and *the Cités An II, An III* and *An IV,* grew up on the four points of the compass.

A town under construction

Even though Burkina Faso's substratum does not contain petrol or uranium supplies that would make the country rich, officials in the capital have nonetheless managed to find enough money to carry out a huge modernisation programme there.

Ultra-modern buildings have sprung up all over the centre of Ouagadougou, for example the *Maison du Peuple* (where galas and large public events are held, including the FESPACO film festival prize-giving ceremony), the new *Rood Woko central market,* large hotels like the "Eden Park" and superb office buildings like the ochre coloured, futurist headquarters of the BICIA (Banque Internationale pour le Commerce, l'Industrie et l'Agriculture du Burkina), the bright white geometric-shaped SNTB offices (Société Nationale de Transit du Burkina), or the tinted-glass BCEAO offices (Banque Centrale des Etats d'Afrique de l'Ouest) opposite Place de la Révolution.

As Ouagadougou is too large to walk round, the best way to find and visit the city's often spread out main sights is by either taking a taxi or, to be like everyone else, by hiring a bike, moped or motorbike from next to the central market.

The National Museum, for example, is right in the east of the town, whereas the municipal Stadium and the Théâtre Populaire Désiré Bonogo are in the south, not far from the cathedral and the Moro Naba's palace.

Masks and craft work

The *Musée National* , which has just been renovated, is well worth a visit. The museum houses a collection of very beautiful traditional masks made by the country's diverse ethnic groups (the Bobo, Mossi, Kurumba, Gourounsi, etc.).

It also displays a large collection of craft works ranging from musical instruments like drums and balafons, to superb baskets, pottery and agricultural tools still made all over the country.

Burkina Faso's flourishing craft activities are greatly encouraged by the authorities who organise the biennial "Salon International de l'Artisanat de Ouagadougou", a show which increasingly attracts professionals, the general public and foreign visitors from all over the world.

The famous Bois de Boulogne

Having gone as far as the Musée National, visitors who like craft works should take the opportunity to press on to the *Manufacture et Centre de Tannage du Cuir (SMBC)* on the Fada N'Gourma road where pyrographic leather goods are made. Otherwise they may head back into town to visit the *Centre National de l'Artisanat d'Art,* well known for its sculptors and batik artists.

From the museum in the *Hôpital Yalgado* quarter, visitors should make a detour to visit the famous *Bois de Boulogne,* where several hotels like the "Silmandé" and the "Ricardo" have been built far from the hustle and bustle of the town. The visitor can stroll along the large dams, enjoying the beautiful landscape and large stretches of calm water that reflect the sky and the forests.

Lost wax bronzes

One of Ouagadougou's other craft specialities is lost wax bronze sculpting. It is still possible to visit these family workshops in the *Niogsin* quarter to the north of the city between dam N° 2 and the station. This very ancient activity was greatly appreciated by the Mossi emperors who frequently ordered bronze jewellery and statuettes from the artisans. One old custom had it that when a Moro Naba died, all his bronzes were melted down and made into new statuettes — sculpted in his and his near ones' effigies — and then placed in his tomb.

One thing that makes a visit to the Niogsin workshops particularly interesting is that visitors can commission any kind of bronze and then watch whilst the piece is being made. The craftsmen will make all sorts of traditional figurines on demand — kings on their thrones, cavaliers, *awalé* players — as well as more modern items like chess pieces. First of all, the piece is modeled in soft wax which, when finished and hardened, is then coated in clay. When the clay is also hard, molten bronze is poured through two little holes pierced in the clay. The hot metal melts the wax and takes its place as the wax runs away. Once the bronze has cooled, the clay mould is broken and the statuette trimmed and polished.

Rood Woko market

In the heart of Ouagadougou, the *Rood Woko central market* is a major attraction for those visiting Africa for the first time. Although it has lost its provincial side a bit since reconstruction work was carried out and the new, modernist market inaugurated in 1989, one nonetheless finds all those perfumes, colours, profuse fruit and vegetables, flour, spices and goods imported from Nigeria and Hong Kong which make these markets so enticing. There are, of course, also plenty of artisanal goods on sale and visitors are bound to

OUAGADOUGOU IN THE 19TH CENTURY

(continued from p. 93)

Naba's residence. I was expecting to find something better than the royal residences one normally finds in the Sudan, as people everywhere had told me of the Naba's wealth and the number of wives and eunuchs he has. It was not long before I got the picture, however, as the very evening of my arrival I noticed that what they call the palace and seraglio is none other than a group of wretched huts surrounded by heaps of rubbish, themselves surrounded by huts serving as stables and housing for the captives and griots. In the courtyard, a few cows, sheep and mules given to the Naba in the course of the day, were attached to posts, offerings that have not yet found a home."

Along with agriculture and cattle rearing, trading and craftwork
play a considerable role in Burkina Faso's economy.
Innumerable arts and crafts products can be found
on sale in Ouagadougou's markets, for example,
some of which make good souvenirs for tourists. (Photo ONTB).

spend a lot of time looking at stalls of hand-dyed material, straw hats, baskets, pottery and thousands of little objects made out of scrap metal and tin cans, like cases, funnels, paraffin lamps and toys…

An unusual restaurant

A large bookshop also selling stationary and newspapers can be found in the market place. A little further on is "L'Eau Vive", one of Ouagadougou's unusual institutions. Run by missionary sisters, "L'Eau Vive" is a high classed restaurant frequented by international businessmen and well-to-do Burkinabè inhabitants. Tables and chairs are set out in an interior garden with a little grotto and statue of the Virgin Mary and an artificial stream. "L'Eau Vive" is a truly lovely place to eat out under the evening starry vault, but it is worth mentioning that after the hors-d'œuvre, the sisters serving the meal suddenly start singing hymns, accompanied in the choruses by most of the customers… (The sisters have set up another similar restaurant of the same name in Bobo Dioulasso).

From the "Centre Méliès" to the "Indépendance"

Visitors passing through Ouagadougou can see old French movie classics or go to jazz concerts, just a stone's throw away from the central market, at the *Centre Culturel Français Georges Méliès* near the Place de la Révolution (the cinema has 200 places, the open-air theatre 500).

It is hard not to notice the various monuments embellishing the squares in the centre of Ouagadougou. One of the most unusual and colourful, situated in *Place des Cinéastes*, where Avenues Nelson Mandela, Abdel Nasser and Mgr. Thévenoud intersect, is dedicated to Burkina Faso's up and coming Seventh Art. Two other monuments mark the beginning of Ouagadougou's "Champs-Elysées" (the grand Boulevard de la Révolution, which leads triumphantly to the Presidential Residence), one of which is dedicated to the United Nations and the other to the Women of Burkina Faso (the latter, by the entrance of a service station, is adorned with a basin).

By taking Avenue Nelson Mandela, where the imposing, futuristic *Maison du Peuple* is located (seats 3,000; used for concerts, conferences and galas), then the "Champs Elysées", visitors will come to the *Hôtel Indépendance,* one of Ouagadougou's most animated places. The "Indépendance" is always in full swing, and its pool-side bar where passing international businessmen, top Burkinabè civil servants, the capital's *zazous* and expatriates meet, is one of Ouagadougou's social hot spots. People often come here for a drink after work, to go for a dip in the pool, or to play tennis in the cool of the late afternoon and evening.

The famous film festival

The hotel is especially lively when the famous Pan-African fespaco film festival takes place every other year, as it then becomes the festival goers' "headquarters" and is frequented by seasoned film directors like Senegalese Ousmane Sembène and rising stars like Burkinabè Idrissa Ouedraogo whose films, notably *Yaaba, Tilai, Samba Traoré,* and *Kini and Adams*, have been selected and awarded prizes at Cannes and Berlin.

All foreigners wishing to visit Ouagadougou would in fact be well advised to come either during the FESPACO film festival, the "Salon International de l'Artisanat", or during the "Dodo" carnival. When these major events take place, Ouagadougou is covered with banderoles and can be seen in all its splendour and at its most jubilant as the inhabitants party late into the night and the cinemas, bars and clubs are never empty.

Towards the Cathedral

South of the town centre, is the large, brick neo-Roman *Cathedral* built in 1934 when Mgr. Thévenoud was the first Bishop of Ouagadougou. On a Sunday, whole crowds of worshippers can be seen flocking to the Cathedral on their "two-wheelers". Mass is usually held in Moré, the Mossi language spoken throughout Burkina Faso, and the service is livened up with traditional music and singing.

A bit further south is the *Moro Naba's Palace,* home of the Mossi emperor mentioned earlier.

After the *Stade Municipal* (stadium) and the *Lycée Bambata* (high school), is the open-air *Théâtre Populaire Désiré Bonogo,* where numerous theatre companies and traditional performers put on shows (seats 2,000 people).

A little way further to the west is the *Gounghin* quarter where it is possible to visit the *Centre de Formation Féminine* (women's training centre). Here the young women's fine artistic talent has earned the centre a great reputation for embroidery and especially for making magnificent thick-pile wool carpets. Inspired by traditional African forms, they decorate the rugs with geometric designs or with stylised masks and sacred African animals.

The crocodile pools

Numerous (and sometimes very unusual!) excursions can be made in the area around Ouagadougou.

On the Nationale 1 heading westwards towards Bobo Dioulasso, visitors will come across two *"sacred Crocodile pools"*. One is at *Bazoulé*, a little village near to *Tanguin Dassouri* (23 km west of Ouagadougou) and the other at *Sabou* (see later section on Sabou).

Foreign visitors are always surprised to see these large saurians crawl out of the water when called by the village children. Having feasted on a live chicken or two, the satisfied and docile crocodiles let the children and tourists climb onto their backs — but still, do watch out for their tails!

"Ouaga 2000"

Further to the south, the new "Ouaga 2000" district was developed on the outskirts of Ouagadougou for the 19th Franco-African summit at the end of 1996. About a hundred North African or Sahelian-style luxury villas were built to accommodate this major event's honorary guests, and will continue to accommodate the guests of other events in the future (for example, the 1998 summit). A 4000 m² conference centre was also built in Ouaga 2000.

The sculpture garden

Equally unusual is the *Laongo* sculpture garden, east of Ouagadougou on the Nationale 4 (follow this road as far as Boudtenga, 31 km from Ouagadougou, then take the track on the left heading in a northerly direction).

From afar, this garden set right in the heart of the savanna looks like a mass of rocks. At closer hand, however, visitors will see that this site otherwise frequented by shepherds and their flocks of goats is in fact bristling with sculptures of all styles, done in 1989 when about twenty artists from all over the world came for a Symposium on Granite. Some of the steles recall ancient Egyptian art, whilst elsewhere, there are surrealist-style groups of people, nudes and women's faces.

Interesting places to see

Further northwards on the Laongo road, is *Ziniaré* village, where the villagers make pottery, tan leather and dye cloth in deep wells dug in the ground.

On the way back to Ouagadougou via the Nationale 3, it is worth stopping at *Loumbila* to visit the market gardening areas around the dam (where it is possible to go for a dug-out canoe ride).

Manega, where the lawyer / poet Frédéric Pacéré Titinga built a very beautiful museum (see later section), can be reached via the *Pabré* seminary road north of Ouagadougou.

In an afternoon, it is possible to take the Nationale 5 southwards from the capital to Pô and the Gourounsi region (see section on Pô and Tiébélé) where traditional, decorated earthen architecture can be seen.

En route, it is worth stopping to visit the *Koubri* Benedictine monastery and the market gardening areas around the dams near *Bazega* and *Kombissiri*. Further to the south, *Toesse* is reputed for its artisanal pottery. At *Nobéré*, visitors will see a huge baobab which is several hundred years old.

(See practical information p. 164).

*In 1989, an unusual, but interesting event
took place at Laongo, east of Ouagadougou.
About twenty artists came together to carve
most of the rocks, thereby creating
a magnificent open-air sculpture museum.*

arli (the national park)

■ Although still unquestionably kings of the vast savanna lands in eastern Burkina Faso, the Burkinabè lions are not given to showing off their power in an ostentatious way. Unlike in the Kenyan wildlife reserves, the king of animals will very rarely be seen obligingly posing at the road side here in Arli, where the huge national park spills over into both the Gourma and Tapoa Provinces. Still, although these animals are extremely discreet, their omnipresence can be sensed. Some signs are unmistakable: the sudden stillness of a herd of antelopes, ears pricked up, ready to bolt at the slightest suspect sound, vultures perched in a lone tree, or an unusual emptiness in the bush, especially near to pools at times when all the wild animals would normally be seen drinking or bathing. Visitors will sometimes chance upon other more tangible, but less obvious signs in the bush which will dispel any doubts about these big cats' presence in the Arli national park: guides will sometimes suddenly point out strange, flower-shaped prints on the tracks and, in the middle of the night, it is not unusual to be awaken with a start by resonant roaring near the camp.

Like the Sioux

Once these clues have been spotted, all that remains to be done is set out to find the big cats. A sturdy vehicle is essential for these wildlife safaris as the tracks in the eastern parks are often in very poor condition. It is also a good idea to take a local guide (they can be found on the spot in Arli) as they will not only stop visitors from getting lost in the savanna where the routes are not always well marked, but above all, as they are most familiar with the animals' behaviour and movements.

Like the Sioux, these guides know how to read the faintest animal tracks and their keen eyes are capable of detecting the presence of animals where the average visitor only sees bush. "Look, there behind the acacia: two waterbucks!", or "Quick! in the rocks, patas monkeys!" Often, it is hard to see the slightest thing move, however hard one might look in the direction the guide pointed.

Fortunately, the noise of the vehicle makes the animals scatter and then you would need to be blind not to see the tail end of antelope herds darting into the savanna, or green monkeys, patas or cynoscephales scrambling up heaps of rocks to scoff at the humans from a safe distance.

Nowadays in West Africa, visitors have to count on their guide's skill and their own luck to come across the increasingly rare lions and elephants, especially as these large mammals do not have fixed roaming grounds and may wander off in search of prey (the lions) or huge quantities of vegetation (the elephants), covering 20 to 30 km in one night.

As both are very fond of water, it is easiest to try to find them near the pools (like Tandougou pool, on the river Doulodo or Tounga pool at Arli) or rivers like the Pendjari, the natural border between Burkina Faso and Benin, to the south of the Arli national park.

A lioness lying in wait

Chance may always befall unexpectedly, however. During our visit to the park, the guide spotted a beautiful lioness right by the track as she lay in wait for a herd of small antelopes. As still as a statue and almost completely hidden in the long grass, she was so absorbed in the sight of her potential prey that she did not move an inch when our vehicle approached… so close that we could almost touch her!

Established in the Fifties, Arli is probably the most beautiful wildlife park in Burkina Faso, both in terms of setting and the numbers of animals that can be seen. In this part of the country, the uniformity of the vast savanna lands is broken by the appearance of the long *Gobnangou* and *Tambarga Escarpments* and by gallery forests which partly cover the rivers (like the Pendjari).

Equipped with good accommodation, the reserve offers visitors a wide range of African savanna wildlife. Many species of antelopes can be seen — sable antelopes, bubals, impalas, Buffon kobs, waterbucks, royal antelopes, bushbucks, oribis, grey duikers and red flanked forest duikers — as can all sorts of monkeys, generally living in groups — cynoscephales (or dog's headed baboons) patas (or red monkeys) and guenons (green monkeys).

Other inhabitants

In the *Ouamou, Tandougou, Tounga* and *Pendjari* pools, families of hippopotami can be seen frolicking in the water and, occasionally, it is possible to spot crocodiles. Whereas buffaloes and wart

banfora

hogs are quite common in the Arli national park, it is often necessary to scour the park from one end to the other before finding elephants and big cats (lions, panthers) — as already mentioned. Many birds, especially birds of prey, also frequent the park.

(See practical information p. 165)

■ Strange mushroom-shaped rocks protrude from the *Banfora Escarpment* overlooking the plain and little town of *Banfora* in south-western Burkina Faso.

According to geographers, rain and wind carrying grains of sand have been eroding away the sandstone escarpment for thousands of years like an abrasive scourer, hence forming these protrusions or "domes". Along with waterfalls and the Sindou "Pèlerins" (see section on Sindou), these rocky mushrooms near *Fabédougou* village are one of the *Comoé* Province's major tourist attractions.

Other than its market, the charming little garden city of Banfora itself does not have a great deal to offer foreign visitors.

Banfora market

Set in a neo-colonial Sudanese style building, Banfora market has one of the best supplies of craft work in Burkina Faso. Effectively, the Gouin, Karaboro and Turka peoples who settled in this region very early on, are highly skilled

AFRICAN MASKS: APPARITIONS

■ *What does the African artist aim to achieve? Life-like resemblance is usually of little interest. Expression, then? Yes, expression that is as specific as musical expression—far from the impassioned facial expression found in Japanese or ancient comedy masks, so different from them that what distinguishes an African mask from a standard European mask at the very first sight is precisely the first's specific expression and the "expressionism" of the latter.*
Black art has rarely sought to suggest via realism, even caricatural or impassioned realism, except when subjected to foreign models (and then not well). The African mask does not capture human expression, it is an apparition... The sculptor does not geometrise an unfamiliar ghost, he creates it via his geometry. The mask works less in the sense where it resembles man, than in the sense where it does not resemble him. Animal masks are not animals; an antelope mask is not an antelope, but the spirit of an antelope, and its the style that conjures the spirit. It is said that for the black sculptor, the best mask is the most efficient; where does its efficiency come from if not the richness of its style?

ANDRÉ MALRAUX
Les Voix du Silence (Gallimard)

bobo dioulasso

artisans. In the dry season, when the harvests are stored and whilst they are waiting for the next rains before starting work in the fields again, they devote their time to craft work.

Their baskets are particularly fine, especially the stacking baskets woven for weddings which may have about ten separate components. Basket workers in the region have the strange habit of working in what could be described as burrows. These underground workshops not only provide them with shelter from the relentless heat outside, but also stop the palm fibres they use from drying out.

Other types of craft work found include: decorated pottery, traditional material (made particularly by the Sénoufo and Dioula people) and all kinds of agricultural tools (billhooks, hoes, sickles) made by blacksmiths.

Beautiful waterfalls

A wide range of excursions can be made in and around Banfora. It is possible, for example, to visit both the vast sugar cane plantations and the SOSUCO sugar works (Société Sucrière de la Comoé). The beautiful *Karfiguela Waterfall* lies a few kilometres north of the town and can be reached via a track that cuts across the sugar cane plantations off the Bobo Dioulasso road from Banfora. The waterfall cascades down from the Banfora Escarpment onto a riot of stunning rocks. Water is channeled off from this river to irrigate the valley plantations. The *Takalédougou Waterfall* east of Banfora, just off the Bobo Dioulasso road, is also worth a visit.

The little village of *Tengrela,* lies further to the west towards Sindou (see later section) and is famous for its "Quiverers" ("Trembleuses"), the young women who dance wildly, shaking their whole bodies. Next to the village is the picturesque Lake Tengrela. Visitors may be able to gently persuade a local fisherman to take them for a very rustic ride in a dug-out canoe.

Following the Sindou road, visitors will come to *Douna,* a large village 43 km west of Banfora, then Sindou (52 km). Before reaching Sindou's famous "peaks", take the route to *Niofila* on the right. Just after Niofila, visitors can walk to the *Léraba Waterfalls* which are perhaps the most beautiful in Burkina Faso.

(See practical information p. 165).

■ According to Salvador Dali, Perpignan's railway station, in France, was "the centre of the world". Had he visited the station in Bobo Dioulasso, however, he might have changed his mind. This immense, neo-Moorish style white "cake" looks like it could have come straight out of a Hollywood film studio from the film "L'Atlantide".

Tired and groggy after their 24 hour-train ride from Abidjan, passengers will think they are seeing things when they reach Bobo Dioulasso. Built in the 1930s, this station incarnates the grandiose dreams that drove the major European powers to build themselves empires in Africa.

During the colonial period, the French also built similar grandiloquent buildings that look like pasteboard sets in Dakar (the former governor's palace, the cathedral and the railway station), Bamako (the main market building, the post office and the administrative headquarters) and Casablanca (the main post office).

This station in Burkina Faso was the terminus of the Abidjan-Niger railway for a long time.

When the railway reached Bobo Dioulasso in 1934, it was considered a godsend in the ancient Gouiriko capital founded by the Ouattara dynasty from Kong, as the town rapidly expanded and at last stood a good chance of becoming Upper Volta's rich and prosperous capital.

It is hard to stop progress, however, and when the Abidjan-Niger railway was extended to Ouagadougou twenty years later, this town in turn underwent rapid growth and supplanted rival Bobo Dioulasso as Upper Volta's (and now Burkina Faso's) capital. Nonetheless, with 300,000 inhabitants and many businesses, Bobo Dioulasso is Burkina Faso's second city and is now considered the country's "economic capital".

Ali Baba's cave

The station is not the only surprise in store for visitors in Bobo Dioulasso. The *grand marché* (market) in the town centre was built in the same architectural vein as the station and is situated right next to the completely different, huge cylindrical-shaped *cathedral* whose grandeur comes from its lack of ornamentation and the simplicity of its shape.

Those who like browsing will soon discover that the market and surrounding bric-a-brac shops are like Ali Baba's cave. Endless artisanal goods can be found there—ranging from baskets, local cloths, jewellery, Fulani covers to printed wax cotton—as well as rarer pieces of African art like Bobo masks, Lobi statuettes, Mossi bronzes...

The most beautiful objects are not usually displayed on the market stalls nor in the bric-a-brac shops, however, but are tucked away at the bottom of an old trunk or stored in the "antique" dealer's home somewhere in Bobo Dioulasso. In order to see such goods, visitors have to first of all show that they are connoisseurs and are ready to pay large sums in cash!

A colourful market

The market area is the town's main attraction, offering both an inexhaustible area for strolling and buying things, and a riot of colours, sounds and smells. This commercial centre is first and foremost a food market and farmers come here from all over the region. Tropical fruit and vegetables that many foreign visitors will never have even seen before are found on sale by the ton: mangoes, cola nuts, yams, cassava, millet, sorghum and strange mixtures used in sauces made from karite kernels, baobab leaves or tamarind pods.

The earthen mosque

Another attraction in Bobo Dioulasso is the famous earthen *mosque* surrounded by the mud houses of the *Kibidoué* and *Sya* old quarters. The beige mosque is a cross between a tiered cake and a modern sculpture. Its pointed cylindrical minarets bristling with posts and the walls' sugar loaf buttresses are made out of laterite.

Unfortunately for photographers, the harmony of this wonderful Sudanese architecture is somewhat marred by the telegraph poles and corrugated iron canopies surrounding the mosque. One can only hope that the authorities—especially those in charge of Burkinabè Historic Monuments—list this remarkable building and clear the surrounding area.

The old quarters, a stone's throw away from the mosque, are also worth a visit. Local children will take visitors to see the *House of the Original Parents* (Sya) of the people who founded the town (the Bobo and Dioula). Inside is a labyrinth

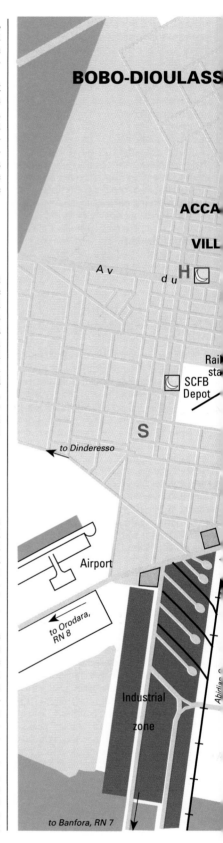

to Mali, RN 9

0   1000 m

Rte de Dédougou

NIENETA

RN 10

H

H

+

S

Avenue

DIARADOUGOU

Jamot

H

général

neur

HAMDALAYE   FARAKAN

DONONA

BINDOUGOUSSO

OUEZZIN-

VILLE

Liberté   Stadium

H

de   la

Avenue   Market

TOUNOUMA

KIBIDOUÉ

du   Pdt

KOMBOUGOU

YOROKOKO

Ouezzin   Coulibaly

H

de   la   Nation

H

H   H

SSO-

RA

+

KOKO

Rue   Vicens

Av   du   général   de   Gaulle

to Ouagadougou, R

M

Châlons-sur-Marne

BOLOMAKOTE

Bd   de

RTB

M   Market

H   Hotel

S   Stadium

+   Hospital

C   Mosque

† Church

KOUNIMA

Military

base

Kounima
protected
forest

F.   Éboué

of innumerable dark corridors and rooms. Hidden staircases lead to roof terraces which, like in the Arabic countries, are linked together and serve as interior courtyards, terraces and even as a place to dry millet and cobs of corn.

Also near to the mosque is the old *Kibidoué* quarter through which the picturesque *Wé* creek flows and where there is a market specialising in clay pots and jars *(canaris)* of all shapes and sizes made on site by the women of the *Dioula, Soba* and *Farakan* quarters. In fact all the town's craft workshops are highly reputed, and the goods made there have not yet been replaced by imported manufactured goods.

Craft workshops

It is possible to visit the very interesting traditional weaving workshops (in the *Diaradougou* quarter in the north, the *Zone 7* quarter where the Diébougou road begins, and the *Accart-Ville* quarter on the other side of the railway), the dyeing workshops (*Koko* quarter in the east) and the bronze workshops where artisans make many bronze sculptures using the "lost wax technique".

It is also worth visiting instrument makers in the *Bolomakoté* quarter in southern Bobo Dioulasso, where griots and traditional musicians come from all over Burkina Faso to buy their balafons (xylophones).

Many of Burkina Faso's craft objects are real works of art and deserve to be exhibited in a museum. This is precisely what has been done in Bobo Dioulasso where the fascinating *Musée de la Province du Houet* was set up to display wonderful collections of works made by the different ethnic groups in the country. Amongst the most beautiful exhibits are the wooden Mossi platter surmounted by a female figurine, wooden Sénoufo and Mossi locks adorned with carvings and engravings, and a beautiful door and lock from Ouahigouya.

There is also a collection of jewellery (Bissa, Gouin and Kassena bracelets, Fulani and Bellah ankle bracelets), spoons and ladles, baskets, gourds, hats and agricultural tools (hoes, picks, adzes, axes).

Several Burkinabè habitations have been cleverly reconstructed in the museum's courtyards and equipped with traditional furniture and domestic utensils. Visitors can thus see a Fulani straw igloo and Bobo and Sénoufo *soukalas* (inside of which they will notice hunting weapons like poisoned bows and arrows, catapults and crossbows).

The *Centre Culturel Français Henri Matisse,* which has a wonderful library, is located near the museum and regularly organises shows and art exhibitions. There is also a bar with a shady terrace ideal for resting after the exhausting walk around Bobo Dioulasso! French newspapers are available there.

Bobo by night

Bobo Dioulasso may well be more provincial than the capital Ouagadougou, but is by no means a ghost town at night. Anyone who likes African dance and music will have ample occasion to lead a particularly hectic nightlife in the many clubs found in Bobo's "hot spot", between the "Auberge" and "Ran" Hotels. The average night out on the town generally begins with an aperitif on the terrace of a popular bar (like the one at the "Auberge", for example), followed by dinner in one of the area's many restaurants and, finally, at about eleven o'clock in the evening, is rounded off by a trip to one of the "in" clubs like— at the moment— the "Big Jack" or "Black and White"...

The Hippo pool

All sorts of excursions are possible in the region around Bobo Dioulasso. One of the most amusing places to visit is the *Hippo pool,* about 70 km north-east of the town.

To get there, take the Dégougou road from Bobo Dioulasso (the Nationale 10) as far as the Satiri crossroads. The Bala track on the left leads to the pool. At the pool, visitors can approach the herds of hippos in boats or dugout canoes nonetheless keeping a respectful distance for safety reasons. Even though these huge animals are quite used to man, they are by no means tame.

Hippos can be touchy animals— especially when their offspring are around or when they feel cornered— and do not like to be disturbed when sleeping. If disturbed they can become very dangerous and have even been known to up-turn boats and crush the occupants with their powerful jaws. Even though hippos are not carnivores, they do have rather formidable canines and incisors. Their essentially vegetarian diet consists of aquatic plants and grass that they look for on land after nightfall.

During the daytime, hippos spend the whole time frolicking about in the water, swimming or walking underwater for up to six minutes. When hippos come up for air, all that you can usually see emerging from the water are their huge heads and the jerky movement of their ears. Sometimes they can be seen yawning their heads off with their mouths wide, wide open, showing off their formidable canines.

Koro : a hillside village

Several of the places east of Bobo Dioulasso along the Nationale 1 to Ougadougou are also worth visiting. The first is the little village *Pala* (track to the right, 6 km along the Nationale 1) at the foot of an escarpment famous for its ancient baobab. Further on, the N1 cuts through the *Poa forest* where, from the road, there is a wonderful view of the whole region and notably the village *Koro* set in the hillside (12 km from Bobo Dioulasso, follow the track on the right, then the path alongside the quarry). Just before the Koro junction, another track on the left leads off the N1 and, about 1 km on, comes to a group of rocks which have been eroded into twisted forms. Another track left of the main road leads to *Boradougou* village. Visitors may be able to get one of the villagers to take them to see the rock shelters which, in theory, are out of bounds to strangers as they are still used for cult practices (some of these shelters also countain granaries and others have rupestral engravings).

Further to the east, the N1 comes to the village *Kotédougou*, famous for its traditional dancers and for its Sudanese style mosque.

Bathing in the Kou

There are also numerous things to see to the west of Bobo Dioulasso. When it becomes unbearably hot, the *Baignade de Kou* is a highly appreciated spot. To get there, take either the Dinderesso and Nasso roads (R34) or the Koumi road (N8) which is possibly less congested. To get onto the Koumi road, leave Bobo Dioulasso via the airfield and head in the direction of Orodara.

After the metal bridge, it is worth stopping off to visit *Koumi*, a little village with typical Bwa (or Bobo-Oulé) mud habitations. Every year, major traditional animist celebrations take place during which large geometric masks representing the village's protecting animals come out. The strange, burrow-like underground workshops, which permit basket makers to work during the dry season without their palm leaves drying out, are also found here.

The track parallel to the River *Kou* on the right just after Koumi, first of all passes the seminary, then *Kokorowé* village before coming to the open-air café at the Kou bathing place. Here the beautiful Kou River's cool, clear waters shaded by the gallery forest, provide an exquisite place to swim!

To get back to Bobo Dioulasso, take the track to the north then, at the junction, the route on the left which passes close to *Nasso* village and a seminary. A little further on, turn right onto the R34 from Dinderesso (a forestry station) which leads back into Bobo Dioulasso.

Burkina Faso's "orchard"

Heading westwards towards Koumi from the Bobo Dioulasso airfield, the Nationale 8 also leads to the *Mouhoun Waterfalls* and *Orodara,* a town 73 km west of Bobo. Just off the Nationale 8 after Koumi, Moami, Tiara and Guena, is the little village *Sidi* (55 km from Bobo). The track on the right heading northwards leads to Banfoulagué (64 km). From here it is possible to walk northwards for about an hour to the waterfall at the *Mouhoun Gorge* (formerly known as the Black Volta), 70 km from Bobo Dioulasso.

About twenty kilometres beyond Sidi, the Nationale 8 comes to the town *Orodara* which lies nestled in a basin. Large fruit growing areas have been developed around the town, earning Orodara its nickname: the "Orchard of Burkina Faso". From Orodara, it is possible to travel in a large loop northwards and back to Bobo Dioulasso, thereby enabling visitors to discover several of the ethnic groups in western Burkina Faso (the Syemou, the Sénoufo, the Tussian, the Samoro, the Sembla and the Bwa).

Along the R35 road, visitors will also pass by some interesting villages like *Tin, Samorogouan* and *Foulasso,* before heading back to Bobo Dioulasso on the Nationale 9 via Dandé and Bama.

*With its towers, pillars and cylindrical minarets,
Bobo Dioulasso's mosque looks like
a cross between modern sculpture
and a fairy-tale castle.*

boromo

The Banfora Escarpment

The main road heading westwards from Bobo Dioulasso leads to *Banfora* (see earlier section) and Côte d'Ivoire. Eight kilometres from Bobo, the track on the right leads to the *Farakoba* agronomic research institute and, a kilometre further, to the *Matourkou* agricultural centre.

The route follows the contours of the *Banfora Escarpment,* affording wonderful views of the region (especially at Dingasso which can be reached via a track to the left before Dar Salami). Before Banfora, the beautiful *Takalédougou Waterfall* cascades down from the escarpment (see section on Banfora).

(See practical information p 165).

■ Nowadays, it is increasingly difficult to catch even the slightest glimpse of a trunk or an elephant's ear without going to the circus or the zoo. This is especially true in Africa, where man still ruthlessly hunts and slaughters these huge creatures just to make a few paltry pieces of ivory jewellery. This is why, having scoured the numerous African nature reserves and wildlife parks in vain to see the elephants, foreign visitors in Burkina Faso will immediately prick up their ears when they are assured that they will definitely see "lots" of elephants (translation,"quite a few") in the protected *Deux Balé Forest* near to Boromo,"without even leaving the Ouaga-Bobo road") !

In search of elephants

Bubbling with this information and impatient to finally see the largest mammal on earth in flesh and blood (and free) no one could be blamed for jumping straight in their car and rushing off to the Deux Balé forest. Alas! Having parked the vehicle at the side of the road and

WHEN THE SKY MOVED AWAY

■ *In the past, the sky* (Ouendé) *was very close to the earth When the people who walked beneath it were hungry, they would take their knives, cut a little piece and eat it.*
One day, a hungry blind man took his daba *(hoe) to break off a few pieces.*
As he struck here, there and everywhere, without reaching the sky, the idea came to him to light a torch as he thought this would be the best way to see.
He walked around, his torch alight, looking for the sky.
The torch burnt Ouendé, who felt the pain and immediately fled upwards. Since then, the sky has remained high up above men.

L. TAUXIER
Le Noir du Yatenga
(Larose)

djibo

having scrutinized the bush for some time in vain, visitors will have to face the facts: not one single elephant has hired a parking lot along the Nationale 1!

Still, the information given is not entirely fictitious. If visitors go with a local guide very early in the morning, they will most certainly come across an elephant or two and sometimes even a whole herd in the protected Deux Balé forest.

Boromo camp

In order to find a competent guide, visitors should go to the nearby *Boromo* tourist camp. With its seven rooms, bar and restaurant, the camp is used to welcoming and showing quite a few tourists round the area. It is an ideal base when travelling around in western Burkina Faso, starting with Boromo where the animist Kô people periodically organise major traditional celebrations.

During the dry season (and especially between April and June, and around October/November) the Kô bring out their large strip and zoomorphic masks (representing hares, sable antelopes, fish, gazelles, crocodiles and even the moon).

Even if visitors miss the time when the traditional festivities take place, they can still go and visit the Boromo village chiefs who will very kindly show the different painted masks hung on the walls of their huts as if in a museum.

From Boromo it is possible to go on wildlife safaris in the *Deux Balé forest*, visit the beautiful earthen mosque at *Ouahabou* (see relevant section) or visit the nearby Bobo region where traditional villages and animist celebrations are stunning (see section on Houndé/Boni).

(See practical information p. 168).

■ Little is known about the origins of the paintings covering the inside walls of the *Aribinda* and *Pobé Mengao* rock refuges to the east and south of Djibo. Archaeologists working on these sites in Burkina Faso and on the Bandiagara Escarpment in Mali where there are also many rupestral paintings, do not yet know who the mysterious artists were, nor when these first inhabitants lived in the *Soum* Province.

Visitors will in turn wonder about the origin of the Aribinda paintings depicting cavaliers, spears and animals, which are one of the main attractions of the journey to the vast Sahelian regions in northern Burkina Faso.

In the mass of engraved rocks around Aribinda and the sacred hills—the main three represent Man, Woman and Child—there is an "inexhaustible" spring and numerous caves where experts have found fragments of pottery and bronze statuettes and the remains of grindstones hollowed into the rock.

The large cattle market

Several of Burkina Faso's ethnic groups live in Aribinda village, for example the Kurumba (or Foulsé), the Mossi and notably the Fulani, whose strange straw igloo-shaped habitations are made of plaited plant fibres. It is definitely worth visiting the Aribinda and Djibo markets held every day or every three days in one locality or the other. On Wednesdays, the Fulani and Tuareg nomadic pastors bring their herds of cattle (cows, goats, camels) to the Djibo market.

Djibo is also a major arts and crafts centre and, when walking round the streets, visitors will inevitably chance upon Fulani jewellery makers (whose speciality are big, gold, twisted ear-rings), weavers making striped covers, blacksmiths, potters and basket workers making mats, matting screens *(sekos)* and cane furniture.

Djibo's earthen architecture is also noteworthy. High walls surrounding square houses with roof terraces that bristle with gables, evocative of the *ksour* in the south of Morocco and Algeria, have been made from wattle and daub bricks. The mosque with its sugar loaf minaret and openwork mud balustrades on the roof terrace is also very interesting.

(See practical information p. 168).

dori

Set in a region where the first few sand dunes and nomads begin to appear, Dori gives a foretaste of the Saharan landscape and life in the oases. Just like the rest of the Sahelian region, this little north-eastern Burkinabè town inhabited by Tuaregs, Fulani and Songhai, periodically suffers the ravages of droughts and relentless annual desertification. This process has been going on for thousands of years and is to blame for having transformed the fertile Saharan region into an immense, arid zone. The yellow, sandy area on maps of Africa is advancing further and further towards the Sub-Saharan countries like Burkina Faso and neighbouring Mali and Niger. It is no surprise that the province in which Dori is the county town is called *Séno*, the Fulani word for "sandy plain".

For the time being, the desert's advance appears to have slowed and even stopped in the Dori region where the dunes are "held back" by the sparse vegetation. Further to the north beyond Gorom Gorom, however, "live" dunes are advancing, carried by the wind.

Tanners and leather workers

Like the Saharan oases, Dori is a major crossroads for the nomadic pastors, especially the Fulani who live in search of pastures and water with their herds of cows. During the dry season, pastors often assemble at Dori as it is surrounded by a large creek and many stay there for several months.

The town's settled population lives mainly from agriculture (farming millet and sorghum), trading and art and crafts, notably weaving, jewellery making, shoe making and leatherwork. The Dori workshops have a convenient supply of cow hides and goat skins direct from the local cattle rearers. Once tanned in the town, they are sold to shoemakers, whose speciality are the *samara* sandals commonly worn by the nomads, and to other leather workers.

Tuareg craftwork

The latter are mainly Tuaregs of the *Inaden* caste who specialise in leatherwork. They make a whole range of richly decorated objects which were particularly sought after in the days of the trans-Saharan caravans, including pillows, bags, saddle bags, wallets, boxes, sword sheaths

The northern regions of Burkina Faso
offer typical Sahelian landscapes:
open, dry savanna lands are dotted with camel drivers
travelling down from the Sahara.

and belts. All are dyed with bright colours and decorated with strips of plaited leather. Like on Moorish leatherwork, the geometric motifs represent the moon, sun, stars and lizards, and some are considered charms against the evil eye.

Whilst walking around Dori, which is a very spread out town with several quarters (notably the "Quartier des Nobles"), it is possible to visit the workshops where tanners, shoemakers, leather workers, weavers and jewellery makers work. Many craft goods are sold in the market, but often come from neighbouring villages, like, for example, woven strips of cloth from *Malléré, Yacouta* pottery, wicker baskets, trays and hats from *Wendou* and *Dantchiali,* and engraved calabashes from *Beguintingui.*

Bani
mosque

When heading along the Nationale 3 from Ouagadougou or Kaya to Dori, it is worth stopping off at Bani (35 km south of Dori) to see its beautiful, imposing earthen mosque. What is interesting is the sharp contrast in architectural style with the other Muslim religious buildings in Burkina Faso. Unlike the mosques in Bobo Dioulasso and Ouahabou (see relevant sections), the Bani mosque does not appear to have been modeled out of clay by a sculptor—or a potter—inspired principally by the shape of sugar loaves and conical cylinders.

The people who built the Bani mosque from uncovered wattle and daub bricks, favoured simple forms and right angles. Instead of being piled up on itself like a huge bibelot, the mosque and its interior courtyards are spread out over a large area enclosed by a crenellated exterior wall. Even the mosque's "telescopic" stacked towers and minarets are different than those characteristic of "Sudanese" earthen architecture, the most beautiful examples of which are the Djenné and Mopti mosques in Mali. Finally, the edifice's white and ochre colouring has Middle Eastern influences and evokes the architecture of the wonderful Yemeni storied houses and mosques.

Camel markets
and gold mines

It is worth visiting several of the places in the Sahelian region around Dori which, it would seem from the large megaliths found at *Kourori* south of the town, has been inhabited since time immemorial. A little way to the north by the border with Niger is *Falagountou* village where a large cattle market is held every Saturday, frequented by nomads who come on foot, on mules, or on camels.

It is also possible to reach the Niger River just over the border along which there are some beautiful villages and big markets selling dromedaries, mules, bovines and sheep. The *Ayorou* market is particularly special as it attracts all the main Niger-Sahelian peoples—the Fulani, the Tuaregs, the Djerma, and the Songhai—to the village. Some, like the Fulani, come herding bovines with lyre-shaped horns and, if necessary, will make them swim across the river.

Hippopotami
and giraffes

Further upstream from Ayorou, hippopotami can be seen at Firgoun. Near to Tillabéri, it is also possible to see West Africa's last remaining giraffes in the savanna land bordering the Niger.

Another of the Séno Province's places of interest are the *Sebba* and *Essakan* gold mines where hundreds of workers sift for gold.

Finally, the *Oudalan* Province, also essentially inhabited by nomadic Tuaregs and Fulani, is situated further northwards (see section on Gorom Gorom).

(See practical information p. 168).

fada n'gourma/pama

■ "Look, that's where he landed when he fell from the sky!" The children from the little village of *Pama* in south-eastern Burkina Faso love pointing out the impression their ancestor's horseshoe is said to have made in the rocks. According to legend, Diaba Lompo, the first Gourmantché king, came down from the clouds on his flying horse and landed at Pama which he designated as the first capital of his kingdom in the 13th century. The oral traditions also have it that this mythical king was possibly the son (or cousin) of Ouedraogo, founder of the Mossi kingdom and hence, the Mossi and Gourmantché have always considered each other cousins.

Gourma was a kingdom of warriors who launched numerous expeditions in all directions from their headquarters in Pama. The first Gourmantché kings built up an impressive empire akin to the Tenkodogo, Ouagadougou and Yatenga empires established by their neighbouring Mossi kinsmen. After having won several battles, however, Gourma suffered a reverse of fortune.

During King Tantiari's reign (in the 17th century), disaster occured when the Tomba from northern Togo, who had previously been defeated by the Gourmantché, reversed the situation and headed to Pama with their army. For a whole night, battle raged in the little burning capital. Defeated, the Gourmantché were forced to leave the ruined Pama buried under corpses. Having taken refuge further to the north, the Gourmantché fought back during Lissoangui's reign (1684-1709), managing to push back the Tomba. It was Lissoangui's successor Yendabri, however, who inflicted the final, stinging defeat on the Tomba at Bassar in northern Togo.

When told by the griots, this final episode takes an epic turn as, according to the African bards, Yendabri stuck his sword in a rock at Bassar and said to his son: "If you come back to this place victoriously one day, you will take my sword" (the sword is still supposed to be there today!).

Fada
supplants Pama

Yendabri, who is considered to have been the greatest Gourmantché king, decided to transer the kingdom's capital further northwards to protect it from the southern Togolese and Beninese invaders. He chose *Fada N'Gourma* as the new capital, thus definitively supplanting Pama. Nowadays, Fada N'Gourma is a sizeable town at the crossroads of the Nationale 4 from Ouagadougou to Niger and the recently surfaced Nationale 18 which heads directly southwards towards Benin via Pama. Fada N'Gourma is both the Gourma Province county town and the Gourmantché Head Chief's seat of power.

Once the capital had been moved, Pama dwindled until it was no more than a small village tucked away in eastern Burkina Faso's savanna lands where little else is fournd other than large African wildlife— lions, antelopes and buffaloes. Life was to remain difficult, however, as in the Fifties, just before Upper Volta (now Burkina Faso) attained Independence in 1960, the French colonial authorities decided to create immense natural parks and wildlife reserves right in the heart of Gourmantché country.

All of a sudden, traditional hunters were forbidden to hunt on thousands of hectares of land. Even today, there is no question that the Gourmantché be allowed to partake in their favorite pastime: the animals living in the strictly protected parks are untouchable, and those in the reserves can only be hunted by European and American hunters who pay a lot in taxes and permits to hunt lions, buffaloes and large antelopes. This provides the country with quite a significant income, and several hunting camps have been set up for these modern day braggarts, notably at *Bigou, Ougarou* (on the Fada N'Gourma-Kantchari road) and Pama. Game hunters can find trackers, guides and four-wheel drive vehicles at Pama.

Hunting lions
with bows and arrows

As the Pama villagers hung up their old European trade guns and bows and arrows a long time ago, they now have to make do with the elders' tales of the good old days when lions were hunted with bows and arrows. As recently as a few decades ago, Gourmantché hunters did not need whole armories of modern shotguns to do battle with the big cats. All it took was their home made bows and tiny arrows that will leave any visitor flabbergasted. Where on earth did they find the courage, armed just with these rudimentary weapons, to affront the packs of ten to fifteen lions that hungrily prowled round the villages during the wet season on the look out for unsuspecting goats or even… pots of millet mush?

The answer is simple: the Gourmantché were not just good archers, but also had expert knowledge of poisons used to harden their arrows and magic spells, which steered the arrows straight to their target.

Less fearsome than their forefathers
who were threatened with foreign invasions
for centuries, the Lobi children immediately
form welcome committees
as soon as a stranger appears.

The night before a traditional hunt, the Gourmantché would go to the seer and make a few sacrifices in return for gris-gris. Thus equipped, they would head into the bush at dawn. Like any other hunter, as soon as they spotted their prey, they too would try to get as close to the animal as possible, but not because they doubted they would miss the target.

A magic potion

As the old hunters in Pama explain: "Even if you shot the arrow haphazardly, up in the air for example, it would not just land anywhere in the bush because a kind of magic potion would righten its path, make it hover just above the animal, before plunging into the target, leaving the animal paralysed." This ingenious explanation will charm ballistic experts as, after all, isn't this magic potion analogous with modern day remote control missiles?

Another of the Gourmantché's strange weapons were the "poupou guns" sometimes used instead of bows and arrows.

Made from an assortment of bits and pieces, these old blunderbusses had a section of piping for a barrel and, often, a bit of rubber from the inner chamber of a tyre for a trigger spring. Stuffed with powder and shot, the main disadvantage with "poupou guns" was their propensity to explode in the owners hands, usually taking an arm or part of the shoulder with it. Nowadays, these old relics are considered museum pieces, reminding of the olden days when for years such guns were the only fire arms used in sub-Saharan Africa for hunting and fighting.

Towards the Arli and Pendjari Parks

Burkina Faso's vast eastern parks and reserves can be reached from both Fada N'Gourma and Pama, especially *Arli National Park* (see relevant section). To get there, follow the track from the *Tindangou* crossroads (16 km south of Pama on the Nationale 18 to Benin). A four-wheel drive vehicle is essential for making this 85 km journey from Tindangou to Arli, but it is well worth it as some beautiful

MYSTERIOUS RUINS

■ *Strange ruins of houses, whose origins go back to the beginnings of time can be found dotted here and there all over Burkina Faso.*
This is how the writer Guilhelm Marcel described one these buildings at Loropéni, near to Gaoua:
"....Several hundred metres northwards by foot across a field— which means that the ruin is about three kilometres north-west of Loropéni—and we were in front of an imposing, vaguely square wall, about a hundred metres in length.
We entered a vast enclosure where tall grass made it difficult for us to advance via a heap of rubble that must have once been a door. Some dozen metres on, we reached a second wall as considerable as the first one that seemed to divide the immense square into two very unequal parts.
We entered the large rectangle and almost immediately were in a compartment a few metres in length: perhaps a warder's room, perhaps a food store. The general form allowed for several of these rooms, either situated against the party wall, or completely detached. The mass of fallen earth and stones have raised the level surrounding the walls. From the vaguely circular kind of opening, which must have once been as tall as a man and today is level with the rest, we tried to evaluate the thickness of the construction. It must have been a metre and a half at its base, tapering regularly to the top. The high quality rubble stones

gaoua

Gourmantché villages can be seen tucked away in the savanna, like, for example, *Sombouali, Singou* and *Madjoari* villages.

Many wild animals including monkeys, buffaloes and antelopes can also been seen en route. In Arli there is a good hotel at the foot of the beautiful *Gobnangou* Escarpment.

From Pama, it is also possible to reach *Pendjari River*, where lions can sometimes be seen drinking. The river forms a natural border between Burkina Faso and Benin. The recently reorganised, large national park in northern Benin is named after the river. When driving from Pama to the Pendjari, it is worth stopping to visit the *Kompienga* dam.

(See practical information p. 168).

■ Fearsome? The word is hardly strong enough to describe the Lobi people living in south-western Burkina Faso and northern Ghana and Côte d'Ivoire who, once warriors, have now converted to farming and hunting. As their region suffered all kinds of wars, raids and invasions, for centuries the Lobi got used to living entrenched in real fortresses, armed to the teeth. Only very recently—perhaps reassured by the peace that now reigns in Burkina Faso—did they deign to lay down their bows and poisoned arrows which they always used to keep close at hand whether they were working in the fields or sleeping!

Lobi architecture

Anyone who has visited the Lobi region and discovered the strange buildings set in the hills around Gaoua and Kampti will soon confirm such stories. At first sight, the Lobi fortified, windowless habitations with thick, cracked walls, look remarkably like mud blockhouses. Just one or two narrow openings are pierced in the walls, like the entrance to a burrow. In the dark

themselves seem to shrink the further up the building they are and, at the highest points, there is an additional layer of clay about fifty centimetres thick. The whole thing is about six to eight metres. The builders wanted to make the walls straight and smooth, without slots or loopholes, windows on the outside, bumps that could facilitate climbing, without any gaps, with no embankment inside, without anything in fact that may suggest the need to defend or attack. The layers of stone are regular and bound with a remarkably hard "cement" made from clay and sand. A roughcast of the same kind covers the inner wall in large patches and seems to go as far as the clay mixture that tops the best conserved tips (...).
... The peaceful Gan villagers living in the area refer to the mysterious ruin as the "house of refusal" and they have always effectively "refused" to use it, as if some curse hung over this silent witness of troubled events. Nothing, in any case, can be more heterogeneous than this huge construction, this match for history, that defies the passage of time, both proud and pitiful, in the heart of the bush near to these huts, that take on the frail dimensions of a man. These remains of a sinister past of servitude do not tie up in any way with things of the present and the soul would like to refuse the sinister evocations of a time when human slaves groaned under the whips of the sordid gold lusting traders".

hallway, one almost expects to see the long barrel of some kind of gun loom out of the shadows! At closer hand, these forts are much less formidable.

Out on the esplanade, children learn to play the balafon, whilst their mother looks for kindling wood to do the cooking and their father inspects his millet and corn plots and there is even a sleeping dog, a few chickens pecking here and there and a couple of amorous pigeons to complete the bucolic picture.

Minotaur dens

Once inside the houses, however, visitors will immediately understand that the carefree impression given outside is deceptive. The Lobi have never dropped their guard in fact, as can be seen from the fact that the layout of their homes has not changed an iota since the days of the heroic, never ending wars. Not even one tiny window has been made to light or air this maze of dark, smoky rooms.

On the contrary, the Lobi appear to be at ease buried away in their minotaur dens. Any outsider who enters immediately finds themselves at a disadvantage. In the dark, unfamiliar surroundings, strangers are forced to grope along like blind men, bumping into the low ceilings and getting lost in the twisting and turning passages. By the time their eyes grow accustomed to the dark, it is already too late. The inhabitants hidden away in the shadows will have had ample time to gauge the visitor's intentions and to put him out of action if he is an enemy.

Magical telecommunications

What is even more amazing is the occult-based warning system that protects the Lobi habitations. A fetish placed on the roof of the house acts like a radar, immediately detecting when a stranger approaches the family compound. A soon as the intruder is spotted, the fetish warns another fetish in the sacred wood about a hundred metres away. This statuette in turn alerts the spirits in the ancestral hut in the courtyard who then contact the various seers in the sky.

This complex, instantaneous circuit also sets off commotion in the whole house where the inhabitants make for their look out posts, ready for action.

In some compounds, like that of the *Kampti* seer, there may be slight variations in this circuit similar to a kind of "magi-cal satellite telecommunications station". Fetishes placed outside also communicate with a huge hippo-shaped rock which in turn transmits the signal to the ancestral hut and the sky. It is possible to visit this seer's residence and the experience is one of the most memorable events during a trip to Burkina Faso.

Having plunged into the depths of his smoky labyrinth, one comes to the ancestral hut where the seer usually receives "customers" who have come for a consultation. A round hole somewhat like a porthole in the passage wall leads to the room if two orders are obeyed: visitors have to take their shoes off (like in the mosque) and enter the room backwards.

Inside, visitors are in for an experience! In the tiny, dark room, a beam of light shines from the roof, lighting the middle of the room where there are two wonderful typical Lobi statues buried up to their necks in a heap of cowry shells. This lighting accentuates and dramatizes the forms of the sculptures which are better displayed here than in any museum. It is like being in the crypt of some sacred sanctuary! As the eye becomes accustomed to the darkness, other statues can be made out at the end of the room along with some wrapped ritual objects and calabashes that are perhaps filled with philtres.

Sat on the ground, the seer begins the session by throwing cowry shells on the ground as if he were playing jacks. According to how they land, he will be able to read whether the rains will fall or not, if the harvests will be good or bad, if a given woman is fertile or not, and if a student in the big city will pass his or her exams!

The Lobi museum

Before leaving Gaoua and the Lobi region, visitors are strongly advised to visit the town's museum devoted to the Lobi people (set up by the French ethnologist Madeleine Père who has lived in Gaoua for many years). This well-stocked museum exhibits numerous objects, weapons and tools used in the various Lobi activities like hunting (bows and old European trade guns), agriculture, forging and even warfare (helmets made out of half calabashes covered with feathers and porcupine spikes). Several very beautiful ancient statues on display bear witness to the Lobi sculptors great artistic skills (see Panorama). One three-legged stool which, like most Lobi chairs, is surmounted by a little carved head, is particularly interesting.

*In the Kampti soothsayer's lair
in the Lobi region, light shining down
from the ceiling dramatises the forms
of the ritual statues that peep out from
under piles of cowrie shells.*

The charmed Lobi bronze or iron pendants and bracelets displayed are also remarkable. The Lobi, who are highly superstitious people, wear these grigris as they are protected by occult powers. Such charms either represent twins, the moon or pairs of overlapping chameleons.

Another of the interesting exhibits are the archive photos taken by Arnold Heim in 1934, as they show the Lobi community as it had probably been for centuries: the men's almost naked bodies were ritually scarified and the women's faces were deformed by lip plates and plugs (either a little stick or a plate inserted in the lips). Here in the photos, the brave Lobi warriors pose obligingly for the camera, displaying their calabash helmets, bows and poisoned arrows.

The Loropéni ruins

Along with *Kampti* and its seer, *Batié*, situated 42 km south-west of Gaoua in Burkina Faso's southernmost region, is another place worth visiting here in the heart of Lobi country. Forming a sort of point that juts into northern Ghana and Côte d'Ivoire, this little enclave with its beautiful hills overlooking the valley of the *Mouhoun* (ex-Black Volta) that flows down into Ghana, with its forests like *Koulbi* forest right in the south, and with its gallery forests whose foliage forms arches over the rivers, will charm visitors fond of green spaces.

In the *Gan region*, 39 km west of Gaoua is the curious *Loropéni* archaeological site (take the Nationale 11 to Banfora). Here the mysterious remains of a family compound (see inset) have raised many questions amongst the experts and have inspired many a tale. Some people have even claimed that they are proof of Phœnician and Egyptian presence (!). Others attribute the remains to the Portuguese or the Moroccans.

According to the historian Jacques Bertho: "A building of this type belonged to slave traders who used to house slaves who were not worth exporting there, instead using them to wash the gold that is still mined in the region where these ruins are located. The building could also have been used as a meeting place where traders could rest after making forays to catch slaves".

Professor Joseph Ki-Zerbo claims, on the other hand, that these ruins date back to earlier than the 16th century: "They correspond more or less with the period when the Mandé were penetrating the forest in search of new sources of gold and were possibly used by Wangara traders and the local gold prospectors as rendez-vous points".

René Mauny esteems, however, that these ruins are quite simply Lobi vestiges as lost wax objects were found there (bracelets, rings and figurines like those still made in the Lobi region today).

Traditional markets

In several of the villages and small towns north of Gaoua, particularly interesting craft objects can be found in the traditional markets, for example in *Bouroum Bouroum* in the Lobi region (wooden sculptures, basketry and pottery), *Diébougou* in the Birifor region (pottery and basketry) and *Dano* in the Dagari region (pottery and weaving).

(See practical information p. 169).

gorom gorom

■ The Gorom Gorom region right in the north of the country where the borders of Burkina Faso, Mali and Niger meet, is very poetically named the "Land of the Blue Tents". In fact, this northern Province is maintly inhabited by Tuareg and Tiguirmalt nomads who settled here in their *ou-dalan* (blue tents) during the 16th century. The tribe and the Province are named *Oudalan* after these tents. Other nomads— the Fulani and the Moors — also live here along with the settled Songhai whose major empire here in the Niger loop was destroyed by the Moroccans in the 16th century after the battle of Tondibi (April, 1591).

Approaching the desert

In this landscape typical of Sahelian regions, Oudalan's sun-burnt steppes stretch into the distance and the first few dunes begin to show as a reminder of the desert's proximity. Many nomadic pastors live in this region, eternally wandering from place to place in search of water and pastures for their herds of bovines and dromedaries. The sight of whole families of Fulani nomads slowly riding along on mules with all their belongings is enough to make one think time has stopped in the Middle Ages.

In the Gorom Gorom region, a new form of tourism based on the human contact between European visitors and the African villagers is currently being tried. The aim is to encourage visitors to discover the real Africa with all its serious development problems, rather than a picture "post card" Africa with deserted beaches, blue seas and palm trees.

By bus, bike or bush taxi

In December 1980, the French company "le Point-Mulhouse" set up its own airline charter company (le Point-Air) and began organising the first cheap flights from Lyons to Ouagadougou. The initiative was a great success, attracting customers who before had been unable to afford the very expensive regular long haul flights, especially those to Africa.

Suddenly groups of students, teachers, families on relatively low budgets and all sorts of travellers passionate about the Third World began arriving in Ouagadougou. Little by little, the Burkinabè capital became a convenient starting point for trips around Upper Volta as it was still then called, and the neighbouring countries of Mali (especially the Dogon region), Côte d'Ivoire, Ghana, Togo and Benin. Making the most of the rough and ready accommodation available—village huts, encampments—these tourists travelled round on even the most uncomfortable local public transport: trains, bush taxis, buses, motorbikes, hired bikes, or simply by foot.

The success of the first charter flights encouraged the owners of "le Point-Mulhouse" to work with the Burkinabè authorities to develop on-site accommodation in small towns in eastern, western, northern and central Burkina Faso. The decision was taken to build the first site in the north at Gorom Gorom, the meeting place of all the Sahelian peoples, especially the nomads. In 1984, the Gorom Gorom hotel complex opened its doors to the public. Built in the same architectural style and in the same materials (mud bricks) as a typical Sahelian village, it offers tourists an initial direct contact with the people of the Sahelian regions, thereby helping them really discover the region.

Understanding the Third World

In order to facilitate contact between tourists and local inhabitants, an interior courtyard was built in the hotel complex as a meeting place, equipped with a "discussion corner" and arts and crafts stalls. Even more original were the on site conferences organised at the Gorom Gorom centre. Tourists who attented these conferences learnt about organic agriculture, the problems of fighting the droughts and desertification affecting the country, about wider geopolitical questions like North-South relationships, and about issues more specific to Africa like traditional medicine and earthen architecture. Tourists who stayed at the Gorom Gorom hotel complex did not just take a classic holiday, but learnt to understand the Third World better and, according to their means and capacities, could then offer solutions to development questions.

This style of tourism, which some called "militant", had the advantage of being based on well-meant ideas and, perhaps for the first time, offered a radically new European approach to Africa: instead of continuing the plundering begun during the colonial period, visitors from Europe established friendly relationships with the African people. This is evident from an excerpt of French tourists' accounts on returning from Burkina Faso, quoted here in an article written at the time by "Le Monde" journalist Alain Faujas:

Although much appreciated by tourists, the magnificent
Oursi dunes are in fact unfortunately a sign of the desertificãtion
taking place in the Sahelian region (Photo ONTB).
The Burkinabè authorities have undertaken large reforestation
campaigns in an attempt to solve the problem.

"It was amazing, Rafael exclaims. The villagers welcomed us in their huts and offered us water and millet. Everywhere we went they begged us to stay with them for two or three days. Oh! Sometimes it was hard, it was so hot! We weren't familiar with the food either, but we did try everything.

I have never met such kind, hospitable people before: we were invited to a wedding and a party. I now understand that African music is inspired by and embodies the rhythm of daily rituals: the rhythm of pounding the millet, the rhythm of carrying water. We really know so little about Africa."

Due to complications with the French authorities (notably the civil aviation authorities), however, "le Point-Mulhouse" was forced to stop its flights at the end of the Eighties and to file its statement of affairs and hence, a wonderful adventure came to an end…

Pink
sand dunes

The Gorom Gorom hotel complex still exists nonetheless and is a perfect base from which to make numerous excursions in northern Burkina Faso's Sahelian Provinces of Oudalan, of which Gorom Gorom is the county town, *Soum* (Djibo) and *Seno* (Dori).

In Gorom Gorom, visitors must go to the main market where all the region's nomadic pastors (Tuaregs and Fulani) come together every Thursday, and the old quarters where it is possible to visit the forgeries and jewellery and leather workshops.

Further to the north-west, the beautiful *Ouri Pool* is surrounded by white and pink sand dunes. Many of the shepherds bring their cattle to drink here amongst the flocks of aquatic birds.

A model
ranch

Another circuit from Gorom Gorom to the north-east passes via *Markoye* village where huge cattle markets are held on Mondays and Tuesdays. There is even a model ranch here, where extensive bovine, sheep and goat rearing are practised. Particularly rich art and craft works can be found in Markoye, for example the beautiful, finely decorated leather saddle bags used by the Tuaregs, traditional *samaras* sandals, jewellery and locally woven covers.

Tambao's
deposits

About twenty kilometres north of Markoye near the border with Niger and Mali, the *Tambao* site has already aroused a great deal of interest due to the important manganese deposit discovered there. The deposit has not yet been exploited as it is not just a case of opening a mine and building an ore processing plant, but rather of building a whole town for the miners and engineers as well as prolonging the Abidjan-Ouagadougou railway to this northern region of Burkina Faso. Without this, it would be impossible to transport the ore at a reasonable price from this landlocked Sahelian region to Abidjan port, from where it would then be exported all over the world by ship.

Further northwards still right by the Malian border, *Tin-Akof* is a pretty Tuareg village near the *Beli* River, that feeds into the right bank of the Niger. As well as meeting nomads there, visitors will also see a huge number of birds as the Beli is a true ornithological sanctuary.

(See practical information p. 169).

houndé/boni

■ All that can be heard at first is the low thudding of drums and the high chiming of balafons. Next, a whole delegation of young people arrive asking us to join them. It is time to quickly break off the long discussion with the kind chief of *Boni*, the little Bobo village near to Houndé: the celebrations are about to begin!

Foreign visitors will soon appreciate that it is a real privilege to be allowed to watch one of these large traditional ceremonies and such occasions are amongst the most memorable moments of the stay in Burkina Faso.

"Cleaning up" the village

The celebrations take place in the dry season, and visitors must first ask the traditional leaders—the chief of the lands and the village chief—for permission to watch.

By following their ears through the maze-like, little Boni streets, visitors suddenly come across a cortege of about thirty extraordinary looking characters followed down the long, narrow trench-like alleys by the traditional orchestra. From afar, they appear to be wearing brown fur coats and bearing huge wooden strips painted with checks, diamonds, and black and white squares of chevrons by conceptual artists.

Then one realises that these voluminous costumes are in fact made from thousands of coarse, rope-like plant fibres.

For over an hour, these traditional Bobo masqueraders rush around the whole village followed by the musicians and crowds of villagers.

According to ethnologists, these dry season celebrations purify the village and regenerate the land so that it will produce plentiful harvests when the rains fall.

Totemic masks

Incarnating the village's protecting spirits, these masks in fact quite simply come to do the cleaning! The scrubbing brush-like fibre or leaf masks brush past the villagers and the walls of their houses collecting up all the "harmful dust" that accumulates every day due to the inhabitants wrong-doings.

They literally and metaphorically "clean" the whole village of its impurities which they carry off into the bush, leaving a regenerated community behind them.

Before retreating into the bush, the masks dance in the centre of Boni village.

Each masquerader mimes the totemic animal he represents. Masks with antelope heads will rear up, paw at the ground and stamp their feet whilst brandishing their horns. Most stunning are the butterfly masks with large wooden wings painted with geometric designs which whirl about, pause a moment as if landed on a flower, then flutter off again exactly as butterflies always do.

Foreign visitors following the cortege will catch lots of glimpses of daily Bobo life. In front of the huts or through their open doors, they will see most of the family absorbed in household tasks like pounding millet, or making shea butter from the karite kernels heaped on the doorstep.

Towards Bobo Dioulasso

Numerous artisans—potters, basket makers, blacksmiths—can be seen working in the villages around Houndé. It may also be possible to find the excellent local sculptors who make the festival masks so sought-after by the museums and private collectors.

To the west, the Nationale 1 leads to Burkina Faso's economic capital Bobo Dioulasso (see relevant section), which is a particularly interesting town to visit.

(See practical information p. 169).

*Bobo masks, amongst some
of the finest pieces of African sculpture,
are first and foremost ritual objects
and feature in many
of the traditional ceremonies.*

kaboré tembi (national park)

■ Nature lovers will approve the Burkinabè authorities' recent decision to rename the Pô national park after Kaboré Tembi, a Forestry Commission employee who was cowardly murdered by a poacher in 1981.

A memorial has also been erected in this park to the south of Ouagadougou which, in the past, was reputed for its large herds of elephants.

Courageous park warders

The courage of these men who risk their lives every day to protect wildlife all over Africa can never be commended highly enough.

The problem is that they are in fact fighting a major international network responsible for setting up huge rackets all over Africa and forming armed gangs who procure the ivory elephants tusks and rhinoceros horns. A continuing battle is going on in different parts of the African continent, and many of the warders in wildlife parks and reserves are hurt or killed every year.

Zoologists like Pierre Pfeffer, author of the book *Vie et Mort d'un Géant, l'Eléphant d'Afrique* (Editions Flammarion), predict that the African elephant will become extinct over the next ten years if draconian protection measures are not taken.

Such claims are substantiated by the fact that tusks weighing less than 5 kg have appeared on the international black market, which means that poachers are now killing baby elephants along with the adults, thereby leaving the species no chance of survival…

But the African countries' vigilance and the Washington Convention (which bans all trade in ivory and rare animal skins) have been efficient, although the dispensations introduced by the June 1997 Harare conference may well constitute a new danger.

Nearly all the big elephants in Burkina Faso's Kaboré Tembi Park have now been poached. If visitors really want to see these huge creatures, they should go to the protected *Deux Balé Forest* near Boromo to the west of Ouagadougou, or to the *Nazinga Game Ranch*.

It is nonetheless worth visiting the 150,000 hectare Kaboré Tembi Park where

THE CAT THAT ATE THE MOON

■ *In his book* Lumière sur la Volta, *the missionnary Father Marcel Paternot recounts a particularly picturesque and poetic scene he witnessed at Diébougou, in the Lobi-Dagari region in western Burkina Faso.*
"The night was calm; not a drum beat in the town, only the savage and raucous howling of the hyena could be heard from time to time, and a lost jackal began to bark sinisterly. It must have been about midnight. All of a sudden noise broke out : it sounded as if someone deranged was banging harder and harder on an old saucepan.
"—What idiot is that?" murmured my bed mate. "As if it's not already hard enough to get to sleep!"
But the banging becam twice as intense, faster. Cries soon broke out, making an incredible din! What was happening?
I jumped out of bed, as did my companions and we went out onto the veranda of the house that looked out over the town.
What an incredible sight! The head chief's hut was lit up by a multitude of dried millet stalk torches, thousands of Blacks were bustling around, gun shots were going off and hundreds of men were furiously beating on drums, old petrol containers, old tin

kaya

large numbers of monkeys, wart hogs and antelopes can be seen.

The Nazinga Ranch animals

To get to the Nazinga Ranch, take the Léo road (D7) westwards from Pô via Tia-kané (see section on Pô). This 100,000 hectare ranch is particularly original in that it is both a natural reserve and a wildlife farm where antelopes are bred for their meat which is then sent to markets in Oua-gadougou.

When driving along the 600 km of tracks, visitors will see lots of elephants, all kinds of antelopes (sable antelopes, bubals, kobs, oribis, bushbucks and dui-kers), monkeys (cynoscephales, patas monkeys and grivets) and warthogs. Although there are buffaloes, lions, pan-thers, hyenas and crocodiles at the ranch, they will be seen less frequently.

All sorts of birds can also be seen and heard, as can the ranch's protected flora, notably the larger species like baobabs, cailcedras and the immense kapok trees. *(See practical information p. 169).*

■ For centuries, the saddlers in and around Kaya supplied harness and saddles to the great Mossi horsemen whose strength help-ed the Mossi kingdoms to perpetuate their power in West Africa. Now that the Nabas are no longer allowed to raise armies, and now that cars and "two wheelers" have replaced horses, these cavaliers have prac-tically disappeared from present Burkina Faso. On rare, important occasions, how-ever, cavaliers wearing helmets and deco-rated tunics rise out of the past on adorned horses like European knights heading off to a tournament in the Middle Ages.

A large leather and hide market

Although Kaya has developed with the times, it has nonetheless remained a large market for leather and hides. Its pictu-resque tanneries are supplied by noma-dic Fulani and Tuareg pastors from the north, and in turn supply leather workers who make shoes, bags, saddle bags and sometimes even attaché cases for the capi-tal's city dwellers. Some saddlers in the area do still make harness for the few

cans and bits of iron. The women accompanied the deafening din by clapping their hands. Then piercing cries rang out. What were they saying? Impossible to make anything out...
The torch lit cortege then began to move to the sound of this new style of fanfare!... They came closer. We finally managed to make out these words: "The cat is eating the moon! The cat is eating the moon!" repeated rhythmically almost as if they were chanting slogans!
Instinctively, we turned our heads to look at the moon... Well, well, an eclipse was taking place and, my gosh, it was very clear, already half of the luminous circle was veiled. As the shadow advanced, the beatings increased, the cries became more and more intense... and the cortege ran through all the streets of the town, constantly swelling with new-comers who had left their huts and rushed to replace those already hoarse from shouting. Then little by little, the moon resumed its normal shape and we heard the cries:"Cat, let go of the moon! Cat, let go of the moon!..." Finally its shine came back, and the din died down, then petered out completely".

kongoussi

horses still living in the Mossi region (the men make most of the saddles and harness whilst the women plait the bridles and decorate them with coloured leather tassels).

Dyers and weavers also work in Kaya. Amongst other things, the weavers, who are regrouped in the same quarter, make covers with black and white geometric designs (diamonds, checks, hatching).

Dugout canoes on Lake Dem

Like Kongoussi (see following section), Kaya is also an agricultural town and survives on fruit and vegetable growing. Large market gardening areas have developed around the town and dams have been constructed on Lake Dem. Pleasant trips can be made here in dugout canoes, offering a wonderful view of this particularly bucolic landscape where Fulani pastors bring their large herds of zebus to drink amongst the flocks of aquatic birds.

From the crossroads town Kaya, it is possible to visit the Burkinabè Sahelian region by either taking the Kongoussi and Djibo roads westwards, or by taking the Nationale 3 which heads up to Dori and Gorom Gorom and on around the north of the country. This latter route passes by the beautiful *Tougouri* and *Yalogo* Lakes where Fulani nomads are found alongside Mossi farmers. About 20 km north of Yalogo is the beautiful, earthen Bani mosque already mentioned in the section on Dori.

(See practical information p. 170).

■ Many of the early fruit and vegetables savoured in both Ouagadougou's restaurants and in Europe come from the little agricultural town of Kongoussi north of the capital in the Mossi region.

The quality and quantity of one of the market gardening crops produced has earnt the *Bam Province* county town its humorous nickname : "the French bean capital".

The largest lake in Burkina

Vast agricultural zones have developed around the town, irrigated by Lake Bam, Burkina Faso's largest natural lake. Well shaded by the large trees that grow on its shores, Lake Bam is especially impressive after the rainy season (from June to the end of October) when it sometimes swells to over 30 km in diameter.

One of the Kongoussi region's specialities is iron work. For centuries, iron ore was extracted from the laterite using earthen blast furnaces. The technique was only abandoned quite recently.

"Saviours of the land"

Nowadays, Burkinabè blacksmiths work using scrap metal found in the towns whether it be old cars or any other kind of old iron.

Blacksmiths—who make arms and tools—have always been particularly appreciated by the Mossi people who consider them indispensable, hence the title "saviours of the land" *(baamoogo)*.

Often married to potters (as they also need a fire for their work), many blacksmiths live in Kongoussi and the surrounding villages of *Darigma, Loulouka* and *Bam*.

Visitors can go and watch them work and will be amazed by the ingenuity of the rudimentary techniques used to make tools (hoes, sickles, knives, etc) from very basic materials.

All they need is a hearth dug into the ground, goat skin lined bellows and a little anvil, often fashioned out of an old bit of railway track.

Other artisans can also be found working in the Kongoussi region. For instance, many weavers work in *Tikaré* and *Zana*, whilst in *Bam*, artisans dye material in cement indigo dye pits dug in the ground.

From Kongoussi, visitors may wish to head northwards to the *Kurumba region* (otherwise known as the Fulse region) which begins about forty kilometres away at *Bourzanga*.

koudougou

Traditional mud huts

Here visitors will be able to see traditional mud huts which, unlike in any other region, are built in twin pairs and are storeyed.

If visitors are lucky, they may be able to watch the animist rites practised by the people, particularly those involving the *adone* masks (representing antelope heads).

(See practical information p. 170).

■ With over 60,000 inhabitants, Koudougou is the third largest town in Burkina Faso and is reputed for its textile industry and its famous "red dancers". These dancers can now normally be seen performing at all festivities and official events ranging from school and hotel inaugurations to VIP visits to this region west of Ouagadougou and the Mossi lands.

As ethnologist Jean-Louis Paudrat points out: "The Koudougou "red dancers" are a sect of Gourounsi former captives. In the past, they were at the service of the traditional chief, the Moogo Naaba of Ouagadougou, and were responsible for looking after his horses, which explains why they are still sometimes called the "red cavaliers".

"The colour of their clothes is the same as the saddlecloth of the sovereign's horse. Their horse hair fly swats are a reference to the fact that they were once grooms and, furthermore, the movements of their dance evokes the animal's movements.

"The calabash helmets the dancers had to wear for nine years to assure the Tengsoba's longevity (the chief of the land) have now been replaced by peaked hats".

EARTHEN BLAST FURNACES

■ *At the beginning of the 1970s, the Japanese ethnologist Junzo Kawada discovered one of Burkina Faso's last remaining blast furnaces at Darigma (8 km from Kongoussi) when he was studying the country's traditional technology. Unfortunately, the weather finally got the better of the furnace, which collapsed during the rainy season in 1977.*
This is what Junso Kawada wrote about it:
"Abandoned about fifty years ago, it is a circular, tapering tower about 5 metres tall. Nine openings have been fashioned here and there in the wider bottom part. According to the somewhat vague accounts given by the village elders, one of the openings, which is three times larger than the others, was used for removing slag or for blasting air inside with bellows, the clay remains of which can still be found on site. The hole further up in the wall was probably for ventilation. According to the village elders, there were seven blast furnaces in the village when they were little."

manega

From the raw cotton to the finished product

Cotton from plantations in western Burkina Faso is brought by train and lorry load to "Faso-Fani" in Koudougou, one of the country's largest industrial complexes. Here bales of raw cotton are used in a complex production process that begins with the manufacturing of cotton thread, passes on to dying, weaving and printing the material and finishes off with making clothes and undergarments (hosiery).

Anyone wishing to visit this large textile factory, one of the jewels of Burkina Faso's still embryonic industry, should contact the director of Faso-Fani first.

A traditional mini-religion

Also of interest here in the *Boulkiemdé* Province county town is the traditional religion *Sukomsé* practised in and around Koudougou alone by the Nyonyosé, Burkina Faso's first inhabitants who, after being defeated by the Mossi, were assimilated into their community. The name Sukomsé comes from *suko,* the phallic stone that serves as a sacrifical altar. Led by a chief (the *firma)* and a priest (the *wilma),* the sect organises numerous meetings for initiates and involves the worship of the ancestors' totemic animals and the villages' protecting spirits like the buffalo, crocodile or antelope.

Like most animists, followers of the sect are not circumcised. They also have to take a vow of chastity. Initiates are considered to have great powers, like the ability to cause or stop ligthtning and rain simply by stamping their feet. After several years—three, six or nine years—the sect dissolves and is only reformed when a new chief is designated after the old one dies.

(See practical information p. 170).

■ Manega, several kilometres north of Ouagadougou, is a difficult place to describe. Created by the lawyer-poet Frédéric Pacéré Titinga, it is a centre for African culture that will satisfy even the most curious visitors.

As soon as one enters the place, it is difficult to decide what to look at first as Manega is a traditional chief's residence, a truly mystical place, has an open-air sculpture park, an ethnological museum and is a place of exchange for all cultures—precisely the kind of amalgam advocated by the poet Léopold Sédar Senghor for such a long time.

Visitors must trust their eyesight to find the place. A long way before Manega itself, a strange sculpted antennae can already be seen from the track poking out from the tree tops. By cutting through the bush, visitors will then come to a roundabout where there is a clearer view of the antennae, which is in fact a totem, the *Karinga* or "Manega Mask", homage to African culture. The tallest of the five pillars is 20 m tall, and the monument bears the inscription-proverb: "If the termitarium is alive, let earth be piled on earth". The other pillars bear the names of the last four Mossi kings.

Further on are brightly coloured, plaster equestrian statues representing these Nabas. One of them is dedicated to Moro Naba Wogbo ("the elephant"), the hero of resistance to French colonisation.

The extraordinary "Maison de la Culture" is found further on in the traditional village and has a large polychrome stucco ceiling sculpted with painted African masks, like the very beautiful Bobo butterfly mask. Right next to it in the village is the modern mausoleum dedicated to the major Mossi kings.

A mini museum of Mankind

In our opinion, the most interesting thing in Manega is the large *museum.* Here, using life-size dummies, the main Mossi animist ceremonies have been reconstituted in a series of cells closed off by grills. Several of the rooms in this real little *Museum of Mankind* opened in 1991 have been devoted to Mossi funeral rites. There are also superb collections of Mossi, Bobo and Gourounsi masks and an extraordinary set of little bronze figurines depicting the entire history of the Mossi empire.

(See practical information p. 170).

ouahabou

■ For those not yet familiar with Sudanese style architecture, the wonderful little earthen mosque in Ouahabou is a perfect showpiece. Although not as imposingly large as Djenné mosque in Timbuktu, Mopti mosque in Mali or Agadez mosque in Niger, this similarly styled mosque is nonetheless equally beautiful with its tapering minaret bristling with wooden posts, pointed cylindrical pillars and pinnacles surmounted by ostrich eggs: in fact the whole building looks like it was modeled out of clay by a cubist artist.

This mosque's beauty yet again reveals the many plastic qualities of this much disparaged mud mixture which is considered a poor building material all over the world and especially in Africa, where people are more and more inclined to use parpen and corrugated iron. Walking around the Ouahabou mosque, however, visitors will be struck by the skill with which the builders did justice to this material, as they modelled it with their bare hands and smoothed off all angles, thus inventing voluptuous, curved forms.

A former capital

During the last century, this little village off the Nationale 1 from Ouagadougou to Bobo Dioulasso was the capital of the Ouahabou kingdom. This ephemeral micro-State was created in 1850 by Mamadou Karantao, a Muslim Marka from Djenné in Mali. With his army of Marka, Mossi, Dagari and Dioula soldiers, Karantao set out to conquer western Burkina Faso.

Before founding the capital Ouahabou, he first of all defeated the Kô people and set up headquarters in nearby *Boromo*, then began to attack the Bwaba people settled north of Ouahabou in the *Mouhoun River* loop. He managed to take control of several of their villages, thereby imposing his supremacy in the region, but did not manage to supplant the Ouattara dynasty based in Bobo Dioulasso, capital of the old Gouiriko empire.

His son Karamokho Moktar continued the trend, sending armies southwards to the Lobi and Dagari regions. After several victories, they were defeated at *Djindermé* in 1887. The Ouahabou kingdom survived nonetheless and continued to exist until all of these West African territories were colonised by the French at the end of the 19th century. The Ouahabou kings did cooperate with the new occupants, however, and even signed a treaty of alliance in 1897.

A village of 700 to 800 inhabitants

A lot is known about Ouahabou and its sovereign the Karamokho Moktar, thanks to accounts written by the French Captain, Gustave Binger in his travel diary *Du Niger au Golfe de Guinée*. Visiting Ouahabou in May 1888, Binger noted that there were no more than 700 to 800 inhabitants left living in the village, in buildings that were "all made out of mud with flat or thatched roofs". He was particularly struck by the mosque whose architecture he described at the time as quite "severe".

Having waited forty-eight hours, Binger was received by the marabout whom he describes in a particularly exaggerated, caricatured manner:

"This holy man made a rather deplorable impression on me. He was dressed in an excessively dirty white *doroké* and wore a tattered tarboosh around which he had wound a strip of equally dirty white cotton material. A rag which must have once been a burnous was draped over his left shoulder; in front of him on the ground lay his iron pilgrim's staff tipped with a copper knob. In his right hand he told the beads at an extraordinary speed, moving his lips from time to time, whilst darting furtive looks at me.

"Karamokho Moktar must be around fifty to sixty years old; the tip of his goatee is beginning to go grey. Although his features and his expression imply that he is more intelligent than the average Black, his whole countenance immediately made me think "This holy man seems to me to be a downright scoundrel". Two little naked captives were crouched on his left and right, each holding pistols that were not very dangerous given that they not only had no hammers, but also had no plates. When all his friends had arrived, he greeted me and apologised for have kept me waiting, then added: "Consider me as nothing other than a friend; you can count on me for whatever you need".

A holy man

"As it was nearly time for prayers at sunset (*fittiri*), he asked me to come back the next day to discuss my departure and the route I wanted to take. As he was about to stand up to go home, assistants rushed forwards and, holding him under the arms, lifted him up whilst others kissed his feet, putting on his sandals. Karamokho Moktar is considered a saint here who prays all

*Several of Burkina's Sahelian peoples,
notably the Samo people,
wear clothes adorned with cowrie shells
(in the past a form of money),
during the rain making ceremonies.*

the time. He sometimes makes those who come to see him wait several weeks, and one rarely obtains a meeting with him before having waited ten days.

"He is well loved, pays little attention to politics and punishes only thiefs and *dolo* drinkers severely. Lacking in energy, he is powerless to suppress any kind of disorder which means that every day the Niéniégué from Pô, the little confederacy next door to Bouki, capture and enslave people from Ouahabou. It is therefore prudent to go no further than a few hundred metres from the village without being armed.

"I gave Karamokho Moktar a small gift which, amongst other trifling objects, notably included a pistol and a fine piece of cloth that he sent back to me saying that it was too much. As I insisted that he would accept the objects, he agreed to keep the pistol, saying that he was very happy to have it as I offered it so kindly, but would not accept the material..."

(See practical information p. 170).

ouahigouya

■ The Sunday strollers and innumerable fishermen who frequent the banks of the huge dams give Ouahigouya a rustic air that is a very far cry from the terrible reputation the city earnt for conquering and war-mongering over the last few centuries. It is now difficult to imagine that for a long time, Ouahigouya was the capital of the sometimes bloodthirsty Yatenga empire founded by the Mossi along with the Tenkodogo and Ouagadougou kingdoms.

Ouahigouya was founded by Naba Kango (1754-1787), the most powerful and most formidable Yatenga Mossi emperor. As he wanted to make his new capital Waiguyo (Ouahigouya) into an impregnable stronghold, he ordered that it be surrounded by gigantic walls. The mortar used to cement the rubble stones was said to be—excuse the horrible detail!—mixed with the blood of the thousands of men, women and children who had their throats cut every morning on the building site. As for his orders concerning his fortress-palace, one cannot help but think of Bluebeard: the most beautiful young women in the kingdom were to buried alive in its pillars!...

Let all sensitive souls be reassured, however: such details were most probably invented by the griots who generation after generation have passed on these tales of the leader's great achievements. If they noticed that their audience was losing interest, the African bards would have absolutely no qualms in making up some shocking anecdote to captivate the listeners again. Once his town was built, Kango called together all the Yatenga chiefs so that they could solemnly claim allegiance to him in his new palace. It was on this occasion that he gave the new capital its name, Ouahigouya, meaning "Prostrate yourselves before me!"

An audience with the Naba

Ouahigouya, county town of the Yatenga Province, is currently the largest town in northern Burkina Faso and is linked to Ouagadougou by a brand new tarred road that then heads on towards Mali. Few vestiges from this now rather modern town's proud history have survived. All that remains of Naba Kango's fortress-palace are a few ruins in a quiet quarter far from the town centre where his descendants now lead a most peaceful existence.

By asking the guards at the gate of the actual residence, it is possible to see the Naba almost immediately. Although unlike his predecessors, he no longer has the right to raise an army, administer justice or demand taxes, in the eyes of his former subjects the Mossi chief has lost none of his prestige nor authority, especially with regards to moral and religious questions. He even still has his court and when he receives foreign visitors, especially tourists, he sits in an armchair in front of the palace, surrounded by the traditional officials, who crouch by him, and his wives and children. Amongst the top officials are the "Ouidi Naba", in the past the head of the powerful Mossi cavalry, the "Gounga Naba", head of the infantry, the "Larallé Naba", in charge of the royal tombs and the "Baloum Naba", the palace intendant who nowadays acts as the interpreter for the Naba and his guests. This old fashioned etiquette and the evocation of the dynasty's major achievements make the audience and in fact the whole visit to the town most charming.

Also of interest in the town are the tanneries and saddlers where horse saddles and harness are made, and the cotton spinners and the weavers' workshops whose strips of white cotton are commercialised throughout Burkina Faso.

Several places along the Ouagadougou-Ouahigouya road are worth stopping off to visit, for example *Yako* (see relevant section) and *Gourcy*, the first capital of the Yatenga Mossi empire. Naba Yadéga, founder of Yatenga, took over this little town thanks to a cunning plot. According to the oral traditions, Yadéga invited the chief of Gourcy, said to have been an excellent tailor, to come to his palace to make him a new outfit. Trustingly, the chief came to Yadéga's palace and, as he entered the courtroom, fell into a pit hidden under the rugs. Yadéga was then able to take over Gourcy without any opposition.

To the north of Ouahigouya, potters and blacksmiths (who in the past used earthen blast furnaces) can be seen at work in *Ronga*, where there is also an earthen mosque.

Finally, visitors are advised to stop off on the D17 towards *Djibo* in the north-east to see the pretty, pinkish clay houses at *You*, the beautiful architecture of *Toulfe* chief's mud house with openwork design, and the rupestral paintings and sacred crocodile pool at *Pobé Mengao*.

(See practical information p. 170)

pô

■ Pô, the last major town on the road from Ouagadougou to Ghana, is famous for its paratrooper barracks rather than for being a frontier town.

It was from here, in fact, that the Burkinabè armed forces moved into the capital in 1983 and overthrew Commander J.B. Ouedraogo, thereby initiating a revolutionary process of change led first by the famous Captain Thomas Sankara and then Captain Blaise Compaoré, Burkina Faso's current Head of State.

Today the town is animated by the incessant comings and goings of trucks and bush taxis that shuttle backwards and forwards between Ghana and Burkina Faso. Drivers and passengers stop off here to complete customs formalities, eat in the little restaurants and fill up with petrol.

Pô is also a convenient stopping place for tourists wishing to visit the *Kaboré Tembi National Park* (see earlier section) and the Gourounsi region.

Cave-like houses

Eighteen kilometres west of Pô on the *Léo* road, the little village of *Tiakané* gives visitors a wonderful insight into Gourounsi daily life.

Here, like in most places around Burkina Faso, the term "village" in fact refers to the isolated groups of farms, not to little agglomerations with houses organised into streets around a central square.

Visitors can ask the children playing in the fields to take them to the village chief's *soukala*, which is one of the most typical in the region. Built entirely from mud, voluminous and apparently without any openings, the house evokes medieval European fortresses.

The resemblance is not fortuitous given that the Gourounsi fortified farms—like the fortified castles built by the Crusaders—suffered innumerable attacks and invasions.

In the 19th century, the Djerma were the first to come from the east to take over the Mossi empire's southern neighbour. Later French troops led by Voulet came to the area, supposedly to stop the Gourounsi from being invaded by Samory. In fact these very cunning arbitrators quite simply intended to establish French supremacy in this part of West Africa as a first step to building the vast French colonial empire.

The interior of the Gourounsi *soukalas* are astonishing. Life goes on in a maze of rooms as dark as caves, which appear to be the ideal habitation for bats.

A maze of dark rooms

Only when their eyes adjust to the darkness do visitors stop bumping into the ceiling's very low joists and the ritual objects—skulls of sacrificial animals, calabash gourds—and hunting arms, hung on the walls in the first few rooms serving as an entrance hall. Having squeezed through narrow openings fashioned in the walls, smoky corridors lead to the various women and head of the family's "chambers". Each wife can effectively lead a semi autonomous existence in her underground room where there is also a kitchen and a granary for storing corn and millet. When pushing open the bamboo door, it feels as if one is about to enter a crypt. In the corner of the room, a beam of light shines down from the ceiling onto an earthen altar. Here the women grind millet to make the flour used in *tô*.

Collections of canaris

A hole in the wall leads to the kitchen where a whole collection of black varnished earthen pots are found stacked behind the hearth. These *canaris* are used either as cooking pots or for storing water and foodstuff. Another opening tucked away in a corner is both as a chimney and, with the help of a tree trunk ladder, the way out onto the roof terrace.

This rough and ready ladder leads outside where visitors will discover a succession of roof areas divided into innumerable platforms. Each wife has at least one of these terraces where she dries maize and ears of millet. The ground is sometimes dotted with a multitude of holes covered by terracotta lids. These are the tops of large millet granaries, some of which are sealed and are only opened during times of great shortage between two harvests especially when there is a drought.

Even though no wars have been fought in Burkina Faso for decades now, the Gourounsi have barely modified the style of their "refuge" habitations and not one window has been fashioned in these mud blockhouses. Like spiders lurking in their lairs, the Gourounsi know that these obscure labyrinths, where even the most formidable enemy would have to grope his way round, once saved their lives. This may be why they are loath to do away with the shadows that have always been so good to them. Still, whatever, today the Gou-

*The walls of the magnificent Gourounsi homes
are decorated with painted geometric motifs
and bas relief representing
highly stylized snakes and crocodiles.*

rounsi welcome visitors with the most unguarded sense of hospitality, especially those first tourists who came here intrigued by these unusual habitations...

Binger's hut

Also of interest in Tiakané is the hut where Captain Binger stayed when he visited the Gourounsi region at the end of July 1888. According to the young people who show visitors around, the French officer used this hut as a refuge from hostilities perpetrated by the Oubritenga Mossi warriors (Ouagadougou kingdom). They also say that Binger established very friendly relations with the village chief during his several month stay in Tiakané, and this is reaffirmed by the inscription on the walls of his hut...

If one reads the entries in the French captain's travel diary, however, it would seem that things were quite different in fact. On the one hand, he had no reason to fear Mossi hostilities as, at that time, he had not even made contact with them. When he did go to the Moro Naba's court in Ouagadougou a little later on, he did not encounter the slightest problem, and was given several totally peaceful audiences there. As for the great friendship between him and the Tiakané chief, it must be said that this is a pure fabrication for the benefit ot tourists.

To quote Jacques Binger's version of events: "The Chief of Tiakané is about thirty years old. He was most kind to me the whole time the Koumoullou men were there, but as soon as they left, his attitude changed and he began to try to intimidate me by speaking in a commanding manner and, after a few hours, he began to make demands. He asked for lots of things like retribution for accompanying me to Kapouri. Realising that he was not succeeding, he made up reasons for delaying my departure. As I wondered what the best way was to make this individual see reason, I had the good idea of playing him at his own game. I immediately became hostile, demanding to know why he had not given my men and animals food as he refused to let me leave. As he did not hurry to do this, I sent two men with bags to get some millet. Meanwhile, as we cleaned my revolver, we sometimes took it out of its holster, sometimes out of a haversack, sometimes out of one of my men's pockets, making him think all my men were armed to the hilt, which soon made him decide to let me go, whilst he himself kept a low profile".

"We left Tiakané at about nine o'clock in the morning. When we were about a hundred metres beyond the last hut, the Tiakané Naba stopped and told me that he was going back to the village if I did not give him two fine boubous forthwith. I did my best to make him understand that he would not get a thing from me that way and explained that if he went back to the village, so would I. He tried this little game several times during the journey. It therefore took us four hours to travel the five kilometres to Kapouri.

"As I did not know the way and, even though we were accompanied by natives, as the terrain made very difficult going, I found myself more or less at the mercy of this scoundrel but refused at all costs to give in to his demands. The slightest weakness would have meant that each time we passed through a village, the chief's demands would become so great that eventually the road would become completely barred."

Towards Tiébélé

From Tiakané, continue westwards along the Léo track to visit the *Nazinga ranch* (see Kaboré Tembi section), or head back to Pô, discovering several of the region's beautiful Gourounsi villages en route, notably *Tiébélé* and *Tangassoko* further southwards (see section on Tiébélé) where the splendid architecture is enhanced by immense wall frescoes with geometric patterns or images depicting the savanna wildlife.

(See practical information p. 172).

sabou

■ "In the olden days, a Mossi hunter lost his way in the bush near to the little village of Sabou on the road from Ouagadougou to Bobo Dioulasso. Overcome by heat and thirst, he fainted. He would have died of thirst, if a passing crocodile had not brought him back to consciousness by moistening his lips with a drop of water and then taken him to the creek close to Sabou. Ever since then, inhabitants in the region no longer hunt crocodiles and worship them like gods."

Sacred caymen

Even though the story the people of Sabou tell is most likely a legend, the sacred "caymen", on the other hand, are alive and kicking and can be found in groups of about ten frolicking about in the briny waters of the *Sabou pool*.

Over the last few years, the cult devoted to these saurians has taken a more profane turn since the "sacred cayman pool" has become one of Burkina Faso's greatest tourist attractions and features amongst the "classics" in all the travel brochures.

Even if the pool has lost some of its authenticity, it is still very picturesque...

Fun and games

As soon as foreign visitors approach the banks of the creek pool, they are assailed by the packs of children. They "officiate" there and ask the visitors to pay for their services and for the sacrificial chicken.

If the pool's silty waters are at first perfectly calm, it is not long before the sacrificial birds' distraught squawking arouses the beast—a solitary crocodile which is said to be over 130 years old. First of all it sticks out its snout, then its back, looking somewhat like a tree stump, then emerges entirely, climbing onto the bank and grabbing the unfortunate bird.

Once satisfied, he obligingly puts up with bearing the brunt of the village children's fun and games. They pull his tail to make him turn around, lie or sit astride on his back. Worse still, some of the children will go as far as perching on the saurian's back as it slides back into the water,

LOBI ROMAN ART

■ *"The Lobi are fearsome warriors but also excellent artists, as can be seen from their sculpture. Within Volta itself, they were considered as frustrated artists, as poor, disinherited relatives in the field of creation. (...) In fact, the secrets of Lobi art are only just being uncovered. Some have no reserves in situating the Lobi amongst the very best African artists, seeing in them the equivalent of the Roman sculptors, the unique creators of works which go straight for the essential and only release a rhythm, or a force when certain to strike the most effective point of impact. With Lobi art, one seems to go back to the origins of Black sculpture, the origins which scorn effects or anecdotes. If one had to define African art, one word would suffice above all others: dignity. Never does one see a form, a gesture or an expression that could be qualified as vulgar or outrageous, nor dominated by the singular expression of sentiment. In their ancestral sculptures, the Lobi take this dignity, this dense and powerful reserve, to its greatest point of tension and concentration. It is the character of the Lobi themselves, whether living or dead, that is outlined, embodied and vigorously expressed. Fiercely introverted, "almost always living an arrow away" from all neighbours, the Lobi are reputed for having never been defeated. This insubordination has found its own plastic laws. Let's observe a Lobi statue, preferably a sculpted head: volume, size, incision and bare skull emphasized by a large bridge: it is as if Egypt were reincarnated."*

IBRAHIMA BABA KAKE
"La Saga des peubles d'Afrique"

*Traditional craft works have become
one of Burkina Faso's main economic activities,
to the extent that the State authorities feel it necessary
to promote their variety and wealth by periodically organising the S.I.A.O.
(Salon international de l'artisanat de Ouagadougou).*

riding for several metres as if they were walking on water.

Included in the price of these cruel games, tourists—who are urged the whole time to throw chickens to the crocodiles—can have their photo taken as they carefully perch on the monster's tail or lined up as if in a family portrait!

Towards Koudougou, Boromo and Léo

As a brand new tourist complex ideal for families and groups has opened in Sabou, visitors can now stay longer to explore the region. To the north is *Koudougou,* land of the traditional "red cavalier" dancers and home of Burkina Faso's largest textile factory (see section on Koudougou); to the west is *Boromo* where elephants can be seen in the protected Deux Balé forest (see relevant section); and in the south is *Léo,* where it is possible to discover the traditions and architecture of the Gourounsi.

In Sabou itself, a craft centre specialising in weaving (table-cloths, covers, scarves, napkins) has been opened near to the tourist complex by the "Association des artisans handicapés du Burkina Faso".

(See practical information p. 172).

■ In the distance, strange tree-like shapes suddenly appear on the crest of the hills on the horizon, forming a sombre long, lacy screen that could have been painted by a surrealist artist. At closer hand, the *Aiguilles de Sindou* look more like a crumbling version of the Great Wall of China or the ruins of an immense fantastical fortress with towers, pinnacles and gables in a style that would have suited the "Facteur Cheval", a French naïve artist.

This superb tiered formation, 52 km west of Banfora, is Burkina Faso's main natural curiosity and is well known to geographers and geologists who think it was once part of the famous Banfora Escarpment that runs in a north-east/south-west direction linking Bobo Dioulasso and Banfora, before continuing westwards far into Mali. Near to the Malian border incidentally, *Téna Kourou,* Burkina's tallest summit, culminates at 749 metres.

The geologic history of this sandstone formation goes back a very long way. Over millions of years, the very ancient land of Burkina Faso has been slowly weakened and eroded away, leaving behind only these carved out areas of highland. Only hard rock like sandstone has resisted this erosion and been left towering up from the ground in the form of escarpments whilst all the other softer areas have crumbled away. The long sandstone frieze has nonetheless also suffered the effects of time.

Like mad sculptors, the wind and rain have eroded stone darts, fairy tale chimneys, or long organ pipes topped with large rocks, processions of twisted "pilgrims", and refuges for eagles and spirits. Further on closer to Banfora (see earlier section), nature's work has fashioned giant steps and a chaos of rocks where rivers and springs cascade down. At *Fabedougou,* between Banfora and Bobo Dioulasso, strange stone "domes" somewhat like sandstone igloos have also been eroded out of the escarpment.

In the Sénoufo region

Remarkable for both its highlands and well preserved traditions, this region in western Burkina Faso is still largely untouched by tourism as it is hard to get to and the poor quality of its tracks means a four-wheel drive vehicle is essential.

As it is obviously not worth searching for hotels and good restaurants here, Banfora, which is well equipped in both, serves as a convenient base (make sure to stock up with enough petrol to make the 200 km journey there and back and take a picnic as it is very hard to find food en route. (An ice box for keeping drings cool is certainly not a luxury!).

The Turka, Gouin and Karaboro people have lived in and around Sindou for a very long time. The Sénoufo live further westwards beyond Sindou, near to the borders with Mali and Côte d'Ivoire.

As the Burkinabè Sénoufo were threatened by foreign invaders for many years, they took refuge high up in the mountains where they built eyrie villages in the impregnable caves. Now that the peace seems more durable, however, they have abandoned these troglodytic habitations (mentioned later) and moved down into the valleys and plains, where they have built superb mud homes which look more like the work of sculptors and potters than architects.

This allusion to sculpture is not purely fortuitous as for several decades now, museums of African art and private collectors from all over the world have been snatching up Sénoufo ritual objects. Particularly stunning are the "fire eater" masks *(waniougo)*, their large statuettes representing mythical ancestors like the "divine mother", and sacred birds (buceros), and their wooden door huts sculpted in bas relief.

All of these ritual objects are used in the large animist ceremonies periodically organised by the Sénoufo—most of which are not open to outsiders—notably the men's very long initiation cycles which begin during childhood and finish when they are adults. The initiation is divided into three seven year cycles, during which the young Sénoufo learn to recognise the superior forces governing nature and how to appease them by respecting certain taboos and by offering sacrifices to the powerful gods and dead ancestors.

From Sindou to Néguéni

Even though visitors are very rarely allowed to attend traditional Sénoufo celebrations, the beautiful landscape alone makes the trip worthwhile. Just beyond Sindou, the track veers to the right away from the escarpment without ever actually losing sight of it. Seven kilometres on, *Kawara* village is home to many potters and their work can be seen on display outside. After the little *Léra* forest where there are many irokos, *Loumana* is surrounded by rice paddies that are particularly pleasant during the wet season. Over the last few years, locals have begun growing cot-

ton as well as rice. The little village of *Baguéra* lies at the end of the Sindou track, where the route then veers off to the north towards *Néguéni* via Niansoroni and Outourou. Although the track is very narrow, with a four-wheel drive vehicle it is possible to force one's way through. Erosion has broken the escarpment into several sections of scattered mounds (inselbergs) out of which tower gigantic sandstone stumps.

Picturesque mud buildings

In both Néguéni and Outourou, the villagers originally built their habitations up on the escarpment before definitively moving down onto the plain. Now deserted, Néguéni-Haut and Outourou-Haut (Upper Néguéni and Upper Outourou) can be reached after an easy 2 to 3 hour climb. Ramblers are rewarded for their efforts at the top where they will discover both the picturesque mud granaries set in the rock face and the wonderful view of the whole region.

The villages on the plain are also worth visiting, especially *Outourou* where the mud walls of each family compound encircle innumerable huts and granaries with courtyards, low walls and hidden stairs leading to roof terraces (*argamasses*). This traditional architecture is highly evocative of the minimalist theatrical sets common in European modern theatre.

If visitors have the time they should leave their vehicles at Néguéni and head for *Klani* further to the north from where there is also a beautiful panoramic view of the region and of *Téna Kourou,* Burkina Faso's highest point, near the Malian border (this excursion involves about half a day's walk).

(See practical information p. 172).

The Sindou rocks west of Banfora
are a natural curiosity
evoking both the ruins of a castle
and a large open-air
sculpture exhibition.

tenkodogo

■ Mossi people still consider "the Old Land" (Tenkodogo) as sacred, as it was here that were born the different dynasties who reigned over the powerful kingdoms of Tendodogo, Oubritenga (Ouagadougou) and Yatenga (Ouahigouya) for over five centuries.

Effectively, Ouedraogo, son of Princess Yenenga of Gambaga in northern Ghana and the hunter Riaré, settled here. According to the oral traditions, his son Rawa then headed northwards and founded Zandoma (embryo of the future Yatenga kingdom), and his grandson Oubri set out to conquer the west and founded the Oubritenga kingdom ("Land of Oubri") and the capital Ouagadougou. These semi-legendary tales have been passed on by word of mouth and the main episodes elaborated by griots and troubadours to captivate audiences better. Unfortunately the dates have not been recorded precisely and, much to the frustration of contemporary historians, it is not known whether Ouedraogo lived in the 12th or the 15th century!

Fundamental laws

Visitors wishing to make a pilgrimage to the Mossi birthplace will be a bit disappointed by Tenkodogo, as nowadays it is no more than a little town devoid of any real signs of its past splendour.

An audience with the Naba will liven up this rather worn past, however. To be sure of a reception, it is worth giving some forewarning rather than just turning up on the spot.

As visitors may learn from the Mossi chiefs themselves, the fundamental laws governing the whole of the empire are said to have been promulgated in Tenkodogo in the 11th century.

They decreed that "Moré" (the Mossi language) be spoken to unify the people, that all dissension between the Mossi be forgotten during times of war so that the Mossi be unified when facing the enemy, and that the kingdom's traditional hierarchy (divided into families, clans, villages, tribes, districts, provinces and led by chiefs and the emperor) be accepted without dissent. These laws also imposed a system of succession that excluded women. Their obedience to these laws meant that the Mossi were one of the few African peoples whose kingdom survived for centuries right up until the modern day.

In spite of its humble appearance, Tenkodogo has nonetheless been the setting for several important historical moments. During the last century, for example, the

French Lieutenant Voulet, who had just forcefully taken control of Yatenga and Ouagadougou (where he had deposed the Moro Naba), and the British Captain Donald Stewart met here. Captain Stewart, who was in charge of a military column that had come from Koumassi in the Gold Coast (now Ghana), was expecting to place a part of the Mossi kingdom under British control. He was forestalled by Voulet, however, who came to Tenkodogo by forced march on 7 February 1897, to let his rival know that he had already taken control of these territories.

Voulet and Captain Stewart meet

As one French newspaper recounted at the time: "Of the four missions launched by our neighbours to conquer the Mossi, this (British) expedition went the furthest north. After laborious negotiations, Captain D. Stewart agreed "in writing" to retreat to Mamprousi, that is 120 km to the south. The Mossi region has thus definitively been evacuated by the English and the freedom of the French mission is intact".

It should be pointed out that this peaceful confrontation was just one of the many encounters to take place between the major European powers after the division of Africa at the Berlin Congress (1885). A year after the Voulet-Stewart encounter, the "Fashoda crisis" was to take place on the Nile (1898), but this time the French, led by Captain Marchand, had to give way to the British under Lord Kitchener...

Important guests

Tenkodogo continued to play host to many important and not so important guests in the 20th century, as "Le Monde" journalist Philippe Decraene pointed out in his "Letter from Tenkodogo" on 13 February 1977: "It was here that the Gascon aristocrat d'Arboussier, then District Officer in the Ouagadougou region, mustered up the Mossi partisans who were sent to victoriously fight in German-controlled Togo during the Great War.

"It was at the District Officer's former residence, at the end of the row of cailcedras in the old administrative quarter, that Maurice Yaméogo, the former President of Upper Volta, met the Ghanaian President Kwame N'Krumah, before they decided in 1961 to symbolically tear down the

barriers that separated the two States. It was also at the top of these stairs shaded by bougainvilleas that General Eyadéma of Togo and General Lamizana of Upper Volta, said to be comrades-in-arms and faithful friends, have held talks on several occasions over the last few years.

"The inhabitants of Tenkodogo talk more often about the humbler destinies of Léonce Combes and "Monsieur Raymond", however. The first was the son of the famous "Petit Père", champion of laicism and ardent partisan for the separation of the Church and State. Having served in the colonial administration, he retired here in 1920, where he died fourteen years later. His wife and daughter unsuccessfully tried to readapt to life in France before coming back to finish their days in Tenkodogo, where they were looked after by a population that had adopted them.

"Monsieur Raymond" was originally from Geneva and had been in trouble with the law in Europe. A trader, transporter and planter, with a reputation for gambling and chasing women, he left behind an astonishing earthen "castle" whose crenellated walls are slowly crumbling under the assault of the tropical rains. Outside the city, staggered rows of superb kapok trees are a proof of "Monsieur Raymond's" activities as it was he who planted them. From the imposing boughs of one of these trees, large snowflake blooms rain down on Léonce Combes' marble tomb stone, which bears the inscription "Passed away in Tenkodogo on 15 November 1934, aged 53".

Line fishing and washerwomen

Visitors travelling round the town and its suburbs will be surprised at the numerous family scenes taking place: young women rhythmically pound the millet, artisan-mechanics repair the famous "two-wheelers" that can be seen darting all over Burkina Faso, children cross millet plantations in their minuscule mule-drawn carts... It is at the dam, however, that the greatest sense of calm reigns as children fish with lines, large herds of zebus drink from the waters, and charming young women do their washing and bathe in the cool waters, splashing about and laughing joyfully.

From Tenkogodo, it is possible to head further westwards into the Bisa region. Cousins of the Samo living in the Tougan region in north-western Burkina Faso, the Bisa (otherwise called the Bousanssé) were originally from Mali. According to the oral traditions, the Bisa and Samo had a family dispute which forced them to separate, one group moving northwards and the other southwards.

The Bisa are skilled artisans, who are equally good at weaving, basket making, pottery and forging. Most of their products can be seen on sale on market days in *Garango* village.

It is also possible to travel as far as the Nakambé (ex-White Volta) where, near to *Lenga*, hippopotami can be seen frolicking in the water.

A well-known pottery centre

On the way back to Ouagadougou from Tenkodogo, *Koupéla* is situated at the Nationale 4/Nationale 16 junction. This little town is a major pottery centre where—unlike most of the other villages in Burkina Faso—the pieces are made by the men, not the women. Their *canaris* (pots) are well known for their beautiful geometric line designs done in white kaolin.

On the Ouagadougou road just after Koupéla, it is worth making a little detour via *Pouytenga* where there is a particularly picturesque and well stocked traditional market. Once nicknamed the "thiefs' market" as a whole range of smuggled or stolen goods could be found on sale there, nowadays it is above all a crafts market specialising in pottery, leather, traditional shoes, leather goods, and locally made tools.

(See practical information p. 172).

THE SAMO RAIN MAKERS

Standing in a semi-circle, armed with whistles and cow bells and wearing extraordinary clothing—headgear bristling with feathers that symbolize the rays of the sun, tunics and long skirts studded with shells—the "rain makers" get ready to serenade the powers above at dawn.
This strange event traditionally takes place at the end of the dry season in the little village of Kiembara, about 30 km north-east of Tougan, in the heart of the Samo region.
Like in most of the animist rites in Africa, the senior initiates are in charge of calling on the divine powers. This time their task is to ask the powers to make the rains fall, without which these farming communities could not survive.
Just to make sure their message is understood, they cover themselves with cowries, the shells that served as money for centuries in Africa, thereby stressing the degree of prosperity they will reach if the rains are plentiful and harvests abundant—a bit like going to ask a bank manager for a loan wearing a dinner jacket covered in gold coins and bank notes! The cowry shells evoke not only wealth, but also fertility as their shape is evocative of the female genitals.
These various symbolic reasons explain why the Samo wear these shell garments that always stun foreign visitors, even if they do not always recognise their full significance.

*Charming, bucolic scenes can be seen
alongside the Tenkodogo dams:
women doing their washing, children swimming,
young women fetching water.*

tiébélé

■ Other than in the Middle East (and particularly Yemen), no builders in the world are as skilled at making public buildings and houses out of mud than in Sub-Saharan Africa.

From Mauritania to Chad, from Mali to Ghana including Burkina Faso, surprising architectural sculpture flourishes, the most beautiful examples of which are the Mopti and Djenné mosques in Mali, the old Hausa quarters from Birni to Zinder in Niger and the house-fortresses in Burkina Faso and northern Ghana.

The men who built these constructions—who are not professional architects but nonetheless have an amazing artistic talent—clearly gave free reign to their imagination, and have thus done full justice to this unfairly despised, cheap material. European visitors will be awestruck as they peruse the dried earthen curves, festoons and pointed cylindrical forms, which have a lacy texture evocative of the work of modern sculptors like Brancusi and Henry Moore.

Fortress compounds

Before going to see the beautiful *Ouahabou* and *Bobo Dioulasso* earthen mosques, it is first worth visiting another example of this mud architecture in Tiébélé, near to *Pô* south of Ouagadougou.

The whole southern part of the *Nahouri Province* is inhabited by the Kasséna, who are related to the Gourounsi people and who also live on the other side of the border in northern Ghana. These skilled builders have constructed what are better described as compounds rather than villages.

The clusters of square or cylindrical huts with roof terraces are linked by solid mud walls and have no external openings. From afar they look somewhat like little forts and it would hardly be surprising if arrows rained down on approaching visitors! Nowadays, however, visitors are welcomed to Tiébélé by the chirping of birds, the bleating of goats and the excited shouts of children.

As the beautiful Tiébélé architecture is now better known to tourists, every year there are increasing numbers of visitors and they are asked to pay the village chief an entry fee as if in a museum (and a fee to take photos) and give a tip to the voluntary guides at the end of the visit.

Increasingly used to tourists, these young guides are highly competent and know how to organise a good visit round the whole compound without encroaching upon the inhabitants' intimacy.

A succession of traps

Built for protection at a time when ethnic wars were raging everywhere, these habitations usually only have one staggered entrance leading into a labyrinth of narrow passages densely packed between the outer ramparts and walls of the huts.

Any enemy who entered would be constantly surveyed by the inhabitants of the compound hidden on the roof terraces. If he came out of these dangerous alleys alive, he would be in for further surprises as the huts he would then try to penetrate were full of traps. The very low hut doors forced the assailant to go down on all fours and thus enter head first—the perfect position to get it chopped off!

If he still made it that far inside, he would immediately bump into a low wall that would force him to raise his head—perfect for getting his throat cut! Finally, if he had managed to get through all these traps, he would find himself plunged into the darkness of the room where his eyes would not have time to adjust before the hut's occupant would bear down on him with a machete!

Interior courtyards and little squares

When visiting the Kasséna compounds, tourists will discover that the area inside is compartmented into a multitude of courtyards and little squares separated by low walls. The whole lot is made from the attractive brick red laterite. Using the same construction material, the Kasséna have built stairs up to the roof terraces, tables for grinding grain—built against the hut walls—platforms and benches where the whole family comes to rest, weave baskets, make pottery...

Whole families live in each of these compounds which gradually spread outwards in concentric circles from an original core (the huts built by the grandparents, the first occupants of the site) to include the children's huts, the grandchildren's huts and sometimes even the great-grand children's huts.

The oldest huts are generally cylindrical, whereas the more recent are rectangular, as they are built by the young generations who have had the chance to "head up" to town where they are inspired by the so-called "modern" houses.

According to the guide, unmarried or newly wed young people live in these huts which do not have kitchens yet. In the older women's huts—whose entrance evokes the female genitals hence implying that by entering the hut, one enters into the "mother's womb"—the first room is equipped with a stone work bench. Two grind stones for grinding millet and a jar for catching flour are set in this earthen table. A very narrow, low opening then leads into a tiny kitchen. The walls of this dark, smoky den are lined with a huge range of black glazed *canaris* (pots) in which the women store their millet. The kitchen hearth, next to this astonishing dresser, looks like a modern clay sculpture.

Hidden reserves

As visitors leave this little room and head back into the larger main room, they will notice a huge pot about the size of a barrel tucked away in the corner. Other reserves are sealed inside and hidden, only to be used as a last resort when prolonged droughts destroy harvests and the whole Kasséna community is in danger of suffering shortages. In the calabashes hung from the ceiling the women hide their most precious belongings, like their savings, from their covetous husbands.

Mention has already been made of the large decorative frescoes painted by the skilled Gourounsi married women. As the paintings at Tiébélé are very fragile and tend to wear away, it is better to go to *Tangassoko* where they can be admired in all their splendour. However, it is difficult to get to this little Kasséna village very close to the Ghanaian border south of Tiébélé. A four-wheel drive vehicle is absolutely essential for this very rough road full of potholes.

After an hour of this gymkhana, however, the more adventurous visitors will be rewarded for their efforts by the sight of beautiful village houses completely preserved from extreme weather conditions (and the pollution of mass tourism).

Beautiful traditional motifs

Here the gabled huts and granaries with pointed straw roofs and decorated walls which do utmost justice to the Kasséna women's artistic talents are superb. Instead of the red and black colours commonly used to decorate the Tiébélé habitations, here a monochrome of sombre browns is mixed with black and white.

The walls are entirely covered in the most beautiful checked, hatching, triangular, diamond-shaped and zigzag patterns inspired by the traditional weaving designs. On one hut by the compound's central square, snakes and lizards are depicted in bas relief and covered in white and brown stippling.

A beautiful view

From up on the roof or from one of the stairways inside the compound visitors will have a wonderful aerial view of the compound's yards and little squares and roofs linked by ladders, which give this architecture an air of a theatre stage with staggered, descending gantries.

From Tangassoko, it is possible to head back to Pô without going via Tiébélé: head for Kaya in the north-west, passing by the foot of *Nahouri Peak* (447 m).

(See practical information p. 172)

tougan

"W" national park

■ Distant cousins of the Samo and formerly related to the Mandé people in Mali, the Marka now live in the *Sourou* (Tougan) and *Kossi* (Nouna) Provinces in western Burkina Faso. Also known as the Dafing, it was they who founded the little kingdom of Ouahabou (see relevant section), where there is a particularly well known mosque.

Sugar loaf mosques

About thirty kilometres south of Tougan, the earthen mosques in *Kougny* and *Gassan* in the Marka region are also worth visiting. Like all of the Sudanese style mosques found in western Burkina Faso (especially in Bobo Dioulasso) and along the Niger River in Mali (particularly the Mopti mosque) the shape of the Kougny and Gassan mosques appear to have been inspired by the pointed cylinders and sugar loaves.

When in Kougny, visitors should also visit the picturesque indigo dye workshops, where deep dye pits are dug in the ground, and the weaving and pottery workshops.

Wild silk spinning

Two short trips can also be made from *Dédougou*, county town of the Mouhoun Province in the heart of Bobo country, to *Nouna* in the north-west (where there is remarkable earthen architecture), and to *Safané* in the south-east. In both of these villages, wild silk is still traditionally spun and woven into the very precious clothing worn only during major ceremonies.

(See practical information p. 173).

■ It was not a tired surveyor who graced this vast natural park with a name summed up by a single letter of the alphabet—"W"—but a poetic cartographer who noticed the convoluted course of the meandering Niger River that forms the park's north-eastern boundary.

Not only does "W" Park have an unusual name, but it is also probably the only multinational park on the African continent. Created in 1954, the approximately one million hectares of park land spill over into three different West African countries: Benin (500,000 ha), Niger (300,000 ha) and Burkina Faso (300,000 ha). It is also one of the largest parks in Africa where all types of savanna fauna can be seen in abundance, including buffaloes, elephants, hippopotami, large antelopes and lions.

From Ouagadougou to Diapaga

The Burkinabè part of "W" park is located in the Gourmantché region in eastern Burkina Faso. For visitors coming from Ouagadougou, it is best to go via *Kantchari* (Nationale 1) and *Diapaga* (N19) rather than via Pama and Arli as the Pama-Tindangou route is particularly rough. From Diapaga, where there is a hotel complex, visitors can take one of three routes to the park: the north-eastern track via *Tapoa Djerma*; the eastern track via *Mangou* and *Koabougou;* and the south-eastern track heading to *Kondio* and on into Benin.

Although their numbers have dropped considerably due to the poachers, some elephants can be still seen in the "W" Park, notably in the *Tapoa* valley in the north-east, and the *Mékrou* valley in the east. With some luck, visitors may come across lions near the Beninese border. Since their numbers have also been decimated by hunters, these big cats have come to fear man and now tend to hunt and move around at night and to sleep hidden away in the bushes during the daytime.

Various kinds of antelopes

West Africa's largest antelope, the sable antelope is usually found near to water points or out in the open and is quite timid, galloping off powerfully whenever disturbed. Other antelopes can also be found close to the water points in the park, including bubales, Buffon kobs, Defassa kobs, bushbucks, royal antelopes and red-flanked forest duikers.

*Burkina Faso's flat relief makes it
the perfect place for "two-wheelers".
The annual round-country cycling race
attracts cyclists
from all over Africa and Europe.*

Also common are the groups of cynoscephale baboons whose society is organised according to military-style hierarchy (see Panorama). Visitors are also likely to come across lone or families of warthogs. When disturbed, the visibly furious African wild boars will bolt off with their tufted tails stuck up in the air, which gives them a rather comical air!

A multitude of birds

"W" Park is also a sanctuary for all kinds of birds, especially aquatic birds in search of water, rivers and creeks: ibises, herons, crowned cranes, geese, etc.

From "W" or from Diapaga, it is possible to continue on to Arli, further to the west, where there is another of Burkina Faso's national parks.

From Diapaga, take either the Tansarga or Namounou routes running along the superb *Gobnangou Escarpment*. At the foot of this high ground, small, scattered Gourmantché villages are signaled by the presence of a weaver working in the shade of a baobab tree, by a pastor herding his bovines or by groups of young women pounding millet.

Arli is situated at the end of the escarpment. Here a comfortable hotel has been built for tourists going on the wildlife safaris (see earlier section).

(See practical information p. 173).

W NATIONAL PARK

La Tapoa Gorge
La Tapoa

NIGER

Mékrou Gorge
Mékrou

Niger

Arli
Kaabougou

BENIN

BURKINA
FASO

Koudou Falls

Kondio

——— park boundary
- - - border
----- road or track

0   45 km

yako

During the last century, a "gold rush" took place in the Yako region, even if it was somewhat smaller than the one in Klondike, Canada. At the *Pelegtanga* site in the bush, a few kilometres from the town, strange groups of people with the "gold bug" scratch away in the soil, digging endless tunnels. Unlike the convicts in the past, here the hundreds of frenzied workers are not out in the Styx serving sentences, but, in complete freedom, are all pursuing the same obsessive dream: to find the right lode or the large nugget that will allow them to leave this hell hole once and for all. The dream rarely comes true, however, and after endless days of digging mine shafts and carting about tons of sand, the workers usually only find a few specks which they carefully put away in old aspirin tubes or pill boxes. Sometimes things take an even more tragic turn. Recently, the sumps—dug any old how and with no props whatsoever—collapsed burying a dozen of the prospectors.

Swindling marabouts

Many of the miners work with their families. Whilst the father or uncle goes down into the pit, the children haul baskets of earth up to the surface, then cart the gold-bearing ore off in wheelbarrows making huge piles. The rest of the family then wash this precious stuff in basins. It takes a very keen eye to spot the few specks of yellowish metal in the bottom of these muddy bowls as they have the same dull sheen as bronze.

A whole lot of middlemen, notably "buyers", operate between the miner who furnishes the raw product (gold specks, dust and nuggets still often mixed with earth) and the end of the line: the highly official "Comptoir Burkinabè des Métaux précieux". The buyers—who live in straw huts and wooden villages thrown together near to the mines—work with the prospectors, smelting the ore to get rid of all impurities before selling it to the "Comptoir". This network is too ideal to be respected.

In fact, scores of parasites and swindlers also haunted by the yellow metal come nosing around the gold-bearing sites. As "l'Intrus", the Burkinabè weekly satirical paper described it: "The gold sites attract all sorts of peoples: prostitutes, prospectors, drug dealers, gold dealers and all kinds of hustlers". According to the paper, in this latter category were marabouts who "claim to have the power to make gold sprout in the holes". In return for money,

these individuals usually get the miners to sacrifice sheep and then pour their blood into the mines to make the gold rise up from the depths of the earth into the pits. Given food, accommodation and paid by the miner, the marabout also gets a supplementary commission if his magic practices do cause copious amounts of gold to well up. Obviously, these performances rarely bring any tangible results, but for the gullable miners—who pay a lot for these services—the marabout's intervention panders to their wildest dreams, giving them new zest in their work. "This is how the marabouts rip off the prospectors"—to quote "l'Intrus"—"going from pit to pit, site to site and prospector to prospector. They buy themselves "Yamaha 100 de Luxes" or "CGs". When the marabouts earn a lot, they become traders, setting up at a site and running shops or transport services. At night they return to their real work as marabouts."

In the heart of Passoré

Even though Yako is only a few kilometres north of the gold mines, it feels like it is light years away from all this turpitude. Set back from the recently tarred Nationale 2, this little town—county town of the Passoré Province—appears to be concerned only with the heavy flow of traffic that has developed between the capital Ouagadougou, the large Mossi town of Ouahigouya and Mali in the north.

The imposing mosque in the centre of the town is a reminder that the Muslim religion is very important for the Yako inhabitants. After all, is it not written in the Koran that only believers will go to heaven where "gold plates and goblets will be passed round to the happy ones"...

(See practical information p. 173).

**practical
information**

Ouagadougou

LOCATION AND ACCESS: Capital of Burkina Faso, Kadiogo Province country town, central Burkina Faso. Approximately one million inhabitants.

356 km of Bobo Dioulasso via the N1, 441 km NE of Banfora via the N1 and the N7, 434 km NE of Gaoua via the N1, D15 and the N12, 97 km E. of Koudougou via the N1 and the N14, 217 km SE of Tougan via the D13 and the N14, 181 km SE of Ouahigouya via the N2, 203 km S of Djibo via the D1 and the D2, 261 km SW of Dori via the N3, 234 km W of Fada N'Gouma via the N4, 183 km NW of Tenkodogo via the N4 and the N16 and 144 km N of Pô via the N5.

By air: Ouagadougou Airport, SE of the town (tel. 30.65.15). Domestic and international flight operators: *Air Burkina* (tel. 30.76.76 and 30.61.44), *Air Afrique* (tel. 30.60.20 and 30.65.18), *Air France* (tel. 30.63.65), *Sabena, Air Ivoire* (tel. 30.62.07 and 30.88.87).

By train: Railway station, Place Naba Kom, town centre, SCFB (Société des Chemins de Fer du Burkina Faso), tel. 30.72.17 and 30.60.48.

By bus: Bus station, Avenue Bassawarga, the Pô road (near to the hotel OK Inn, behind the airport).

Group transports: Régie X9, tel. 30.42.96/ 33.46.69; SOGEBAF, tel. 36.36.27; *Sans Frontières,* tel. 30.46.75; *Egi-Voyages,* tel. 31.02.62.

Taxis: City Cab (tel. 31.20.93) ; Taxis Rapides Radio (tel. 31.43.43).

CAR HIRE: *Faso Tours* (tel. 30.65.13), *OK Raids* (tel. 30.40.61), *Burkina Auto Location* (tel. 30.68.11).

TOURIST INFORMATION: Office National du Tourisme Burkinabè, avenue Léon-Frobénius, Immeuble de la Caisse de Stabilisation des Prix, BP 1311 (tel. 31.19.59 and 31.19.60; open from 7:00 to 12:30 and from 15:00 to 17:30).

TRAVEL AGENTS: *Faso-Tours* (tel. 30.65.13), *OK Raids Vacances* (tel. 30.40.61), *Armelle Voyages* (tel. 31.17.60).

ACCOMMODATION: *Silmandé**** L,* 172 rms., including 10 suites, bar, restaurant, pool, tennis, courts, disco, conference rooms, shops (tel. 30.01.76/30.00.96/ 30.01.88 à 89/30.03.20/30.02.01 to 03, BP 4733, telex 5345, fax 30.09.71) ; *Eden Park*****, 100 rms., 10 suites, conference rooms, bar, restaurant, pool, disco (BP 2070, tel. 31.14.86 to 92 and 31.11.14, telex 5224 BF, fax 31.14.88) ; *Indépendance****, 139 rms., including 3 suites, bar, restaurant, pool, tennis courts, conference rooms, casino, shops (BP. 127, tel. 30.60.60, telex 5201, fax 30.67.67); *Ran Hôtel****, 26 rms., bar, restaurant, pool (tel. 60.61.06/07); *OK Inn****, 25 rms., bar, restaurant, pool (tel. 30.40.61, fax 30.48.11), *Nazemse****, 58 rms., bar, restaurant (tel. 33.53.28); *Relax Hôtel**** (tel. 30.89.08); *Belle Vue***, 30 rms., bar, restaurant (tel. 30.84.98); *Ricardo***, 23 rms., bar, restaurant, pool (tel. 30.70.72); *Tropical***, 26 rms. (tel. 31.27.37/38); *Le Continental*** (tel. 30.86.36); *Don Camillo I***, 14 rms., bar, restaurant, disco (tel. 30.22.36); *Don Camillo II*, 11 ch., bar, restaurant, disco (tel. 30.29.50 and 51); *Le Provence***, 16 rms. (tel. 33.51.63); *Central**, 8 rms. (tel. 31.02.48 to 50 and 30.51.63); *Riviera**, 11 rms., bar, restaurant (tel. 30.65.59); *Le Grillon**, 22 rms. (tel. 31.11.84); *Kilimandjaro*; 36 rms. (tel. 33.64.74).

Little hotels and boarding houses: *Idéal*, 18 rms. (tel. 30.65.02); *Oubri*, 22 rms. (tel. 60.64.83); *Amitié* (tel. 33.30.23); *Yennenga*, 24 rms. (tel. 30.73.37); *Guigseme*, 10 rms. (tel. 33.46.98); *Siguin Vousse*, 10 rms. (tel. 31.04.64); *Yeela*, 23 rms.; *Entente*, 20 rms. (tel. 31.14.97); *Pavillon Vert*, 15 rms. (tel. 31.06.11); *Kadiogo*, 15 rms. (tel. 30.69.44); *Weend Kuuni*, 17 rms. (tel. 30.80.79); *Yamba* (tel. 30.89.17); *Le Dapooré*; *Ouidi* (tel. 33.39.37).

Campsites: *Ouaga-Camping* (Pô road);. *Poko Club* (Bobo-Dioulasso road).

RESTAURANTS: In the large hotels and: *Al Andalos* (Lebanese); *Le Belvédère* (Italian and Lebanese food); *La Chaumière*; *L'Eau vive* (international food); *L'Escapade* (international); *Le Safari* (French); *Le Pub* (international); *Le Vert-Galant* (French); *Ougarit* (Oriental); *L'Harmattan* (African); *Le Wapassi* (international) ; *Le Trocadéro* (African); *La Grotte* (African); *Arc-en-Ciel* (African and international); *La Forêt* (African and international); *Allah Barka* (African); *Wassa Club* (African); *Le Baguem*; *Le Tam-Tam* (Austrian); *Le Dapoore* (international); *La Paillote*; *Hamburger House* (fast-food); *Le Colibri* (African and international); *Le Terminus* (international); *La Paix* (international); *Le Gigot d'Or* (snacks); *Le Major* (snacks); *Le Vietnam* (Asiatic).

LEISURE: *Sports* : tennis (Silmandé and Indépendance hotels, Asecna);swimming pools (Silmandé, Indépendance, Eden Park, OK Inn, Ran and Ricardo hotels, La Forêt and La Grotte restaurants); horse riding (Le Cheval Mandingue, L'Etrier Club); gymnasium (Super Gym Club).

Discos: In the large hotels (La Tapoa in the Silmandé, La Rive Gauche in Eden Park, Le Rim in the Independance, the Ricardo and Don Camillo)

Casino: The Independance hotel.

Overleaf:
*In Africa, hairdressers usually cover their stalls
with brightly coloured signs
showing the different hairstyles on offer:
the "afro", the "Marlon", "zazou", "cock", "calypso", etc.*

Cinémas: Burkina, Neerwaya, Rialé, Oubri.

CULTURAL EVENTS: Centre Culturel Français Georges Méliès (tel. 30.60.97/98).
Concerts, galas and other shows can be seen at the Maison du Peuple, at the Théâtre Désiré Bonogo and at the Stade du 4-Août.
National Museum (tel. 31.09.28); open every day, exception Sundays and Mondays, from 8:30 to 12 and from 15:30 to 18 h.

AMENITIES: Rood Woko central market, petrol stations, garages/repairs, banks, bookstalls/stationers/newspaper shops, pharmacies, food stores, doctors, hospitals and clinics, post office (PTT).

Arli
(national park)

LOCATION AND ACCESS: Tapoa Province, the Arli hotel is 72 km SW of Diapaga via the N19, 101 km E of Pama via the N19 and the N18, 210 km SE of Fada N'Gourma via the N19 and the N18, 435 km E of Ouagadougou via the N19, the N18 and the N4.
Airfield at Fada N'Gourma and a light aircraft runway at Arli.

FOOD AND ACCOMMODATION: *Arli Safari-Hôtel*, 20 rms., bar, restaurant, pool.
Hunting camps at Ougarou, Bigou, Pama and Diapaga.

ARLI NATIONAL PARK: Open for wildlife safaris from December to April (the intense heat in May diminishes water supplies and the rains from June to October leave the tracks in very bad condition). Permits are issued to visitors at the Diapaga and Arli entrance points.
Hunting is unauthorised in different zones in the region: "big" game hunting is open from 15 December to 15 March; hunting for smaller animals is open from 15 December to 30 May. Permits must be obtained from the Service de la Faune et des Chasses, in Ouagadougou, BP 7044, tel. 33.24.77.
Wildlife safaris and hunting safaris are organised by Ouagadougou travel agents.

BIBLIOGRAPHY: *Guide des grands mammifères d'Afrique*, by Jean Dorst and Pierre Dandelot, Editions Delachaux et Niestlé.
Carte touristique des Parcs nationaux des Pays de l'Entente (Arli, Pendjari, « W », Comoé, Kéran), Edited by the Institut Géographique National, Paris.

Banfora

LOCATION AND ACCESS: Comoé Province county town, 85 km SW of Bobo Dioulasso via the N7, 441 km W of Ouagadougou via the N7 and the N1 (tarred), 197 km W of Garoua via the N11.

FOOD AND ACCOMMODATION: Hotels: *Canne à Sucre*, 12 rms. (tel. 88.01.07); *Comoé*, 20 rms. (tel. 88.01.51); *Fara*, 17 rms. (tel. 88.01.17).
Restaurant : hotel *Canne à Sucre*, *La Croix du Sud*, hotel *Fara*.

AMENITIES: BP, Shell, Texaco and Total petrol stations, market, food stores, banks (BIB, BICIA), cinemas, Nadon pharmacy (tel. 88.01.66), hospital (tel. 88.00.11).

Bobo-Dioulasso

NAME: After the Bobo and Dioula people who live there.

LOCATION AND ACCESS: Houet Province county town, Burkina Faso's second town (after Ouagadougou), pop. 300,000.
85 km NE of Bafora via the N7, 356 km W of Ouagadougou via the N1 (tarred), 76 km E of Orodara via the N8, 179 km SW of Dédougou via the N10.
By air: Air Burkina (tel. 97.13.48/97.01.40) operates frequent flights between Bobo Dioulasso and Ouagadougou.
By rail: the SCFB (Société des Chemins de Fer du Burkina) (tel. 98.29.22) operate a frequent service from Abidjan to Ouagadougou via Banfora, Bobo Dioulasso and Koudougou.

FOOD AND ACCOMMODATION: *Ran-Hôtel*, opposite the station, BP 50, 37 rms., bar, restaurant, pool (tel. 98.18.45/46); *Relax*, BP 115, 19 rms., restaurant (tel. 97.00.96); *Watinoma*, 22 rms., restaurant (tel. 97.20.82); *l'Auberge*, BP 329, 40 rms., bar, restaurant, pool (tel. 97.14.26); *Casafrica*, Sikasso road, bar, restaurant (tel. 98.01.57); *Soba*, BP 185, bar, pool (tel. 97.10.12); *Hamdallaye*, near to the bus station (tel. 98.22.87). Others: *l'Okinawa*, *le Royal*, *l'Unité*, *la Paix*, *le 421*, *Commerce*, *Amitié*, *Renaissance*, *Liberté*, *Soma*, *Entente*, *Sigui-Noghin*, *Mazawan*.

RESTAURANTS: *l'Auberge*, *Ran-Hôtel*, *l'Eau Vive*, *la Cantine*, *Nathalia*, *Tharkay*, *Restaurant le Transfo*, *la Boule Verte*, *Central*, *le Troquet*, *le Restaurant Africain*,

Like the one in Bobo Dioulasso, the Ouahabou mosque
near to Boromo, is worth visiting.
Made entirely from daub, it looks more like
it was modeled by a potter or a sculptor,
than designed by an architect.

Chez Mme Diallo, la Carafe, Black and White, le Rêve, le Touba, la Concorde.

TOURISM: Direction Régionale de l'Office National du Tourisme Burkinabè (ONTB) (tel. 97.19.86).

TRAVEL AGENTS: *Faso Tours,* BP 18 (tel. 98.11.40).

LEISURE: Pools (Ran-Hôtel, l'Auberge) ; tennis courts (Ran-Hôtel) ; discos (Black and White, Le Touba-Ran Hôtel, 421, Big Jack) ; cinemas (Guimbi, Houet, Sya).

CULTURE: Centre Culturel Henri Matisse (tel. 98.17.19 and 97.06.60). Musée Provincial du Houet (tel. 97.20.80).

AMENITIES: Large market, shops, food stores, bric-à-brac, petrol stations (BP, Mobil, Shell, Texaco, Total), garages, bus stations, banks (BIB, BICIA, BND), bookshops, pharmacies l'Entente (tel. 97.19.16), Houet (tel. 97.10.80/81), du Levant (tel. 97.03.33), Moderne (tel. 97.02.50/51), Siyara (tel. 97.13.73), Soudia (tel. 97.14.49), Hereso (tel. 97.09.95), Relwende (tel. 97.09.15), Solidarité (tel. 97.17.26); hospital (tel. 97.00.44/45/97.00.47) ; doctors : Dr Duvalet (tel. 98.25.36), Dr Guigemde (tel. 97.04.57), Dr Sama (tel. 97.10.49), Dr Schutz (tel. 98.14.43), Dr Zei (tel. 98.24.28).

Boromo/Deux-Balé (conservation forest)

LOCATION AND ACCESS: Mouhoun Province, 176 km W of Ouagadougou via the surfaced N1, 88 km W of Sabou via the surfaced N1, 79 km E of Houndé via the surfaced N1, 183 km E of Bobo-Dioulasso via the surfaced N.

FOOD AND ACCOMMODATION: *Relais touristique,* bar, restaurant, hotel (tel. 44.06.84).

TOURISM: Délégation du Tourisme et de l'Environnement (tel. 44.06.37).

AMENITIES: Total petrol station, pharmacy, hospital (tel. 44.06.39).

BIBLIOGRAPHY : *Guide des grands mammifères d'Afrique,* by Jean Dorst and Pierre Dandelot, Editions Delachaux et Niestlé,

Vie et mort d'un géant, l'Eléphant d'Afrique, by Pierre Pfeffer, ed. L'Odyssée/Flammarion.

Djibo

LOCATION AND ACCESS: Soum Province county town, northern Burkina Faso, 91 km N of Kongoussi via the D2, 203 km N of Ouagadougou via the D2 and the D1, 109 km NE of Ouahigouya via the D12, 188 km W of Dori via the D12. Airfield.

FOOD AND ACCOMMODATION: *Hôtel Massa, Centre Populaire des Loisirs, Auberge Populaire.*

AMENITIES: Shell and Total petrol stations, post office (PTT), food stores.

Dori

LOCATION AND ACCESS: Séno Province county town, NE of Burkina Faso (near the border with Niger). 53 km S of Gorom Gorom, 78 km S of Markoye, 265 km W of Niamey (capital of Niger) via Téra and Gotheye, 163 km NE of Kaya, via the N3, 261 km NE of Ouagadougou via the N3, 188 km E of Djibo via the D12. Airfield.

FOOD AND ACCOMMODATION: *Campement* (tel. 66.01.87), *Campement de la Coopération Italienne* (tel. 66.01.47).

TOURISM: Direction provinciale de l'Environnement et du Tourisme (tel. 66.02.65).

AMENITIES: Bank (BIB), Shell and Total petrol stations, Welinde cinema, food stores, hospital (tel. 66.02.48), pharmacy (tel. 66.01.75).

Fada N'Gourma

LOCATION AND ACCESS: Gourma Province county, eastern Burkina Faso. 97 km E of Koupéla via the tarred N4, 234 km E of Ouagadougou, via the tarred N4, 104 km N of Pama via the tarred N18, 143 km

E of Tenkodogo via the tarred N4 and N16, 151 km SW of Kantchari (border town near to Niger)via the tarred N4, 207 km W of Diapaga, via the N4 and the N19.

FOOD AND ACCOMMODATION: Hotels: *Yemama*, 8 rms., bar, restaurant (tel. 77.00.39) ; *Nungu* (tel. 77.01.93) ; *Auberge Populaire*, 13 rms. (tel. 77.01.69).
In Pama, *Safari Codeba*, camp, 17 rms., bar-restaurant.
In Diapaga, camp, 8 rms., bar-restaurant.
In Kompienga, *Hôtel de La Kompienga* (Reservations: ONTB-Ouagadougou, tel. 31.19.59/60).
Restaurant de la Paix in Fada N'Gourma.

TOURISM: Délégation provinciale de l'Environnement et du Tourisme (tel. 77.01.30).

AMENITIES: Shell, Texaco and Total petrol stations, banks (BIB, BND-B), cinema (Yendabli), hospital (tel. 77.01.00/39/83), Noungoun pharmacy (tel. 77.01.08).

Gaoua

LOCATION AND ACCESS: Poni Province county town, SW Burkina Faso, bordering on northern Côte d'Ivoire and Ghana. 186 km SE of Bobo-Dioulasso via the N6 and the N12, 74 km S of Diébougou via the N12 (unsurfaced), 210 km S of Pô, via the D15 and the N12, 258 km S of Boromo via the tarred N1 and the unsurfaced N12, 42 km NE of Kampti via a track, 39 km E of Loropéni via a track, 66 km N of Batié via a track.

FOOD AND ACCOMMODATION: *Hôtel Hala*, BP 76, 14 rms., bar, restaurant (tel. 87.01.21) ; *Hôtel du Poni*, BP 69, 9 rms. (tel. 87.02.00).
In Diébougou : *Relais* (tel. 86.02.88) and *l'Auberge Populaire*.

TOURISM: Direction provinciale de l'Environnement et du Tourisme (tel. 87.01.90).

AMENITIES: Shell petrol station, bank (BIB), Poni cinema, food stores, post office (PTT), hospital (tel. 87.00.96), pharmacy (tel. 87.04.15).

BIBLIOGRAPHY: *Les Lobi, tradition et changement*, by Madeleine Père, Editions Siloë.

Gorom Gorom

LOCATION AND ACCESS: Oudalan Province county town, to the far north of Faso (at the border with Mali and Niger). 53 km N of Dori, 37 km SW of Markoye, 76 km E of Aribinda, 318 km NE of Ouagadougou, via the N3.
Airfield.

FOOD AND ACCOMMODATION: *Hôtel-campement* (tel. 66.01.87).

TOURISM: Direction provinciale de l'Environnement et du Tourisme (tel. 66.00.65).

AMENITIES: Post office, petrol station, pharmacy (tel. 66.01.69).

Houndé

LOCATION AND ACCESS: Houet Province, western Burkina Faso, 104 km E of Bobo-Dioulasso via the N1 (surfaced), 31 km W of Pô, 79 km W of Boromo via the N1 and 255 km W of Ouagadougou via the N1.

FOOD AND ACCOMMODATION: *Auberge Populaire* or in Boromo (79 km away) or Bobo-Dioulasso (104 km away).

AMENITIES: Bank (BIB), post office, medical center (tel. 11 at Houndé).

Kaboré Tembi (national park)

NAME: The old Pô National Park was recently renamed after Kaboré Tembi, a park warden who was killed by poachers.

LOCATION AND ACCESS: Situated in southern Burkina Faso, the park spills over into both the Nahouri and Zoundweogo Provinces. Approx. 110 km S of Ouagadougou via the surfaced N5 (the Ghana road).

FOOD AND ACCOMMODATION: The small *Mantoro* (tel. 39.00.41) and modest restaurant *L'Auberge* in Pô.

AMENITIES: Petrol stations, food stores, a hospital and pharmacy are found in Pô, further to the south).

BIBLIOGRAPHY: *Guide des grands mammifères d'Afrique,* by Jean Dorst and Pierre Dandelot, Editions Delachaux et Niestlé; *Vie et mort d'un géant, l'éléphant d'Afrique,* by Pierre Pfeffer, Edition Odyssée/Flammarion.

Kaya

LOCATION AND ACCESS: Sanmatenga Province county town, central Burkina Faso. 98 km NE of Ouagadougou via the N3, 163 km SW of Dori via the N3, 55 km SE of Kongoussi via the N15, 161 km SE of Ouahigouya via the N15.

FOOD AND ACCOMMODATION: *Auberge Populaire* (tel. 45.30.45). Restaurants at the *Auberge Populaire,* and the *Désert* and *Sandaogo* bars.

TOURISME: Direction provinciale de l'Environnement et du Tourisme (tel. 45.32.34).

AMENITIES: Shell and Total petrol station, bank (BND), post office, hospital centre (tel. 45.30.36), pharmacies Nouvelle (tel. 45.30.55) and Wasongma (tel. 45.32.40).

Kongoussi

LOCATION AND ACCESS: Bam Province county town, central Burkina Faso. 112 km N of Ouagadougou via the D1, 91 km S of Djibo via the D2, 106 km E of Ouahigouya via the N15 and 55 km NW of Kaya via the N15.

FOOD AND ACCOMMODATION: Hotels: *Le Major* (27 rms.), *Pouwende* (4 rms.). Restaurants in the hotels and the *Faso* bar.

TOURISM: Direction provinciale de l'Environnement et du Tourisme (tel. 45.71.82).

AMENITIES: Shell petrol station, post office, pharmacy, medical center (tel. 45.71.58).

Koudougou

LOCATION AND ACCESS: Boulkiemdé Province county town, 13 km SE of Réo via the N14, 21 km NW of Sabou, 97 km W of Ouagadougou via the surfaced N1 and the N14.
Railway station.

FOOD AND ACCOMMODATION: Hotels *Toulourou*, 9 rms. (tel. 44.01.70); *Yéléba*, 14 rms. (tel. 44.00.91); *Photo-Luxe*, 24 rms. (tel. 44.00.87); *Espérance*, 10 rms. (tel. 44.05.59); *Oasis* (tel. 44.05.23); *Relais de la Gare* (tel. 44.01.38) and l'*Auberge Populaire. Centre d'Accueil et de Formation* (tel. 44.00.28). Restaurants in the *Oasis* and *Toulourou* hotels, *Okinawa* bar-restaurant-dancing.

TOURISM: Direction provinciale de l'Environnement et du Tourisme (tel. 44.07.72).

AMENITIES: BP, Mobil and Total petrol stations, Nelson Mandela cinema, Quatre Vents bookshop, market, food stores, pharmacies: Laafia (tel. 44.00.60) and Provinciale Faag Yooré (tel. 44.02.30), l'Amitié hospital (tel. 44.00.99/44.01.19/44.02.04 and 05/44.07.20 et 21), banks (BIB, BICIA, BND).

Manega

LOCATION AND ACCESS: Oubritenga Province, approx. 50 km N of Ouagadougou via the D1.

FOOD AND ACCOMMODATION: A Ouagadougou.

AMENITIES: None.

Ouahabou

LOCATION AND ACCESS: Mouhoun Province in western Burkina Faso. 21 km W of Boromo via the N1, 197 km W of Ouagadougou via the surfaced N1, 154 km NE of Bobo-Dioulasso via the N1.

FOOD AND ACCOMMODATION: In Boromo (21 km away).

AMENITIES : None.

Ouahigouya

NAME: Means « Prostate before me " (see

*Of the innumerable and flourishing arts
and crafts products in Burkina Faso,
the little "lost wax" bronzes made in
the family workshops of Niogsin, Ouagadougou
are particularly noteworthy. (Photo ONTB)*

(section on Ouahigouya).

LOCATION AND ACCESS: Yatenga Province county town, northern Burkina Faso, near the Malian border (50 km). Small town of approx. 42,000 habitants, the fourth in the country after Ouagadougou, Bobo-Dioulasso and Koudougou respectively.
181 km NW of Ouagadougou via a very good tarred road (the N2) and 165 km N of Koudougou via the N10 and the R14.

FOOD AND ACCOMMODATION: Hotels: *de l'Amitié*, 19 rms., bar, restaurant (tel. 55.05.21); *Dunia* (tel. 55.05.95); *du Nord* (tel. 55.01.94); *Mandela*; *Le Recueil*, boarding house (tel. 66.00.09); *Auberge Populaire* (tel. 55.01.84). Restaurants: *hôtel de l'Amitié*, *Sougri*, *Le Caïman*.

TOURISM: Direction provinciale de l'Environnement et du Tourisme (tel. 55.02.76), Faso Tours travel agency (tel. 55.03.10).

AMENITIES: Banks (BICIA, BIB, BND), Shell, Texaco and Total petrol stations, Nyolsba pharmacy (tel. 55.00.05), regional hospital centre (tel. 55.00.50 and 55.02.86), Eco bookshop/stationers, post office (Onatel, ONP).

Pô

LOCATION AND ACCESS: Nahouri Province county town in southern of Burkina Faso, border town between Burkina and Ghana, 144 km S of Ouagadougou via the tarred N5.

FOOD AND ACCOMMODATION: Small hotels: *Auberge Agouabim*, bar, restaurant, 6 rooms (tel. 39.01.42); *Mantoro* (tel. 39.00.41) and modest restaurants (l'*Auberge*, le *Lido*, bar-restaurant *Koubassare*). *Nazinga Ranch camp* (like the reserve, open from December to June). Reservation at OK Raids, Ouagadougou, tel. 30.40.61).

AMENITIES: BP, Total and Texaco petrol stations, pharmacy, hospital (tel. 39.00.05), food stores.

Sabou

LOCATION AND ACCESS: Boulkiemdé Province, 20 km S of Koudougou and 88 km

W of Ouagadougou via an excellent surfaced road).

FOOD AND ACCOMMODATION: *Tourist complex.*

AMENITIES: Clinic (tel. 5), post office (public phone, tel. 3).

Sindou

LOCATION AND ACCESS: Comoé Province to the far west of Burkina Faso (near the Malian and Ivoirian borders), 51 km W of Banfora via a track and 136 km SW of Bobo Dioulasso via the surfaced N7 and via a track.

FOOD AND ACCOMMODATION: Only in Banfora (51 km).

AMENITIES: None.

Tenkodogo

NAME: « The old town », in Moré.

LOCATION AND ACCESS: Boulgou Province county town, 46 km S of Koupéla via the N4 and 183 km SE of Ouagadougou via the N16 and N4.

FOOD AND ACCOMMODATION: *Auberge Populaire Djamou* (tel. 71.01.98), *Wend Kuuni*. In Koupéla: *Bon-Séjour*, *Wend Waoga* and *Avenir*. Restaurant: *Auberge Populaire*.

AMENITIES: Banks (BIB), Shell and Total petrol stations, Koulbalé cinema, l'Avenir pharmacy (tel. 71.00.67), post office (Onatel, ONP), hospital (tel. 71.00.12).

Tiébélé

LOCATION AND ACCESS: Nahouri Province in southern Burkina Faso (near the Ghanaian border), 29 km E of Pô via a track, 173 km S of Ouagadougou via the surfaced N5 and a track.

FOOD AND ACCOMMODATION: Although there are no hotels, it is possible to stay with the inhabitants (ask the village chief). No restaurants. The nearest hotels and restaurants are in Pô (29 km).

AMENITIES: None.

Tougan

LOCATION AND ACCESS: Sourou Province county town, NW Burkina Faso, 88 km N of Dédougou via the N10, 264 km NE of Bobo Dioulasso via the N10, 94 km SW of Ouahigouya via the N10, 120 km NW of Koudougou via the D13 and the N14, 217 km NW of Ouagadougou via the D13 and the N14.

FOOD AND ACCOMMODATION: *Auberge Populaire*, or in Dédougou (88 km away) and in Ouahigouya (94 km).

TOURISM: Direction provinciale de l'Environnement et du Tourisme (tel. 53.40.24).

AMENITIES: BP and Shell petrol stations, post office, bookshop, food stores, bank (BIB), pharmacy (tel. 53.40.73), hospital (tel. 53.40.91).

W (national park)

NAME: Due to the "w" shaped meanders in the Niger River.

LOCATION AND ACCESS: Tapoa Province, right in the east of Burkina Faso, near the border with Niger and Benin. Diapaga, the county town, is 56 km S of Kantchari via the N19, 207 km E of Fada N'Gourma via the N4 and the N19 and 441 km E of Ouagadougou via the N19 and the N4.

FOOD AND ACCOMMODATION: At the *campement de Diapaga* (8 rms., bar, restaurant).

VISITING THE PARK: Visitors must enter via the Diapaga, Tapoa Djerma, Koabougou or Kondio check point where they will pay an entrance fee. The park is open during the dry season from October to the end of May (it is closed from June to the end of September).

EQUIMPENT: Safari clothing (no bright colours); hat and sun glasses; binoculars; cameras with telephoto lenses.

BIBLIOGRAPHY: *Guide des Grands Mammifères d'Afrique*, by Jean Dorst and Pierre Dandelot, Éditions Delachaux et Niestlé. *Carte touristique des Parcs nationaux des Pays de l'Entente*, Ed. by l'Institut Géographique National, Paris.

Yako

LOCATION AND ACCESS: Passoré Province county town, 108 km NW of Ouagadougou via the surfaced N2, 73 km S of Ouahigouya via the surfaced N2, 127 km W of Kaya.

FOOD AND ACCOMMODATION: *Auberge Populaire* (tel. 30.90.86), restaurant *Le Carrefour* (Cristal chain).

AMENITIES: Shell, Texaco and Total petrol station, hospital (tel. 30.90.12), Populaire pharmacy (tel. 30.90.55).

TOURISM: Direction provinciale de l'Environnement et du Tourisme (tel. 30.90.38/85).

the journey

before leaving

■ Burkina Faso's tourist industry was tentatively launched in the Eighties, and is now really beginning to take off thanks to the country's many attractive qualities: the beautiful Sahelian landscape, the diverse ethnic groups' fascinating traditions, the abundance of wildlife in the national parks... and above all, the sense of hospitality and kindness innate in the inhabitants of this "Land of Honest People".

Burkina Faso may not be able to offer the pleasures of the seaside and its lazy life given that the nearest beaches are on the Atlantic coast at least 500 km southwards, but enjoyable holidays do not always have to entail seaside activities and visitors will soon feel consoled when they are invited to attend a large traditional celebration at the ends of the harvests or when, after a long trip to the Arli or "W" park, they see their first lions or elephants ambling along in the savanna.

Furthermore, as initial efforts have been made to develop a tourist industry over the last few years, a good little hotel network has also been established. No longer limited to large towns like Ouagadougou and Bobo Dioulasso, hotels now cater for the main tourist sites and natural attractions, for example in the north at Gorom Gorom, to the east near the national parks and in the west near the superb waterfalls in the Banfora region.

Finally, the good, ever expanding network of surfaced roads now means that it is easy to travel on main roads in the country. As the unsurfaced tracks are generally "smooth", visitors can head into the depths of the "bush" to see natural attractions (like the Bobo Dioulasso "hippo pool") without having to hire a four-wheel drive vehicle.

Which season?

Situated in the Sahelian region, Burkina Faso's climate poses few problems as it is warm and dry almost all year round (with a rainy interlude similar to European summer time). Burkina Faso experiences three main seasons each year: the relatively cool dry season from November to February, a warmer but shorter dry season between March and June, and a rainy season from June to October with maximum rainfall in August.

The best time to visit Burkina Faso is therefore from November to February.

Vaccination requirements

Whenever travelling in Africa and especially in Burkina Faso, visitors must have an international vaccination certificate which Health officials will ask to see on arrival at Ouagadougou airport. This must certify that visitors have been vaccinated against yellow fever (yellow fever jab) before leaving Europe. It is a good idea to be vaccinated at least ten days before leaving, as some people may have a reaction to the injection for up to a week after (fever or headaches). The yellow fever jab lasts for ten years.

Where to get vaccinated

Principal registered vaccination centres in London include:
— the Hospital for Tropical Diseases Travel Clinic, 4 St Pancras Way, London NW1, tel. 0171 387-4411. Open Monday-Friday from 09.00 to 16.40.
— the British Airways Travel Clinic, 156 Regent St, London W1, tel. 0171 439-9584 or 439-9585. Open Monday-Friday from 09.30 to 17.15 and from 10.00 to 16.00 on Saturday.
– West London Designated Vaccination Centre, 53 Great Cumberland Place, London W1, tel. 0171 262-6456, open from 09.00 to 16.45 Monday-Friday.

Average temperatures and rainfalls:

	Jan.	Feb.	Mar.	Apr.	May	June	July	Aug.	Sep.	Oct.	Nov.	Dec.
Av. temp. (in °C)	25	28	31	32	31	28	27	26	27	29	29	26

Light rainfall   Maximum rainfall

Rainy season   Dry season

Overleaf:
*Burkinabè women living in the bush
are not only in charge of the home,
but are often traders and labourers
in the fields as well.*

Medical centres in Britain and the US

Other centres in the major French towns are equipped to give the various jabs:

US travellers can contact specialist travel clinics, which tend to be very expensive, or their local health departments. The Centre for Disease Control and Prevention can be contacted for advice and information: tel. 404 332-4565, fax 404 332-4559.

In Britain, local GPs will often be able to give advice and administer vaccinations. Yellow fever jabs will usually be given in specialist clinics (contact your local health authority). Outside London, tropical disease centres include:
— The Department of Communicable and Tropical Diseases, Birmingham Heartland Hospital, Bordesley Green Road, Birmingham B9 5ST, tel. 0121 766-6611. — Liverpool School of Tropical Medicine, Pembroke Place, Liverpool L3 5QA, tel. 0151 708-9393. — Communicable Diseases Unit, Ruchill Hospital, Glasgow G20 9NB, tel. 0141 946-7120.

Tropical diseases

If visitors have the slightest query about health matters and notably the risks of catching tropical diseases in Africa, consult a specialised information centre before and after travelling:
— MASTA (Medical Advisory Services for Travellers Abroad) at the London School of Hygiene and Tropical Diseases, Keppel Street, London WC1E HT, tel. 0171 636-8636.
— The Hospital for Tropical Diseases Travel Clinic, 4 St Pancras Way, London NW1, tel. 0171 387-4411. Full check-ups will be given on return if referred by your GP.

Some diseases have a long incubation period (malaria for example), and symptoms may not be felt until well after the visitor has gone back to Europe. It is therefore crucial to consult a doctor if even the slightest unusual symptoms occur (fever, nausea, digestive upsets, any kind of skin rashes or blemishes), even if it is several weeks after the journey to a tropical region.

STRANGE STONES IN THE LAND OF THE MOSSI

■ *Up until the end of the 19th century, thousands of sculpted tomb stones ("Ya-Kouga") could be seen dotted about the Burkinabè bush. Most were highly stylized, or abstract effigies of the deceased dignitary they represented. They appear to have been erected several hundred, or even thousand years ago by the Younyosse, the first inhabitants of Burkina Faso, then by the Mossi. Unfortunately, there are practically no ya-kouga left today. Only a handful have been preserved far from prying eyes the tomb stones were often destroyed during the colonial era as they thought to be paganistic. Burkina Faso's rare remaining examples of the ya-kouga thus urgently need to be collected and preserved. Several researchers have taken an interest in these stones, notably the Burkinabè lawyer Titinga Frédéric Pacéré who stresses that "These tomb stones are museums, archives of the lives of the people concerned; each one is part of the sacred domain of life, which can now be reconstituted. Their complete collection in a designated milieu, their dating and their interpretation will bring unquestionable historic truths to light. These stones contain information on political and social organisation, cultural elements, mocurs, and hairstyles at each period of major change." Moreover, the sculpted stones' aesthetic beauty can be inscribed in the long tradition of African statutory. Indeed, the stones are all the more interesting as very few African sculptors worked in stone, tending rather to carve their masks and ritual statues out of wood.*

ADMINISTRATIVE DIVISIONS

MALI

Dji

29

YATENGA

● Ouahigouya

BA

27

Tougan

● Yako

SOUROU

PASSORE

13

Nouna
●

BOULKIEMDE

KOSSI

Koudougou

● Dédougou

Réo
●

●

OUAGADOUG

22

5

MOUHOUN

SANGUIE

15

KENEDOUGOU

25

SISSILI

10

12

HOUET

3

Léo
●

● Bobo-Dioulasso

BOUGOURIBA

Orodara
●

● Diébougou

GHANA

● Banfora

Gaoua
●

COMOE

PONI

6

21

IVORY

COAST

19
OUDALAN

26

Gorom-Gorom
●

SOUM

N I G E R

Dori
●

SENO

SANMATENGA

23   24

Kongoussi **NAMENTENGA**

●   17   **GNAGNA**
Kaya

Bogandé
●

UBRITENGA   Boulsa
                                  8
● Ziniaré   ●

              Zorgho 14
KADIOGO 7   ●   9
  GANZOURGOU ● Koupéla

● **BAZEGA KOURITENGA**   **GOURMA**

2 Kombissiri   Fada N'Gourma
                              ●

Manga   **TAPOA**
  ● 30   ●   Diapaga
             Tenkodogo   ●
ZOUNDWEOGO 4   28

NAHOURI BOULGOU

  ● Pô 16

B E N I N

TOGO

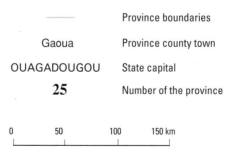

———————— Province boundaries

Gaoua   Province county town

OUAGADOUGOU   State capital

25   Number of the province

0   50   100   150 km
|——————|——————|——————|

Make sure the doctor is aware of the countries the patient stayed or travelled in.

Nota Bene

When visitors return home from Burkina Faso, they must continue to take their antimalarial tablets for another six weeks. If any unusual symptoms arise, it is essential to consult a doctor and inform him/her of the visit to a tropical country.

Entrance requirements

Foreign visitors wishing to travel to Burkina Faso must hold a valid passport and a visa which can be obtained from the Burkinabè embassy in their country or from the Burkina Faso Embassy, 159, bd Haussmann, 75008 Paris, in France, tel. 01.43.59.21.85. Visitors must take their passport and two passport photos. Visas have to be paid for (check the price with the embassy) and are usually delivered on the spot although there can be occasional 24 hour delays.

Further information in Burkina Faso

As there is no Burkinabè tourist bureau in either France or Europe, contact the different embassies.

Maps of West Africa and Burkina Faso can be purchased from the "Institut Géographique National" in Paris (107, rue La Boétie, 75008, tel. 01.43.59. 10.83).

The Michelin map of North and West Africa (n° 95, on a scale of 1:400 000) is an excellent up-to-date map that indicates the states of the roads (useful if visiting other countries too) and the « Carte touristique et routière de la Haute-Volta » (now Burkina Faso) on a scale of 1:1 000 000 is sufficiently detailed to not get lost. The latter includes two little maps of Ouagadougou and Bobo Dioulasso, a map of the administrative divisions and a map of the distribution of the ethnic groups.

Various documents, works, travel diaries and geographic maps can be found in specialised bookshops like: the *Africa Book Centre*, 38 King Street, WC2E 8JT, tel. 0171 240-6649, fax 0171 379-4929; *Stanfords*, 12 Long Acre, WC2E 9LP, tel. 071. 836-1321, fax 0171 836-0189; the *Travel Bookshop*, 13 Blenheim Crescent,

W11 2EE, tel. 0171 229-5260, fax 0171 243-1552; *Astrolabe*, 46, rue de Provence, 75009 Paris, tel. 01.42.85.42.95; *L'Harmattan*, 16, rue des Ecoles, 75005 Paris, tel. 01.43.26.04.52; *The Complete Traveler Bookstore*, 199 Madison Ave, New York, NY 10016, tel. 212 685-9007; *Travel Books Unlimited*, 4931 Cordell Ave, Bethesda, MD Downtown, tel. 301 951-8533.

Interesting museums

It is also worth going to visit local African art and ethnology museums before travelling. Paris has a particularly good range of museums like the Musée de l'Homme, Place du Trocadéro, Paris, or the Musée des Arts Africains et Océaniens, Porte Dorée, Paris, where there are numerous objects, tools, sculptures and masks made by the various ethnic groups in Burkina Faso. There is also a good range of books on ethnology, African art, history and natural science in the Musée de l'Homme bookshop.

Finally, visitors should try to see the films *Yaaba* and *Tila* by Burkinabè director Idrissa Ouedraogo for an especially moving foresight into day-to-day life in Burkina Faso's villages.

Clothing and equipment

Although it is always warm in Burkina Faso, like in most tropical countries, evenings can sometimes be a little cool, especially during the rainy season (July to September). In the day time cotton clothing (and not synthetic materials) are the best for affronting the blazing heat.

What to wear in town

In town, people usually wear trousers or longish skirts, light short-sleeved shirts, sweat shirts and tee-shirts. If walking in the sun for a long time, a cotton hat, sun glasses and light-weight walking shoes (for example canvas boots) are essential.

Safari equipment

On wildlife safaris in eastern Burkina Faso's national parks, long, light clothing is best (not shorts or skirts because of the undergrowth and insect bites). Bright colours are easily spotted by the animals and should therefore be avoided. Remember to take binoculars as it is difficult to get close to many of the large mammals (elephants, lions and antelopes) who, easily frightened, bolt when they hear a motor.

Specialised agencies

When hunting in the assigned areas in the east, shoes suitable for the bush (sturdy canvas boots, for example) and camouflaged clothing should be worn. Arms and munition vary depending on whether hunting small game (game birds) or big game (large mammals). Visitors should consult the specialised agencies in their home country that organise safaris in Burkina Faso. They will know that equipment is necessary and the formalities to be completed before taking hunting arms into the country (carriers, hunting permits, etc.).

Useful things

On all other excursions, sturdy, slightly thicker clothing like jeans should be worn, especially if walking in tall grasses and undergrowth in the savanna. A hat and sun glasses are essential.

Other useful equipment includes: a pocket torch and a pen knife with several blades (a Swiss army knife, for example), a fork, a bottle and can-opener, which will be useful if picnicking or staying in a bush camp.

Photographic equipment

Burkina Faso's landscapes (escarpments, savannas, creeks and waterfalls), traditional festivities and large savanna wildlife are ideal subject matter for photographs and home movies.

A good telephoto lense with a focal length of at least 300 mm (like the "sniper" lense) is essential for taking photos of animals in the vast eastern reserves. For traditional festivities, a standard wide angle lense (approximately 50 mm) is appropriate, plus a little telephoto lense (135 to 200 mm) for focusing in on finer details. A wide angle lense is useful for photographing landscapes.

When taking photos, visitors must pay attention to the sky in Africa as it is often very white and extremely luminous due to the intensity of its ultra-violet rays! A UV filter is recommended. In order to avoid the over-harsh lighting of the midday sun, professionals advise that when possible, photos be taken early in the morning or at the end of the day as the sun sets. Cameras should be protected from the heat and from being knocked about by using a robust, stiff photographic bag that ought not be left in direct sunlight.

Due to the intensity of the light in Burkina Faso, moderately sensitive film should be used: 64 ASA is appropriate for all day time photos. It is advisable to take a sufficient supply of film or video tapes to Burkina Faso as photo and video equipment sold in duty free shops in the airports is much cheaper than in Ouagadougou or Bobo Dioulasso.

Other precautions

Whenever stopping in a hotel in Burkina Faso, visitors should make sure that equipment is clean of sand and humidity, cleaning it with a soft cloth (in order not to scratch the lenses, blow on them first). If there is a fridge, use it for storing film and/or video cassettes.

When travelling by car, photographic material should never be left on the back shelf in direct sunlight, but put in the shade and covered. Once home, visitors should not wait too long before developing their films.

Health and hygiene

Visitors are advised to take a toilet case and a small medical kit. It does not matter if toothbrushes or common medicines are forgotten as shops and pharmacies in Ouagadougou are as well stocked as those in Europe and North America.

A medical kit is essential, especially in case visitors feel ill at night or when out in the bush far from a big town or a clinic.

The essential medical kit

It should contain:
— Antimalarial tablets: Nivaquine, Paludrine, Halfan or Lariam (before leaving, ask a doctor or at one of the tropical illness information centres already mentioned which tablets to take when in Burkina Faso and back in Europe, and for how long).

— Alka Seltzer.

— Medicine to calm stomach upsets, like the bouts of diarrhea caused simply by the change of climate and food: for adults, Intétrix, Imodium capsules or Diarsed pills, and for children, Imodium drops.

— Possible antibiotics (on prescription): Bactrim tablets (for adults) or soluble Bactrim (for children) and an antiseptic: Intétrix (already mentioned).

— Aspirin, paracetamol.

— Talc.

— Surgical spirit or Dakin solution.

— Sterilized compress, plasters.

— Antiseptic eye lotion (Chibroboraline or Biocidan).

— Mosquito repellant (spray) and anti-histamine cream for soothing insect bites (mosquito bites for example).

— Mercurochrome.

Also take high factor suntan lotion for protection against Burkina Faso's intense sun and after sun in case of sunburn.

*This young man from Banfora is lucky enough to live
in a particularly cheerful area in the west of Burkina Faso,
where water flows in abundance.
This has enabled the development of immense rice,
sugar cane and fruit plantations.*

getting to burkina faso

Getting there by plane

By plane (Boeing 747, Airbus) – the safest and quickest way to travel – it takes just over 5 hours to fly the 4058 km direct from Paris to Ouagadougou.

Of the main international airline companies flying to Ouagadougou airport (1 km from the town centre), the multinational company *Air Afrique*, of which Burkina Faso is one of the eleven member states, and *Air France* offer regular services from Paris to Ouagadougou.

Air Afrique and *Air France* fly both directly and with stop-overs to Ouagadougou several times a week.

Other companies like *Sabena* also fly to Burkina Faso.

Travel classes and reductions

Air Afrique and Air France offer a choice of three classes on their flights: "First" (F), "Business" (J) and "Economy" (Y). Passengers with reduced price tickets will be in Economy class as, in order to help Burkina Faso's economic development, Air Afrique has created a certain number of reductions on "Economy class" places. Special "Visite" tickets are available to anyone and "Haute Compétition" tickets (Air Afrique) or "Super Challenge" tickets (Air France) to young people, pensioners, families, immigrant workers, church people and students. These reductions are offered only a certain time of the year, and entail certain constraints: the ticket must be reserved and bought the same day, departure and return dates cannot be modified (otherwise a forfeit, like the full price of the ticket, must be paid), unusued return tickets are not reimbursed.

It is absolutely essential to confirm return flights (whatever the tariff!) at the Air Afrique or Air France agency at least 72 hours (3 days) before the departure date.

Agencies in Europe, North America and Burkina Faso

Addresses: *Air Afrique*:
Britain: 4th Floor, 86 Hatton Gardens, London EC1 N8QQ, tel. 0171 430-0661.
France: 26, Avenue de l'Opéra, 75002 Paris, tel. 01.44.21.33.33 and 01.44. 21.32.32 (reservation service Monday-Friday from 08.00 to 21.00, Saturday-Sunday and public holiday from 09.00 to 17.00
USA: 1350 Ave. of the Americas, NY 10019, tel. 212 541-7474 or 1-800 456-9192.
Ouagadougou: Av. du Général-Nasser, tel. 30.60.20 and 30.65.18. Bobo-Dioulasso, tel. 98.19.23/97.13.53.

Air France:
Britain: 10 Warwick Street, London W1R, tel. 0171 742.6600.
France: 74 Bd Auguste Blanqui, 75013 Paris, tel. 08.20.80.28.02 (flight information).
Ouagadougou: Avenue Nelson-Mandela, BP 116, tel. 30.63.65.

Sabena:
Britain: Swiss Centre, c/o Swiss Air, 1 Swiss Court, London W1V 4BG, tel. 0171 494-2629.
France: 4 Rue Ferrus, 75014 Paris, tel. 01.53.80.59.49.
USA: Swiss Centre, 608 5th Ave, NY 10020, tel. 212 2477-8390.
Ouagadougou: CCP Building, 31st floor, BP 6214 Ouagadougou, tel. 30.58.80.

Charters flights

Some travel agents organise very low cost charter flights with certain conditions: dates cannot be changed, both outbound and return flights are on fixed days (passagers must fly out on either Wednesdays or Thursdays, and return on Wednesdays, Thursdays or Fridays, depending on the different flights).

Visitors should not wait until the last minute to reserve such flights as these very cheap places are snatched up quickly (especially before the summer holidays!).

Discount travel agents

All countries offer a range of discount travel agencies. Addresses include:
Britain: *The Africa Travel Centre,* 4 Medway Court, Leigh Street, London WC1H 9QX, tel. 0171 387-1211, fax 0171 383-5512. *STA Travel,* 74 Old Brompton Road, London SW7, tel. 0171 937-9962.
France: *Nouvelles Frontières,* 87, Bd de Grenelle, 75015 Paris; information, booking and telephone sales: 08.03.33. 33.33 and by Minitel: 3615 or 3616 NF. *Forum Voyages,* 49, Av. Raymond Poincaré, 75016 Paris, tel. 01.47.27.89.89.
USA: *Maharajah Travels,* 393 Fifth Ave. at 37th Street, New York, NY 10016, tel. 1-800 223--6862; *STA Travel,* Head

Office, 48 E 11th Street, New York, NY 10003, tel. 1-800 777-0112. *Nouvelles Frontières*, 12 E 33rd Street, NY 10036, tel. 212 779-0609, fax 212 777-1006.

Organised tours

In Burkina Faso itself, the Ouaga-dougou based travel agents *Faso-Tours* and *OK Raids* offer a large range of services including the organising of tour itineraries and trips, notably in the eastern parks, big and small game safaris, car hire, hotel bookings, etc.

Addresses in Burkina Faso: *Faso-Tours* (Ouagadougou, BP 1318, tel. 30.65.13, Bobo-Dioulasso, tel. 98.11.40; Ouahigouya, tel. 55.03.10; Fada N'Gourma, tel. 77.01.52); *Vacances OK Raids* (01 BP 5397 Ouagadougou 01, tel. 30.40.61, fax 30.48.11).

Getting there by sea and over land

Beware! This journey is a real expedition and should only be undertaken by the most adventurous travellers fond of cross-country driving! A four-wheel drive vehicle (a Land or Range Rover for example) is indispensable for crossing the Sahara.

From Paris, Lille, Bordeaux or Lyons head to Marseilles where a boat goes to Algiers. From Algiers, drive directly southwards into the Sahara via Blida, Laghouat, Ghardaïa, El Golea, Aïn Salah and Tamanrasset (customs formalities). The road, or rather the track, goes to the border with Niger (the In Guezzam post), from where there is the good, surfaced "Route de l'Uranium" to Arlit. At Arlit go via Agadez, Tahoua, Birni N'Konni, Dogondoutchi and Dosso to the capital Niamey. From here, it is another 130 km to Burkina Faso. Cross the Niger River at Niamey and head in the direction of Torodi and Makalondi in the south-west. Just after the Burkinabè border, is the first Burkinabè town: Kantchari, on the main road that heads westwards to the capital Ouagadougou, via Fada N'Gourma and Koupéla.

A perfectly working vehicle

It is essential that the vehicle is in perfect working order before making this trip and is equipped with spare parts (especially tyres and inner chambers), all the tools necessary to make temporary repairs and plates and spades for digging the vehicle out of sand drifts when crossing the Sahara. Ample food supplies and plenty of water (3 to 4 litres per day per person are needed when crossing the desert) are also essential.

Several things are required of the vehicle's driver if the expedition is to be a success, especially when driving through the Sahara: the driver must know how to drive in sand, to read a map and recognise land-marks (or be helped by a "navigator"), to stop if there is a sand storm, to inform the local authorities of the group's whereabouts, to travel in convoy whenever the terrain becomes difficult, not to travel at night and at each stop, to enquire about difficulties that may be encountered on the next stage of the journey.

Covering for problems

Several insurance companies will cover for all risks in Burkina Faso. Cover for potential problem encountered on the journey comes into effect as soon as the plane ticket is bought, as these companies cover for cancellation of the trip if unforeseen circumstances force travellers not to leave Europe or to defer departure at the last moment. Theft or loss of luggage are also covered. The companies' most spectacular role, however, is in assisting wounded or ill travellers by sending them medication or a medical plane. Obviously, such major intervention does not take place in all circumstances.

What to expect from insurances companies

Here is a summary of the insurance offered to travellers and their vehicles in the companies' brochures and guides; if an ill or wounded traveller's condition necessitates, he/she will be flown home and taken by ambulance to the hospital nearest to his/her place of residence (under constant medical supervision). The ill/wounded policy holder may be accompanied home by another person. If hospitalised in Burkina Faso, a near relative can be flown from their home country to visit the patient at the company's expense; and if the patient is accompanied by children, they will be flown home accompanied by one of the company's hostesses. If medical costs

GETTING TO BURKINA FASO
(the major air, overland and sea routes)

ATLANTIC

OCEAN

Canary Islands

Tropic of Cancer

20°

40°

20°

0°

Brussels ● BELGIUM

PARIS

Zurich

Geneva ● SWITZERLAND
Lyon
Bordeaux ● FRANCE ● ITALY

● Marseille

Rome ●

SPAIN
Madrid

PORTUGAL

Lisbon ●

Tunis ●

Algiers ●

MOROCCO

TUNISIA
Tripoli ●

Ghardaia ●

El Goléa ●

ALGERIA

LIBYA

In Salah ●

S   A   H   A   R   A

Tamanrasset ●

Nouakchott ●

MAURITANIA

Arlit ●

Agadez ●

MALI

NIGER

Dakar ● SENEGAL
GAMBIA

Bamako ●

BURKINA FASO
Niamey ●
Tahoua ●

Bissau ●
GUINEA BISSAU
Conakry ●
GUINEA

Bobo Ouagadougou
Dioulasso ●

CH

N'Djamena

BENIN

Freetown ●
SIERRA LEONE

IVORY
COAST

GHANA

TOGO

NIGERIA

Lagos ●

Monrovia ●
LIBERIA

Abidjan ●

Accra ●

Cotonou ●

Lomé ●

CAMEROON

Douala ●

Cabinda (Angola)

Libreville ●

GABON

CONGO

Brazzaville ●

Kinshasa

ANGOLA

- - - - - By road and by sea

Railway

AIR AFRIQUE

AIR FRANCE

AIR ALGÉRIE

AÉROFLOT

0   1000 km

*Petrol pumps can now be found
in the heart of the bush where they fill up
not only the large trucks,
but also the innumerable "two-wheelers",
now kings of the road.*

are incurred in Burkina Faso, up to 25,000 FF will be reimbursed per policy holder (on top of any other insurances policies that may be held).

If problems arise in Burkina Faso, the insurance company will advance up to 40,000 FF in bail and 5,000 FF for a lawyer.

Vehicle troubles

If a traveller's vehicle breaks down or has an accident, repairs and towing charges are covered, as are unforeseen hotel costs consequently incurred. If spare parts cannot be found on site, they will be sent from Europe. If the vehicle is immobilized in Burkina Faso for more than 5 days, or if it is stolen, policy holders can be flown home along with the vehicle if it cannot be repaired on site. A driver can also be sent to Burkina Faso to bring back the vehicle if the policy holding driver cannot drive back (hurt, ill...) and if the passengers do not know how to drive.

DISTANCE BETWEEN THE TOWNS (IN KILOMETRES)

	Banfora	Bobo-Dioulasso	Diapaga	Fada N'Gourma	Gaoua	Gorom-Gorom	Kaya	Koudougou	Léo	Nouna	Orodara	Ouagadougou	Ouahigouya	Pô	Tenkodogo
Banfora	–	85	872	666	197	762	539	361	358	320	161	441	456	485	624
Bobo-Dioulasso	85	–	787	581	211	677	454	276	273	235	76	356	371	400	539
Diapaga	872	787	–	206	864	752	529	529	656	713	863	863	431	575	340
Fada N'Gourma	666	581	206	–	658	546	323	323	450	507	657	225	406	369	134
Gaoua	197	211	864	658	–	754	531	365	208	446	287	433	530	336	616
Gorom-Gorom	762	677	752	546	754	–	223	419	546	603	758	321	423	465	504
Kaya	539	454	529	323	531	223	–	196	223	380	530	98	200	242	281
Koudougou	361	276	529	323	365	419	196	–	157	184	352	98	165	242	281
Léo	358	273	656	450	208	546	323	157	–	321	349	225	302	127	408
Nouna	320	235	713	507	446	603	380	184	321	–	311	282	248	428	465
Orodara	161	76	863	657	287	758	530	352	349	311	–	432	447	476	615
Ouagadougou	441	356	431	225	433	321	98	98	225	282	432	–	181	144	183
Ouahigouya	456	371	612	406	530	423	200	165	302	248	447	181	–	325	364
Pô	485	400	575	369	335	465	242	242	127	426	476	144	325	–	327
Tenkodogo	624	539	340	134	616	504	281	281	408	465	615	183	364	327	–

getting around burkina faso

Travelling by plane

The little domestic airline company *Air Burkina* assures a regular service between the political and economic capitals, Ouagadougou and Bobo Dioulasso (333 km, 35 minutes flying time in a Fokker 28), Gorom Gorom in the north-east of the country and the capital cities in neighbouring countries: Abidjan in Côte d'Ivoire, Bamako in Mali, Cotonou in Benin, Lomé in Togo, and Niamey in Niger. It is also possible to charter out light aircraft from Air Burkina and fly to the other numerous airfields in the Burkinabè bush (*Air Burkina*, Avenue de Loudun, Ouagadougou, tel. 30.76.76 and 30.61.44. In Bobo Dioulasso: tel. 97.13.48).

Travelling by road

Driving round Burkina Faso is not problematic as most of the main roads are tarred, like, for example, the Nationale 1 from Ouagadougou to Bobo Dioulasso (356 km), Burkina Faso's backbone. From Bobo Dioulasso, the route continues to Banfora in the south-west and on to the border with Côte d'Ivoire (N7), whilst east of Ouagadougou, it continues to Fada N'Gourma (N4) and the border with Niger. This long, 900 km east-west road system crosses the whole of Burkina Faso, passing close by to many of the country's natural attractions and tourist sites.

Other secondary, tarred roads link up with the principal road, like the Pô road (N5) that heads southwards from Ouagadougou and cuts through the Kaboré Tembi national park and the Gourounsi region (see the beautiful village of Tiébélé) to the border with Ghana.

The Ouagadougou-Dori-Gorom Gorom road (N3) is interesting for several reasons and leads, possibly for the first time, to the region where the Sahelian-Saharan Fulani and Tuareg nomads live.

The brand new N2 from Ouagadougou to Ouahigouya cuts through historical Mossi lands, linking the ancient Mossi empires of Ouagadoudou and Yatenga.

The Lobi and Sénoufo regions (Gaoua and Sindou-Orodara respectively) in the south-west of the country are harder to get to, but are worth visiting nonetheless, even if it means taking the sometimes very bumpy earth tracks.

The N19 that crosses Arli park in eastern Burkina Faso is also in rather poor condition, but visitors are unlikely to complain as one can hardly imagine driving along a motorway in an air conditioned coach to see African wild animals.

Travelling by taxi

Visitors can get round Ouagadougou and Bobo Dioulasso in taxis which can be found parked in front of the hotels and at the airport or, like all over Africa, hailed as they cruise through the town. People often share taxis which reduces the price for everyone (roughly 150 FCFA per person, that is, 3 FF for any trip round the town), and is a unique opportunity to get to meet the locals. From the bus stations in the major towns, it is possible to take a bush taxi (a Peugeot 404) anywhere in the country for a very modest sum. This is a practical but somewhat uncomfortable way to discover Burkina Faso.

Travelling by bus

Two bus companies also run regular services and have a fleet of more comfortable vehicles. Given that the number of places is limited, passengers must book at least 48 hours in advance in order to get a seat (*Faso-Tours*, BP 1318, Ouagadougou, tel. 30.65.13; *X9*, BP 2991, tel. 30.42.96/33.46.69.

Car hire

Car hire is still a recent phenomenon in Burkina Faso and visitors need to be on their guard when dealing with local private hirers. Visitors should not hesitate to discuss prices if they seem too high and above all must check the state of the vehicle before hiring it (check the state of the tyres, and whether or not the car has a jack and a spare tyre). Remember that for most of the unsurfaced circuits, it is imperative to hire a four-wheel drive vehicle with a driver.

The "two-wheelers" (bikes, mopeds, motorbikes, scooters) commonly used in Burkina Faso can also be hired for periods varying from a day to several weeks from the specialised cycle shops near the Ouagadougou central market.

Of the various car hire companies based in Ouagadougou, we especially recommand *Nis-Location de voitures* (at the Hôtel "Silmandé" : Monsieur Inoussa Nana, tel. 30.02.03).

The "two-wheelers" (bikes, mopeds,

COMMUNICATIONS

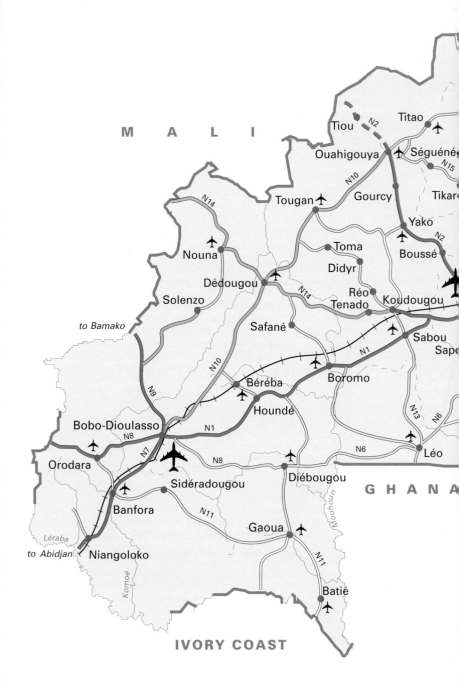

to Ansongo

| 0 | 50 | 100 | 150 km |

Markoye

Gorom-Gorom

Aribinda

D12

N3

to Niamey

Dori

N I G E R

Barsalogho

oussi

N3

Sebba

Kaya

Pissila

Bogandé

to Niamey

Boulsa

N15

D10

Kantchari

Zorgho

GADOUGOU

Koupéla

Fada N'Gourma

Diapaga

Kombissiri

N5

Garango

N4

Manga

Nakambé

Tenkodogo

N17

Pendjari

Arli

Ouargaye

N18

N19

Pô

N16

Zabré

Pama

B E N I N

Tiébélé

to Lomé

to Accra

T O G O

Railways

⊢—⊢—⊢   Existing track

⊢ ⊣ ⊢ ⊣   Planned route

Airports

✈   International standard

✈   Landing strips

Main roads

━━━   Permanent, surfaced

━ ━ ━   Surfacing planned or in process

═══   Permanent, unsurfaced

Secondary roads (unsurfaced)

═══   Permanent

═══   Temporary

motorbikes, scooters) commonly used in Burkina Faso can also be hired for periods varying from a day to several weeks from the specialised cycle shops near the Ouagadougou central market.

Street plans and road maps

A good 1:100 000 map of Burkina Faso's roads edited by the Institut Géographique du Burkina Faso (Boulevard de la Révolution in Ouagadougou) is available from bookshops and the hotels' newspaper stands. It is sufficiently detailed to travel round the country without getting lost and attractions like the Sabou crocodile pool, the Kou bathing spot, the Bobo Dioulasso hippo pools, the Banfora falls and the national parks are marked.

A large, detailed map of Ouagadougou, sometimes with a little booklet that serves as a practical guide to the town, is also available from the same establishments.

Travelling by train

Trains running to and from Abidjan in Côte d'Ivoire reach the terminus in Ouagadougou 1,200 km away, approximately 36 hours later. The trains stop at many stations in Burkina Faso, notably Banfora, Bobo Dioulasso and Koudougou. Each stop is a highly entertaining and colourful event as hundreds of petty traders and vendors descend on the station to sell passengers refreshments and other bits and pieces. If visitors have some time to spare and fancy an adventure, they can always take the train from Ouagadougou to Bobo Dioulasso (train tickets sold at the station only).

Address: *SCFB-Société des Chemins de Fer du Burkina,* BP 192 Ouagadougou, tel. 30.72.88/30.60.48. In Bobo Dioulasso: tel. 98.29.22/98.23.91.

Walking in Burkina Faso

It is possible to organise innumerable rambling trips all over Burkina Faso, with the exception of the natural parks where it is dangerous to leave the vehicle due to the presence of wild cats (furthermore, the rules forbid this).

The best places to go walking are along the Banfora Escarpment between Bobo Dioulasso and Banfora in south-western Burkina Faso where there are beautiful waterfalls and splendid panoramic views of the whole region; westwards beyond Banfora in the Sénoufo region; around the ragged, eroded Sindou rocks, Léra forest, and the Outourou, Néguéni and Klani hillside villages; the Lobi region around Gaoua south-east of Bobo Dioulasso; and around the beautiful traditional villages in the hills, and the Loropéni and Gaoua archaeological sites (where there are remains of buildings).

Organised tours

In Ouagadougou, several travel agents organise trips and hunting safaris all over Burkina Faso and offer voyages around Burkina Faso and on into Mali (the Dogon region, Mopti, Djenné, Timbuktu), Niger (Niamey and the Niger valley, Agadez, the Aïr Massif and the Ténéré desert), Benin (Pendjari park, the Somba region, Abomey, Ganvié), Côte d'Ivoire (the north) or Togo (Lomé, Kpalimé, the Bassar region, Kéran park, the Tamberma region). OK Raids also organises mountain bike tours in the area around Bobo Dioulasso, Banfora and the Lobi region in western Burkina Faso, and in the Gourounsi region and in the Nazinga Ranch south of Ouagadougou.

Agencies in Burkina Faso

Agencies: Ok Raids Vacances, tel. 30.40.61, fax 30.48.11 ; *Armelle Voyages,* tel. 31.17.60 ; *Faso Tours,* tel. 30. 65.13.

In Ouagadougou, you will find all the information you need to prepare your journey in the country at:
– The *Office National du Tourisme Burkinabè* (ONTB), avenue Léo Frobenius, Immeuble Caisse de Stabilisation, 01 BP 1311 Ouagadougou 01, tel. 31.19.59/60, fax 31.44.34.
– The *Direction Régionale ONTB de l'Ouest,* BP 2725, tel. 97.19.86, Bobo Dioulasso.

Ideas for trips and excursions

Here are a few ideas to help visitors choose from the different itineraries possible depending on how much time they have at their disposition:

● **Half a day:**

Visit to the capital Ouagadougou (museum, market, the bronze casting areas, taxidermist workshops).

● **A day:**

Visit to Ouagadougou in the morning, trip to the Sabou sacred crocodile pool (west of Ouagadougou), to the Nazinga Ranch (to the south), or to the Manéga museum (in the north) in the afternoon.

● **Two days:**

Visit to Ouagadougou. Excursions to the Nazinga Ranch and the Gourounsi region south of the capital (superb traditional painted habitations in Tiébélé).

● **A week:**

Ouagadougou and the national parks in the east: wildlife safari in Arli or "W" park (accommodation in Pama or the hotel-camp at Arli). From Ouagadougou westwards to: the protected Deux Balé forest (elephants), the Ouahabou mosque, the Bobo region and Bobo Dioulasso (market, large mosque, old quarters, cathedral). From Ouagadougou northwards to: the Mossi region of Yatenga (Ouahigouya), then the Fulani and Tuareg regions (Dori, Gorom Gorom).

● **A fortnight:**

Ouagadougou and the eastern reserves, then Bobo Dioulasso and western Burkina Faso (Banfora and the Sénoufo region, Gaoua and the Lobi region).

Inter-State tours

Over the last few years, the *Maison de l'Afrique* in Paris has set up in Paris (of which Burkina Faso is a member) has set up a certain number of inter-State tours in West Africa, which include Burkina Faso. Their advantage is that they permit travellers to discover not only beautiful landscapes and interesting wildlife, but also the great variety of ethnic groups living in these countries. Here are some examples of the trips offered:

From Ouagadougou to the Niger River

Departure from the Burkinabè capital for Porga and Pendjari park in northern Benin, on to Arli national park in Burkina Faso and "W" park in Niger, Benin and Burkina Faso. Back up to Niamey (visit to the national museum) and on to Ayorou where dugout canoes take travellers for a trip down the Niger River, followed by a detour to see the gold mines in western Niger.

From the Atlantic to the Sahelian region

Departure northwards from Lomé, the capital of Togo situated on the Atlantic coast. First stage: the Fazao reserve and then on to the Atakora Chain (Naititingou) where the Tamberma live. Visit to the Pendjari reserve in northern Benin, then the Arli park in Burkina Faso (stop over at the Arli camp). The tour ends in Niger with a visit to Niamey (National Museum), a trek to the Ayorou camel market in the Sahelian region, a dugout canoe trip on the Niger River and a visit to the gold mines.

"Rencontres africaines"

This tour begins in Niamey, the capital of Niger, heads up along the river to Ayorou (camel market) and the gold mines. Next, back down a stretch of the Niger in a dugout canoe and on to Niamey. From the capital of Niger, visit to "W" park, then over the border to Arli park in Burkina Faso and on to the Pendjari reserve in Benin. In northern Benin, a trip in the Somba region where this hunting and farming people live in strange, fortified mud farms in the Atakora Massif. The tour then continues on to the Fazao reserve in Togo, then back to Cotonou, the capital of Benin, to see the large village of Ganvié raised up on stilts on Lake Nokoué. From Cotonou the coastal road leads back to Lomé, the capital of Togo, via the beautiful Grand-Popo beaches in western Burkina Faso.

The Sahelian round trip

The most beautiful part of another tour organised by the "Maison de l'Afrique" is the part in Burkina Faso. The "*Boucle sahélienne*" goes from Ouagadougou to Kaya and Gorom Gorom (where Fulani and Tuaregs live) then head on into Niger via Dori and Téra. In Niger, travellers visit a gold mine and head on to the capital Niamey (National Museum). Return via the south-east of Burkina Faso where a wildlife safari is organised in the Arli

TOURISM

1   W National Park
2   Kourtiagou National Park
3   Arli National Park
4   Singou Reserve
5   Pama Partial Reserve
6   Kabore Tembi National Park (ex-Pô NP)
7   Nazinga Game Ranch

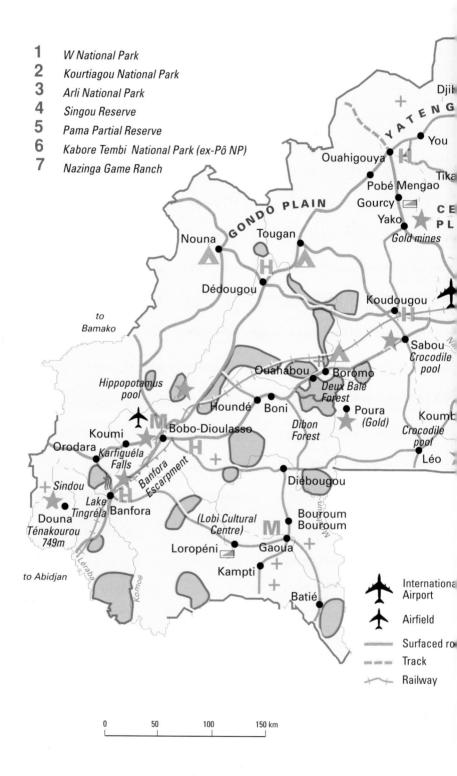

to Ansongo

SAHEL*RVE*

Soum Pool

Darkoy Pool

Tin Akof

Tambao

Oursi Pool

Dunes

Markoye

PARTIAL

Gorom-Gorom

Essakane (Gold mines)

RESERVE

Aribinda

Falagountou

Dori

Bani

Bam Lake

Kongoussi

Tougouri

Dem Lake

Kaya

Bogandé

AL AU

nega

Boulsa

Ziniaré

Laongo

Kantchari

L I P T A K O

G O U R M A

JAGADOUGOU

Koupéla

Fada N'Gourma

Ougarou

Diapaga

Kombissiri

Tenkodogo

Gobnangou Escarpment

1

4

3

2

5

Arli

Tiakané

Tiébélé

Pama

Kompienga

Singou

Pô

Tindangou

Tangassoko

to Lomé

Nakambé

to Accra

★	Natural curiosity or tourist attraction
⬙	Forest, reserve or national park
)))	Waterfall
▱	Archaeological site
+	Outstanding architecture
M	Museum
H	Hotel
▲	Campsite or inn

national park. Trip into northern Burkina Faso and Ouagadougou via the Gourmantché region.

Other inter-State trips are feasible from Ouagadougou or Bobo Dioulasso, especially southwards into *Côte d'Ivoire* to visit the Sénoufo lands (Korhogo region) and the Comoé national park. From here, it is possible to head southwards to Abidjan by the lagoons and the Atlantic, via Bouaké and Yamassoukro (the new capital). In Abidjan, it is worth visiting the National Museum and the east of Abidjan, the ancient capital Grand Bassam (colonial style architecture) and its beaches. To the west are the stilt village of Tiegba, the ancient town Grand Lahou, the Sassandra beaches and Grand Béréby. The beautiful Man mountains and the Dan-Yacouba region (masks and traditional dances) are also located in western Côte d'Ivoire.

A very good road links Ouagadougou and Abidjan and it is also possible to take the plane (Air Burkina or Air Ivoire) or train (SFCB - Société des Chemins de Fer du Burkina Faso) from Ouagadougou via Bobo Dioulasso, Ferkessédougou and Bouaké.

Burkina Faso-Mali circuit: From Ouagadougou, the Ouahigouya road leads to one of Africa's most beautiful tourist spots: the Bandiagara Escarpment, recently classed a place of "world cultural heritage" by UNESCO. It is here that the fascinating Dogon people live, who were studied and revealed to Westerners by the ethnologist Marcel Griaule before the Second World War. A track leads from the escarpment to Mopti (earthen mosque, river port) in the west where the Niger and Bani meet, then on the capital Bamako (National Museum, markets) via Ségou (ancient capital of the Bambara kingdom). From Koulikoro, 70 km downstream from Bamako, it is possible to catch a boat that makes the approximately week long journey down the Niger calling in at Ségou, Mopti, Lake Débo, and Kabara-Timbuktu, amongst other places, before finally stopping at Gao.

From Ghana to the Ténéré

Burkina Faso-Ghana circuit: The Pô road (national park) southwards from Ouagadougou heads into northern Ghana, an area reputed for its decorative mud houses and mosques. The most interesting places on this journey are Kumasi, in central Ghana (the Ashanti emperor's palace and several museums), the capital Accra on the Atlantic coast (National Museum) and the innumerable European forts that date back to the slave trading days along the coast of the Gulf of Guinea (Cape Coast and Elmina are especially worth visiting).

Burkina Faso-Ténéré Desert circuit: From Ouagadougou eastwards to Niamey, the capital of Niger, then directly northwards to Agadez, gateway to the Aïr Massif. After Aïr cross the Ténéré, the "most beautiful desert in the world", via the salt caravans route, the "Arbre du Ténéré" (Ténéré Tree), the Fachi and Bilma oases and salt marshes. Back through the Ténéré via the Djado (ghost towns) and the north of the Aïr Massif.

daily life

■ Although, like all over Sub-Saharan Africa, a rural exodus is well underway and major urban centres like Ouagadougou and Bobo Dioulasso are growing, Burkina Faso has nonetheless remained a predominantly rural country.

It is in the bush villages that the charming traditional African hospitality is really felt and understood: visitors are always greeted like VIPs and led in cortege to the village chief's hut. Then, once installed in a reclining chair shaded by a mango tree, and offered cola nuts and cool water or millet beer, the elders, surrounded by groups of giggling children, will talk about the harvests and the lack of rain, the ancient kingdoms and their legendary kings, hunting lions with bows and magical arrows... and the delighted visitor will savour the experience until nightfall.

The charm of rural Africa

This is typical of the kind of situation experienced a hundred times during a trip to Burkina Faso, "Land of Honest People", but also "land of hospitality". It speaks for itself why many of the Westerners who have been coming to Africa for years now, tend to flee the comfort of the large towns in search of the simplicity and charm of this traditional, rural Africa where life is harsh, but where the people are refined and sensitive.

One can only hope that increasing flow of visitors today and in the future does not cause the already fragile village traditions to disappear.

Foreign visitors are advised not to take photos without asking permission from the village chief first; not to enter the huts without being invited; and not to give money to the children (if visitors do wish to give them money or sweets, they should give them to the village chief who will share them out afterwards).

Entrance formalities

As already mentioned, a valid passport and international vaccination card certifying that the visitor has had the yellow fever jab in the past ten years must be shown when entering Burkina Faso (either at the airport or the road border towns).

Customs permit visitors to bring a camera, a radio, cigarettes and a bottle of alcohol along with their personal effects into the country.

Hunters must have permission to carry arms and permission to bring hunting arms and munition into the country (ask at the hunting agencies).

Visitors must then get their permit from the Direction de la Faune et des chasses, tel. 33.24.77.

Taking photographs

Beware! People wishing to take photos or film in Burkina Faso must first get permission from the Ministère de l'Environnement et du Tourisme in Ouagadougou (tel. 30.63.98). It is forbidden to photograph any official and public buildings (airports, ministry buildings, railways stations, military bases).

Currency

Like most of the French-speaking African countries, Burkina Faso is part of the zone where the Franc is used and therefore uses the same currency as these other countries: the CFA Franc (Communauté Financière d'Afrique).

The advantage of the FCFA for the French is that it has a fixed parity with the French Franc, which means that the exchange rate remains constant except in exceptional circumstances like when the CFA Franc was devalued in 1994.

All over the franc zone, 1 FF always = 100 F CFA.

• Exchange value:
the following table gives the exchange values of the two currencies:

1 FF = 100 F CFA

10 F CFA = 10 centimes
10 FF = 1 000 F CFA

100 F CFA = 1 FF
50 FF = 5 000 F CFA

1,000 F CFA = 10 FF
100 FF = 10,000 F CFA

10,000 F CFA = 100 FF
500 FF = 50,000 F CA

Paradoxically, the International Visa Card is not accepted by shops in French-speaking countries like Burkina Faso. American Express is preferred but even

*This view of Tenkodogo, "the Old Land",
birthplace of the Mossi empire,
exudes the peaceful nature
of country life.*

the use of this card is very limited, serving mainly to pay classy hotel bills in Ouagadougou, for plane tickets and car hire. It is therefore essential to carry enough cash or traveller's cheques for the whole holiday. Several of the major international banks have agreements or subsidiaries in Burkina Faso (in Ouagadougou). In some banks—like the large BICIA bank in Ouagadougou and other Burkinabè towns and the BIB—it is therefore possible to cash a cheque by showing one's passport, cheque book and international Visa card.

When shopping (in the markets, for example) or taking taxis, be sure to carry small notes or coins as most of the petty traders rarely have change.

The cost of living

The cost of living varies enormously depending on whether one stays in the large towns (especially Ouagadougou) or in the "bush". If visitors intend to stay in the capital's large hotels, to always eat out in the town's classy restaurants (frequented mainly by passing businessmen) and especially if intending to pay the often astronomical car hire prices, be sure to plan a large holiday budget.

In the "bush", on the other hand, it is a completely different story. In the smaller towns and national parks very reasonably priced accommodation is available (camps, small hotels), and small restaurants offer a meal and a cool drink or two at low prices.

Haggling

All over Africa, Burkina Faso included, haggling is the norm whenever buying something in the traditional markets or from artisans. Visitors should not be afraid to lower the price by, often laboriously, discussing the first sum suggested by the trader or artisan. The latter always begins very high and will not understand your attitude if you accept such high prices without haggling. You will be considered a dupe and immediately a multitude of petty traders will swarm in trying to sell their bits and pieces.

On the contrary, you have to throw yourself into the haggling game with gusto, pretend to be most indignant when the

USEFUL PHONE NUMBERS

■ *Ouagadougou:*
Airport: 30.65.15/19. Air Afrique: 30.60.20/30.65.18.
Air France: 30.63.65. Air Burkina: 30.76.76.
Railway Station (SCFB): 30.63.73.
Hôtel Silmandé: 30.01.76/30.02.02.
Hôtel Indépendance: 30.60.60.
Tourist Board: 31.19.59/60.
Firemen: 30.69.48/47.
Police Emergencies: 30.63.83.
Police Station: 30.66.24/30.45.42.
Ambulance: 30.66.44/45.
Hospital: 30.66.43/44/45.
Pharmacies: see list p. 202.

Bobo Dioulasso:
Airport: 98.03.68.
Air Afrique: 97.13.57.
Air Burkina: 97.13.48.
Railway Station (SCFB): 98.29.22/98.23.91.
Tourist Board: 97.19.86.
Road Safety: 98.21.48.
Ambulance/Hospital: 98.00.79/98.00.82.
Pharmacies: 98.19.43/98.05.58/98.12.10.

trader gives his or her "exorbitant" price and then suggest your own, obviously much lower price. This will cause the trader to start shouting, but then to lower the price a little. In turn, the potential buyer will raise the offer a little, and, so on until the two parties' prices get closer, one lowering the proposed price, the other raising. If the negotiation comes to a deadlock ("it's my last price", the trader may declare), do not hesitate to act up a little, walking off as if offended. This will most probably resolve the situation: the trader will come after the client with a lower offer.

Haggling is a real art and a game and livens up a trip to the traditional markets or the antique shops.

Working hours

With one or two slight variations, office hours (Tourist Information Bureau, banks, ministries) are more or less the same: people start work early in the morning (at around 07.00/07.30 until 12.30), then avoid the midday heat (from 12.30 to 15.00) when it is time for the sacrosanct siesta. Almost all activity in the town stops at this time and then resumes between 15.00 and 17.30.

Shops open later in the morning and shut later at night. The traditional markets—both in town and in the bush—do not shut at midday.

Local time

Burkina Faso's local time is the same as Greenwich Mean Time (GMT). When it is midday in Ouagadougou, it is 13.00 (GMT+1, during the winter) or 14.00 (GMT+2, during the summer) in Paris.

Public holidays

Public holidays fall either on civil or religious occasions (both Muslim and Christian):
1 January, 8 March, 1 May, 4 and 5 August, 15 October, 11 December, Ramadan or Aïd el Seghir, Tabaski or Aïd el Kebir, Christmas, Easter Monday, Ascension Day, Assumption Day and All Saints' Day.

Furthermore, a certain number of traditional festivities are still celebrated by the animist peoples (see p. 212).

Post and telecommunications

All the large towns have a post office and a telephone network. International connections are very good.

To phone abroad from Burkina Faso, to France for example, dial 00 (international code)—wait for the dialling tone—then dial 33 (code for France), and then the correspondent's telephone number.

Dialling codes for other European countries are: 49 (Germany), 32 (Belgium), 39 (Italy), 44 (Great Britain).

To phone Burkina Faso from France, dial 19 (international code)—wait for the dialling tone—then dial 226 (code for Burkina Faso), followed by the correspondent's telephone number.

Medical services

Medical services are quite good throughout Burkina Faso: the cities and regional county towns have hospitals and clinics, whilst in the smaller localities in the bush, one usually finds clinics.

Ouagadougou has a modern hospital (Yalgado Ouedraego hospital, tel. 31.16.55/56/57) and several clinics: Dispensaire urbain (tel. 30.60.04), Dispensaire de Dapoya (Avenue de la Liberté, tel. 30.69.93), Dispensaire Ophtalmologique de la Mission (Avenue Bassawarga, tel. 33.35.03), Dispensaire de Gounghin (Avenue du Kadiogo, tel. 33.22.77), Dispensaire de Samandin (tel. 33.60.65), Dispensaire Larlé (tel. 30.65.60), etc.

Pharmacies throughout the country

There are many pharmacies in all the towns and especially the capital Ouagadougou: Pharmacie Benkadi, tel. 31.46.50/51; Bethania, tel. 31.31.41; Pharmacie de l'Amitié, tel. 30.52.36; Pharmacie de l'Avenir, tel. 30.08.72; Pharmacie de l'Espoir, tel. 34.80.47; Pharmacie de la Fraternité, tel. 30.11.84; Pharmacie de la Jeunesse, tel. 31.37.68; Pharmacie de la Savane, tel. 31.13.47; Diawara, tel. 31.30.56/30.61.68; Pharmacie du Carrefour, tel. 34.02.62; Kadiogo, tel. 33.36.54; Pharmacie du Progrès; Pharmacie du Sud, tel. 30.42.82; Dunia, tel. 36.20.51; Kabore Dominique, tel. 30.48.84; Kamin, tel. 30.24.31; Pharmacie de la Paix, tel. 30.73.68; Maignon, tel. 31. 01.20; Pharmacie Natio-

*Although cars are certainly the most practical way
of getting round Burkina Faso, bicycles and mopeds
are a better way of really getting to know the country...
as long as visitors have the time to take
the same back routes as the school children!*

nale, tel. 30.66.45; Pharmacie Nouvelle Traoré Amadou, tel. 30.61.33; Talba, tel. 36.22.25; Wend Denda, tel. 31.09.64; Wend Kunni, tel. 36.20.15.

Health and hygiene tips

There is no point in being so worried about catching a tropical disease when on holiday in Burkina Faso that one ends up doing nothing. A few precautions are sufficient.

One thing worth being careful of is the risk of malaria, an illness that rages throughout Sub-Saharan Africa. It is caused by a parasite transmitted to man when bitten by a certain species of mosquito: the anopheles. Not all mosquitoes carry malaria. To avoid catching this illness, visitors should use the air conditioning when staying in hotels or camps. If there is not air conditioner, spray insect repellent in the room. When outside, visitors are advised to put mosquito repellent on any uncovered parts of the body (mosquitoes usually come out at night rather than in the daytime and are particularly fond of humid places, especially stagnant pools). If eating outside in the evening on the terrace of a restaurant or bar, pay attention! Once bitten, put antihistamine cream on the bites to calm itching.

Regular protection

The body is more resistant to malaria if the quinine based antimalarial tablets are regularly taken when in Africa and for at least six weeks after returning to Europe. In the past, one Nivaquine pill a day was sufficient protection against malaria. More recently, however, a new Nivaquine-resistant parasite has appeared, and so now it is necessary to use stronger medication: a combination of Nivaquine and Paludrine, Halfan, or Lariam. But beware! Some people have an unpleasant reaction or suffer side effects from these pills, so it is essential to consult a doctor or an information centre about tropical diseases (see section "Before leaving") before taking them. They will know the exact dose to take (this varies according to age and depending on which area exactly is visited: " plasmodium falciparum ", which can be fatal, does not exist everywhere in Africa).

Stomach upsets are very common when travelling in hot countries. This intestinal complaint is due to the change of food and climate and is often provoked by drinking too many ice-cold drinks, especially fruit juice. If hot and thirsty, visitors should avoid gulping down too much pineapple or mango juice as they have a diuretic effect! Several glasses of ice-cold fruit juice is like eating green European plums!

Visitors need not panic and call a doctor or rush to the hospital: it is not the dysentery the explorers suffered from (after having been forced to drink polluted creek water), but a harmless, if painful, stomach ache that will calm by stopping drinking cold drinks, avoiding sudden changes of temperature (do not lie in the sun and then jump straight into a cool swimming pool, or go into an air conditioned room dripping wet) and taking Intérix tablets and eating rice.

Avoid sunburn and sunstroke! Visitors should wear a hat and protect their skin with suntan lotions...

The media

Burkina Faso has several daily newspapers, all of which are in French: the "Observateur", "Le Pays" and "Sidwaya". The "Observateur", which first appeared some twenty years ago, is the veteran of the Burkinabè press. Printed in Ouagadougou by Sonepress, it covers national and international political and economic affairs. There are also editorials, readers' letters, sports and arts columns, adverts, puzzles, cartoons and sometimes even a serialized story.

Several newspapers

Created in 1984, "Sidwaya" aims to be "a news daily to mobilise the people". This Ouagadougou-based, government-owned paper (the Director of Publications is the Minister of Communications) offers a wide range of domestic political and economic news. Other pages are devoted to sport, games and foreign affairs.

The newest paper, "Le Pays", is entitled "the independent general Burkinabè news daily". Like the other dailies, its twelve, tabloid size pages, cover national and international politics and economics, sports and games. Various specialists like historians, magistrates, computer scientists, pharmacists, researchers, etc. also write columns. Several articles and insets—cartoons, recipes, important historical dates—add a little spice to "Le Pays".

souvenirs

A Burkinabè television channel does exist, but does not have a very wide audience as televisions are expensive and there are barely over 50,000 sets for a population estimated at over 9 million people. Radios are very popular, on the other hand, and people in Burkina Faso can often be seen sporting portable radios and sometimes even walkmans.

■ Still barely industrialised, Burkina Faso has remained a predominantly rural country where artisanal crafts are still prevalent. Although manufactured products imported from Nigeria and Hong Kong are trying to penetrate the market, traditional Burkinabè basketry, pottery, wood and iron work have not yet been supplanted. This becomes evident when travelling across the country where a whole range of locally made objects, tools and utensils can be found on sale in the innumerable bush and remote village markets.

Thriving crafts

The thriving craft industry—whose goods can be seen on display in several shop windows in Ouagadougou and Bobo Dioulasso—offers foreign tourists an inexhaustive supply of souvenirs to take back to Europe. Here are a few ideas of what to look out for in the country.

Bronzes

Statuettes made by Ouagadougou master craftsmen who use the "lost wax technique" are now amongst Burkina Faso's best known craft objects. A wide choice of these bronzes, ranging from rings and bracelets to chess pieces and statues of cavaliers, can be found in the airport, in Ouagadougou market and in the hotels' craft boutiques.

Rather than buying a finished product, it is more interesting to jump in a taxi and go to the Niogsin quarter in the north of Ouagadougou. Here it is possible to commission a piece and watch whilst it is modeled in wax, and then removed from the mould after the metal has set.

Wood carving

As already seen in the chapter on arts, the Burkinabè are amongst the greatest sculptors in Sub-Saharan Africa. Although it may not always be possible to find museum pieces in the Ouagadougou and Bobo Dioulasso antique stores, there are beautiful copies (which are also much cheaper and which can be taken out of the country) of Bobo strip masks and Sénoufo masks.

Traditional musical instruments are also much sought after, especially balafons (wooden xylophones), drums of all shapes and sizes, and the very elegant lute (kondé).

Rugs and embroidery

The high quality, beautifully designed thick pile wool rugs made at the Gounghin Artisanal Centre in Ouagadougou are becoming very popular. They are at least 2 cm thick and have over 40,000 stitches per square metre.

The young Burkinabè women have always been greatly encouraged to embroider by the missionary sisters who set up specialised workshops ("ouvroirs") in Ouagadougou. The young women skilfully embroider table linen (table cloths, place mats, serviettes) and other items.

Leatherwork

As Burkina Faso is a major cattle rearing country, for years now the hides of bovines and sheep have been used to make leather. The leather is then used to make bags and pouches of all sizes, sandals and trimmings on baskets. The Fulani and Tuareg nomads from northern Burkina Faso, particularly skilled in this domain, plait strips of coloured leather to decorate wallets, bags and hats.

The Tanning Centre in Ouagadougou specialises in making suede-like items decorated with pyrographic designs: caskets, chess sets, bags, wallets, blotters, etc.

Basketry

Burkina Faso's many basket workers continue to make traditional goods like baskets and hats of all kinds. At the same time, they have also adapted to meet the needs of the modern world, making slippers, "panama" hats, bread baskets and shopping bags.

Pottery

Pottery is the most widespread artisanal activity in the country and is very much the women's domain (in the villages, potters are often married to the blacksmiths, as they both need fire to work). Whole villages have become renowned for their pottery, for example Dalgan in the Dagari region, Tcheriba in the Dafin region, Sikiana, etc. Like the basketry goods, Burkinabè pottery comes in all shapes, colours and sizes, ranging from the little ashtray-sized pots to the immense *canaris* jars used for making and storing millet beer. The pots may be one colour, terracotta or glazed black, engraved, or painted with white, black or brown geometric patterns (the pots are found on sale in the traditional markets).

Weaving

Traditional weaving on tiny looms that make just one narrow strip of material still goes on in Burkina Faso. Using just this rudimentary loom, the weavers are capable of producing wonders, notably the splendid coloured covers with geometric motifs (if visitors cannot find these in Ouagadougou's craft shops, they can order them directly from a weaver. They take several weeks to make, so be sure not to leave it until the end of the stay!).

Painting

In the larger traditional markets all over the country, visitors will notice tiny traditional hairdressing "salons", most of which have wonderful, primitive style painted signs showing the different hairstyles available. By haggling a bit, it is possible to buy them quite cheaply, collecting the best to hang on walls once back home.

Fruit

Burkina Faso's grafted mangoes—especially those grown in the Banfora region—are delicious and are exported all over Europe. If visitors are in the country when mangoes are being harvested, they would be well advised to go and buy a basket full in the Ouagadougou market.

Stamps

Anyone who likes or knows someone who likes stamp collecting, can buy current stamps and thematic collectors' series from the main post office in the capital Ouagadougou.

Some addresses

In Ouagadougou, it is possible to find a wide range of artisanal goods at the airport, in the capital's large hotel boutiques (the "Silmandé" and the "Indépendance"), in the central market, at the Centre National de l'Artisanat (Avenue Dimdolobsom), in the blacksmiths' quarter (Niogsin, in the north of Ouagadougou), at the Centre du

Traditional statues
are a favourite amongst
the thousands of souvenirs
foreign visitors
like to bring back from Burkina Faso.

bibliography

Tannage (bois de Boulogne, BP 7033, tel. 33.44.57), at the Direction des Arts (batik, bronzes, sculptures, BP 544, tel. 33.31.25), at the Centre Artisanal of Gounghin (rugs, embroidery, BP 358, tel. 33.32.21), at the Centre des Handicapés of Cissan (pottery, BP 1509, tel. 33.67.28).

■ As few works have been devoted specifically to Burkina Faso up until now, anyone wanting to find out more about the country will have to consult encyclopedias and general works on Africa.

General works

— *The Jeune Afrique Atlas du Continent*, Editions du Jaguar.
— A long chapter on Burkina Faso is found in volume XI of the *Grande Encyclopédie du Monde* (Editions Atlas). This offers a succinct but well documented look at the country's political organisation, geography, history, art and economy.
— A whole section is also devoted to Burkina Faso's economy in *Atlaséco*, the world economic atlas periodically published by Editions SGB and sold in news-stalls in France at the beginning of every school year.
— *Burkina Faso: New Life for the Sahel*, Robin Sharp (Oxfam Publications).
— *Rapport annuel sur l'Etat de l'Afrique* (Annuaire Jeune Afrique).
— *Atlas du Burkina Faso*, Jeune Afrique, coll. 2nd edition, 1993.

MOSSI PROVERBS

■ *A woman's mouth is her quiver.*
If the swap amounts to a gift, let each keep what belongs to him.
A house built from saliva will not withstand the damp.
Do not dismember what is not yet dead.
If water is not disturbed, it will not lie still.
The stone and the egg do not dance together.
If a mule kicks a rock, it will break its hooves.
When the camel's hump is swollen, one should not lance the mule.
If the bird hesitates before taking flight, it will fly off with an arrow.
Do not ask a deaf man the way.
If the mule is too docile, its back will break.
One cannot bore a well in a day.
A dog can be made to lie down by force or by kindness, but it cannot be forced to close its eyes.
Even if the chick is protected with a magic potion, it will not go to visit the sparrowhawk.

History

— *Modern Africa*, Basil Davidson (Longman).
— *African Civilization Revisited: From Antiquity to Modern Times*, Basil Davidson (Africa World).
— *General History of Africa*, ed. Joseph Ki-Zerbo, UNESCO.
— *The Making of Modern Africa*, A.E Ahigbo, R.J Gavin, R. Palmer, E.A. Ayandele and J.D. Omer-Cooper (Longman).
— *Francophone sub-Saharan Africa 1880-1985*, Patrick Manning (Cambridge UP).
— *Topics in West African History*, Adu Boahen (Longman).
— *Contemporary West African States*, Donald Cruise O'Brian (Cambridge UP).

Art, traditions, ethnology

— *A Short History of African Art*, Werner Gillon (Penguin).
— *The Dance, Art and Ritual of Africa*, Michael Huet (Random House).
— *Smashing Pots: Feats of Clay from Africa*, Nigel Barley (British Museum Press).
— *African Traditional Architecture*, Susan Denyer (Africana Publishing UK).
— *African Textiles*, J. Picton and J. Mack (Icon Editions).
— *Black African Cinema*, Nwachukwu F. Ukadike (California UP).
— *African Experiences of Cinema*, eds. I. Bakari and M. Cham (BFI Publishing).
— *African Rhythm and Sensibility*, John Miller Chernoff (Chicago UP).
— *African Religions and Philosophies*, J.S. Mbiti (Heinemann).
— *African Music, A People's Art*, Francis Bebey (Lawrence Hill & Co).

Literature

— Frédéric Pacéré Titinga, *Refrains pour le Sahel* (P.J. Oswald, 1976); *Ça tire sous le Sahel* (P.J. Oswald, 1976); *Quand s'envolent les Grues couronnées* (P.J. Oswald, 1976); *Poèmes pour l'Angola* (Silex, 1982); *La Poésie des Griots* (Silex, 1982): *Du lait pour une Tombe* (Silex, 1984).
— *Poèmes Voltaïques*, Yé Vinu Muntu and J. Boureima Guégane (NEA).
— *Nouvelles du Burkina* (Ouagadougou, Ministère de l'Information et de la Culture).
— *Champ d'Août*, J.H. Bazie (Imprimerie de la Presse écrite, Ouagadougou).

— *Une Récitation du Bagré*, Jack Goody et S.W.D.K. Gandah (les Classiques africains, Armand Colin).
— *La Fille volage et autres Contes du pays San*, Suzanne Platiel (Armand Colin).
— *L'arbre à Palabres*, an essay on the traditional tales of Africa, Jacques Chevrier (Hatier).
— *Littérature du Burkina Faso* (special issue of "Notre Librairie").

Zoology

— *A Field Guide to the Birds of West Africa*, W. Serle and G. Morel (Collins).
— *A Field Guide to the Mammals of Africa*, T. Haltenorth and H. Diller (Collins).

leisure and local festivities

■ All sports enthusiasts and nature lovers should scratch the name Burkina Faso into their memories. This is a country where visitors will rarely have the time to "lie about getting a suntan", as everything is geared to getting up and moving. Almost as soon as visitors get off the plane, they will already feel compelled to go shopping in Ouagadougou central market. After a few days in the capital, one already begins to feel the call of the large open spaces, these immense savanna lands dotted with little traditional villages, sometimes surmounted by picturesque escarpments where one can climb up to enjoy the splendid view of the country.

The beautiful Sahelian landscape is the perfect place for going on energetic rambles or trips, especially as en route, visitors may chance upon a traditional festivity or one of the numerous national parks where large savanna wildlife can be seen roaming freely.

Rambling and wildlife safaris

Rambling is one of the most popular leisure activities in Burkina Faso and all sorts of fascinating walking or mountain bike excursions can be organised, notably in the west of the country along the Banfora Escarpment (waterfalls) and around Sindou where little Sénoufo villages are found perched in the rocks. Other trips are also possible in the Bobo region (east of Bobo Dioulasso), the Lobi region (around Gaoua) and in the Gourounsi region (south of Ouagadougou).

Visiting the national parks

The richness of the country's fauna has led the authorities to set up large national parks in the east, notably the Arli and "W" parks. Here all sorts of large savanna wildlife can be seen, including elephants, lions, buffaloes, hippopotami, panthers, antelopes, warthogs, monkeys, etc. Wildlife safaris are not walking trips, however, as walking in the parks can be dangerous. Visitors are only allowed to drive around and are forbidden to leave their vehicles or the track. To maximise on chances of seeing the animals, visitors should go to the park very early in the morning or late in the evening before nightfall. Visitors should also drive slowly, looking carefully at the copses, groves and bushes where the animals try to hide when frightened, keeping perfectly still and thanks to their natu-

ral camouflage (mimesis), eluding their predators.

In order to be able to observe the animals better (both mammals and birds), take a pair of binoculars. Photographers should use a telephoto lense with a focal length of at least 300 mm. Two books provide indispensable bedside reading: *Guide des grands Mammifères d'Afrique* and *Les Oiseaux de l'Ouest Africain* (both published by Editions Delachaux et Niestlé). Visitors who know nothing about wildlife are advised to find a guide on site: not only will they identify all the animals, but also know where to find them and have very keen eyesight, sometimes spotting animals that are several hundred metres away. They will also stop visitors from getting lost in the park and will give a hand if ever a vehicle breaks down.

Hunting

Burkina Faso is one of the rare countries in Sub-Saharan Africa where hunting for small (game birds), medium (warthogs) and big game (buffaloes, lions and antelopes) is permitted. Several partially protected wildlife reserves—Arli, Pama and Kourtiagou—have been created in the east of the country near the Arli national park.

Big game hunting is open every year from 15 december to 15 March (during the dry season) in an area of over 110,000 hectares. Hunters stay in camps built near the wildlife reserves: either the Codeba-Safari at Pama, south of Fada N'Gourma (by the partially protected Pama reserve), or the Ouagarou camp between Fada N'Gourma and Kantchari, to the north of the Pama and Arli reserves.

Once hunters have their big game permits and have paid a shooting tax, they can kill up to three animals of different species per week (lions, buffaloes, sable antelopes). Led by a professional guide and a registered tracker and accompanied by porters, the hunters go to the hunting zone in four-wheel drive vehicles and then track and approach the animals on foot, looking for fresh trails of solitary animals or herds. (Beware! It is forbidden to hunt female and young animals and threatened species like elephants, leopards, panthers, crocodiles and hippopotami).

Big and small game

The hunting gun recommended for big game is a 375 HH or an equivalent model; for medium game: a 300 magnum or equi-

The women of Sabou, near to Koudougou,
excel in the art of cooking
delicious doughnuts and other delicacies
that can be munched upon
at any time of day.

valent model (hunters must bring their own ammunition to Burkina Faso and settle the relevant taxes with the Burkinabè customs officials).

The small game hunting season runs from 15 December to 30 May. Hunters shoot at birds that happen to pass by (francolins, turtle doves, pigeons, guinea fowl), wait for others in the evening near the water points (fowl, turtle doves, pigeons) and stalk small mammals also found in the small game zones (warthogs, baboons, oribis, duikers, African hares). The best areas for small game hunting are the areas right in the east of Burkina Faso near the large parks and reserves around Pama, towards Diapaga and Kondio, where the vast savanna lands are rife with game birds.

Permits must be obtained from the Direction de la Faune et des Chasses in Ouagadougou, tel. 33.24.77/30. 63.98.

Traditional festivities

Most of Burkina Faso's sixty or so ethnic groups have conserved their traditions, some of which are particularly spectacular, notably the animist rites in which masqueraders come out dressed in leaf, shell and raffia costumes. These ceremonies generally take place after the harvests and before the rainy season begins when the villagers are not so busy in the fields (around April/May).

Of the most beautiful celebrations are the Samo festivities (west of Ouahigouya) in which the people cover themselves in shells and dance at the end of the dry season to summon the rains; the Bobo festivities (Bobo Dioulasso region) during which the large strip and "leaf" masks come out to clean the village of wrong doings at the end of the dry season so that the rains will come and harvests will be plentiful; and the Lobi initiation ceremonies and after harvest festivities (Gaoua region), which involve most of the men in the villages.

Sporting activities

It is possible to go swimming both in the pools of the large hotels in Ouagadougou

OUAGADOUGOU'S "DODO" CARNIVAL

Every year at the end of the Muslim fasting period (Ramadan or Aïd-el-Fitr), Ouagadougou's different neighbourhoods get into the party spirit: it's "Dodo", or Ouagadougou carnival time. All the young people make masks for the occasion, using any bits and pieces they can get their hands on—material, cardboard, plastic, wood, barbed wire, etc.—and according to all sorts of themes, with inspiration ranging from the African animist traditions to current international affairs.
Masks representing bush animals are references to the secular divinities of Burkinabè ethnic groups like the Bobo, Sénoufo or the Kurumba. Others will dance calmly sporting masks straight out of our modern day mythology, representing cosmonauts, for example. Unlike the big Rio de Janeiro and Nice carnivals, the "Dodo" in Ouagadougou is much more modest, and does not have the same floats, bands and groups of costumed dancers jubilantly parading through the streets. The carnival is more like an interneighbourhood contest, the most exciting moment of which is the competition between the masquerading groups on stage at Ouagadougou's Maison du Peuple. There, in front of several thousand people, the jury will choose the best group, ie., the group that danced the best and wore the most imaginative costumes.

and Bobo Dioulasso and out in the bush at the Kou bathing place near to Bobo Dioulasso (swimming is allowed and is not dangerous). All the large hotels (notably the "Silmandé" and the "Indépendance" in Ouagadougou) have tennis courts, where it is pleasant to play early in the morning or late in the afternoon when it cools a little. The capital also disposes of a golf course, which is especially popular with business people, and the Cheval Mandingue riding centre on the Bobo-Dioulasso road (in the Zongo district) which organises horse riding trips in the country and in Mali.

Burkina
by night

Since Ouagadougou became one of the world's film capitals, more and more people in Burkina Faso appear to prefer going to the cinema than to the numerous clubs and discos, where dancing is nonetheless still the rage. Held for the first time in 1969, the now famous Ouagadougou Pan-African film festival (FESPACO) attracts not only film enthusiasts from all over the world, but has considerably stimulated Burkina Faso's own film industry, notably by increasing the number of cinemas open to the general public and by highlighting Burkinabè film directors. This major biennial event (odd years) held in February is certainly worth seeing.

Even if visitors do not come to Ouagadougou during the festival, they can still go to see African films at the cinema, notably those by Burkinabè director Idrissa Ouedraogo.

The "Dodo" company from the Ouidi quarter in Ouagadougou was recently selected and, in reward, was invited by the authorities in Niger to go on a trip to Niamey and to take part in the 37th anniversary of Niger's independence.
The roots of Ouagadougou's "Dodo" in fact go back to Niger, as the carnival was originally the invention of young Hausa children whose parents had left Niger to settle in the Burkinabè capital. It was apparently their idea to organise a neighbourhood party with dance, music and masquerades to celebrate the end of the long Ramadan fast. At the beginning of the 1970's, the event's popularity and the beauty of its masquerades captured the imagination of M. Triandé, director of Ouagadougou's National Museum. He therefore decided to support and help organise the carnival, notably by instigating the idea of having an official jury and of putting on a major show at the Maison du Peuple.

*This stunning example of colonial architecture
is not a mosque nor an oriental palace,
but rather Bobo Dioulasso railway station,
on the Abidjan-Ouagadougou line.*

language and vocabulary

■ Burkina Faso is made up of about sixty different ethnic groups, all of whom speak their own language. There are three or four national languages, however: French (the official language), Moré (the language spoken by the Mossi, the main ethnic group), Dioula (spoken by traders all over West Africa) and Fulani (the language of the Fula or Fulani). Here are some phrases in Moré and Dioula to help visitors get by when in the bush or shopping in the large urban markets.

Phrases in Dioula: Phrases in Moré:

GOOD MORNING: *a ni sòròma;* ni movinn diga/nii yiboro.

GOOD AFTERNOON: *a ni wula;* ni gaara.

HELLO (AT WORK): *i ni baara.*

DID YOU SLEEP WELL?: *hèrè sira?;* fogann laafi?

HOW ARE YOU?: *i ka kènè?;* fokié mamé?

FINE, AND YOU?: *ònhòn, ilé don?;* laafi béhémé?

YES, FINE: *ònhònn ka kènè;* laafi béhémé.

AND YOUR WIFE?: *i muso don?;* para gaassi?

FINE, THANKS: *a ka kènè;* laafi béhémé.

AND THE FAMILY?: *somòrou ka kènè?;* fosakrama?

THEY ARE ALL WELL: *ònhòn o byè ka kènè;* laafi béhémé?

YES?: *ònhòn;* nyé.

NO: *òn òn;* ayo.

THANK YOU: *i ni tye;* na pouss baraka.

SORRY: *sabari;* malsougouri.

WHO IS THAT?: *dyon lo?;* nyaon ouin yaagne?

HOW OLD IS HE?: *a bè san dyoli?;* foyoumdé?

WHAT'S YOUR NAME?: *i tòrò bè di?;* foyou oulé?

I DO NOT UNDERSTAND: *n ma a mèn dè;* mka oumyé.

SPEAK SLOWLY: *kuma dòoni dòoni;* gom bilfou-bilfou.

CAN YOU REPEAT THAT: *segi a kan;* gom mpaacé.

WHAT DOES IT MEAN?: *a kòrò bé di?*

In the market:

THE MARKET: *lò ròfè;* rà-ra.

A TRADER: *féérèkela;* ràbizi.

COME HERE: *na yan;* oua-ka.

I WANT A LOT: *n bè a tyaman fè;* m'data oussro.

HE WANTS A LITTLE: *a bè a dòoni fè;* mam'data bilfou.

DO YOU WANT ANYTHING?: *i tè foyi fè?;* m'karatié?

THEY'VE GOT TOO MANY: *a ka tya u fè kodyugu;* oum'tala oussro.

I DON'T HAVE MUCH MONEY: *wari tyaman tè n fè;* oum'man kata liguidi ousré.

I WOULD LIKE TO BUY: *n bé a fè ka a san;* m'data nda mal.

HOW MUCH IS IT?: *dyoli lo?;* nya ouin awana?

IT'S EXPENSIVE: *a sòngò ka gbèlè;* yà torou.

LOWER THE PRICE!: *dò bò a la!;* bô bilfou!

GIVE IT TO ME!: *a di n ma!;* kôn mam!

In restaurants:

I'M HUNGRY: *kòngò bè n na;* kômeta rama.

DO YOU WANT SOMETHING TO EAT?: *i bè a fè ka dumuni kè wa?;* fona mdi boiun!

I'M THIRSTY: *minnòrò bè n na;* komioudou tarama.

DO YOU WANT SOMETHING TO DRINK?: *i bè a fè ka ji min wa?;* forata komiou?

I'D LIKE SOME WATER: *n bé dyi fè;* hé mdata komiou.

HE LIKES ALCOHOL: *dòlò ka di a yé;* anongaram.

HE DOESN'T LIKE ALCOHOL: *dòlò man di a yé;* akarat damié.

IT TASTES GOOD: *a ka di;* ya soma.

HE WANTS SOME MORE: *a bè dò fè tugun;* aratamé mpassé.

THERE'S NONE LEFT: *a banna;* sahamé kalébé.

FISH: *dyègè;* zima.

RICE: *malo;* malo.

GROUNDNUT: *tiga;* si-kàm.

CHILI: *foronto;* kipéressé.

YAM: *ku;* kou.

PINEAPPLE: *dyabidi;* ananas.

BANANA: *baranda;* banane.

IT'S MINE: *n ta lo;* yama mousso.

IT'S YOURS: *i ta lo;* yafo mousso.

THE HOST: *dyatigi;* saàna.

I'M A FOREIGNER: *lonan le bè n ye;* mamya saàna.

WHERE ARE YOU FROM?: *i bòla min?;* foyi ta temboro?

Travelling:

BUS: *bisi;* caré.

HERE'S THE BUS STOP: *yan le bè bisi lòyòrò ye;* yaka lilora yassa.

CAR: *mòbili;* voiture bila.

DON'T DRIVE TOO FAST!: *a boli dòoni!;* rasué oussoyé!

THERE ARE A LOT OF PEOPLE: *mògò-u ka tya;* ne baya ousrou.

TOWN: *duguba;* teignepoura.

QUARTER: *karice;* saka.

VILLAGE: *so;* mbahiri.

HOUSE: *bon;* yiri.

COURTYARD: *lu;* zaka.

VILLAGE CHIEF: *dugutigi;* teigne naba.

WHERE'S THE CHIEF'S HOUSE?: *dugutigi ta bon be min?;* naàba zakbéyé?

SCHOOL: *lekoli;* école.

HE GOES TO SCHOOL: *a bè taa lekoli la;* akien école.

SHOP: *butigi;* boutique.

MOSQUE: *misiri;* mihiri.

MARABOUT: *karamògò;* morré.

ROAD/TRACK: *sira;* souré.

LET'S GO!: *an tara!;* tiengué/tienn tao-tao!

WHEN ARE YOU LEAVING?: *a-u bé tara tuma dyuman na?;* rabouré liyam lauda?

GO TO THE VILLAGE: *tara fo dugu la;* tiengne bahiri.

COME BACK: *segi ka na;* leb-rowa.

TURN RIGHT: *sira ta kinibolo fè;* rik-ritoro.

RIGHT: *kinibolo;* ritouro.

LEFT: *numanbolo;* wabara.

IN THE MIDDLE: *tyé;* tensouka.

OPPOSITE: *nya fè;* taoré.

HERE: *yan;* ka.

OVER THERE: *yen;* hâlka.

IT'S FAR: *a uòrò ka dyan;* zâramé.

IT'S CLOSE: *kòrò;* yam-yamka.

ON TOP: *kan;* yigniri.

UNDERNEATH: *dyukòrò;* tiengnéré.

IN: *kònò;* pouré.

STRAIGHT AHEAD: *nya fè;* tirera.

BEHIND: *kò fè;* poré.

STOP: *i lò;* yalaska.

ABOVE: *san fè;* yinnguiri.

BELOW: *dugu ma;* tiengbéré.

TODAY: *bi;* rouna.

YESTERDAY: *kunu;* zàamé.

TOMORROW: *sini;* buoro.

THE DAY AFTER TOMORROW: *sinikènè;* rayita.

MORNING: *sòròma;* ibuoro.

NIGHT: *su;* youngo.

AFTERNOON: *wula;* wountôoro.

WHEN WILL YOU COME?: *i bè na na tuma dyuman?;* outara boulé?

STRAIGHT AWAY: *sisan;* mahamassa.

WHEN DID HE COME?: *a nana lon dyuman?;* raboulé foata?

THE SUN IS RISING: *tle bè bòla;* zingna nièredamé.

THE DRY SEASON: *tléma;* cépolro.

THE WET SEASON: *saminya;* céoro.

Health:

IT'S HOT: *funteni bè;* ya touloro.

I'M TIRED: *n sègèla;* m'yaamé.

I'M SLEEPY: *sunnòrò bè n na;* wem talma natougoussamé.

HE HAS A HEADACHE: *a kun bé a dimi;* zougou zabdé.

I'VE GOT STOMACH ACHE: *n kònò bé n dimi;* por zabédé.

Family:

FATHER: *fatyè;* bâaba.

MOTHER: *bamuso;* ou'mma.

CHILD: *dentyè, denmuso;* mbiiga.

ELDEST BROTHER: *kòròtyè;* mkiéma.

YOUNGEST BROTHER: *dòròtyè;* miaowa.

ELDEST SISTER: *kòròmuso;* mkié pouaka.

YOUNGEST SISTER: *dòròmuso;* yobiboubla.

HUSBAND: *tyè;* assida.

WIFE: *muso;* abara.

OTHER WIVES: *sinamuso;* mam paraba.

HOW MANY CHILDREN DO YOU HAVE?: *den dyoli bè i fè?;* fotara kam mawana?

I'VE GOT TWO CHILDREN: *den fla bè n fè?;* kama yibou.

BABY: *denmisèn;* bipelra.

Days of the weeks - Dioula:

MONDAY: *tènèn;* TUESDAY: *tarata;* WEDNESDAY: *araba;* THURSDAY: *alamisa;* FRIDAY: *dyuman;* SATURDAY: *sibiri;* SUNDAY: *dyumansi.*

Days of the weeks - Moré:

MONDAY: téné; TUESDAY: tallata; WEDNESDAY: arabata; THURSDAY: lamoussa; FRIDAY: ajouma; SATURDAY: sibiri; SUNDAY: ato.

Numbers - Dioula:

ZERO: *fu*; ONE: *fu*; TWO: *fla*; THREE: *saba*;
FOUR: *naani*; FIVE: *looru*; SIX: *wòorò*;
SEVEN: *wolonfla*; EIGHT: *seegi*; NINE:
kònòntò; TEN: *tan*; ELEVEN: *tan ni kelen*;
TWELVE: *tan ni fla*; TWENTY: *mugan*;
THIRTY: *bi saba*; FORTY: *bi naani*; FIFTY:
bi looru; ONE HUNDRED: *kèmè*; ONE THOU-
SAND: *waa kelen*.

Numbers - Moré:

ZERO: zalam; ONE: yemelé; TWO: ibo;
THREE: taabo; FOUR: naassé; FIVE: nou; SIX:
yevé; SEVEN: yopoué; EIGHT: nii; NINE:
wouai; TEN: piiga; ELEVEN: pila emmblé;
TWELVE: pila yi; TWENTY: kissi; THIRTY:
pista; FORTY: pisna-lé; FIFTY: pihi-nou;
ONE HUNDRED: pabra; ONE THOUSAND:
toukouli.

Pronunciation: all vowels in Dioula have
a nasal pronunciation (an, en, in, on, un).
The vowel "u" is pronounced "ou" and the
letter "r" is sometimes rolled vigorously
(according to the lexicon compiled by
Marie-José Derives and Paule Thomas).
 In Moré, the tonic accents are very
strong, the letter "r" guttural and rolled,
the vowels very long and pronunced.

An elegant Burkinabè woman and her family
popping off to market on the eternal moped,
no doubt a gift from her husband
which is why it is nicknamed "My-husband-is-able"!

the food

■ Like in all frequently drought-stricken Sahelian States, Burkina Faso is not a country of great feasting. Although somewhat frugal, Burkinabè food can be very tasty, however, and thanks to the predominance of farming and cattle rearing, one could not hope for more "natural" food produce: chickens raised in the bush have not been fed hormones, market gardening produce (tomatoes, French beans, salads) is not oozing with pesticides, and fish come from unpolluted rivers...

African cereals

Furthermore, Burkinabè farmers grow cereals that are uncommon in Europe and which really should be tasted to discover and appreciate their true flavour: millet, sorghum (or coarse millet) and corn. These African cereals are the basic ingredient of the national dish: the "cake" ("tô", in Burkinabè). In spite of its name, this dish eaten in the family is not a dessert, but a savoury main course. The dish comprises of a millet, sorghum or corn paste, as thick as the famous dollops of yam eaten in neighbouring countries. When served in the bottom of a plate, the children call it the "33 tours" (LP). Depending on the region, it is then coated with a fish or meat sauce and sometimes even with a sauce made from crushed baobab leaves.

Rice is also very common in Burkinabè cooking. Steamed or boiled, it is often served just with a very spicy, groundnut paste sauce. Rice is also sometimes eaten like couscous with meat and a sauce.

More traditional is "riz au gras": rice fried in the oil that was used to cook the meat (diced beef or game cooked with onion, tomato and chili).

Soup or stew?

The soup dishes served in the little, cheap restaurants (aubergine leaf or "gohio" soup, bean soup, soup with bones, etc.) are also common in Burkina Faso. These very consistent soups are in fact more like stew than European soup. "Guinea fowl soup", for example, will consist of large pieces of meat—wings, carcass, drumsticks—and a broth served in a soup bowl.

The grilled dishes served in most of the little restaurants in towns and villages and sold along the roadsides are simple but delicious. Every day all over Burkina Faso thousands of guinea fowl and bush chickens (nicknamed the "poulet-bicyclette" as its huge claws make a rapid pedaling movement when it flees from oncoming danger, the cook, for example!) are barbecued.

Fish and meat

In the capital Ouagadougou, grilled fish from the lakes and rivers is becoming increasingly popular along with chicken and guinea fowl. Another speciality found is grilled piglet (Paspanga quarter in the north of the town).

Finally, the chapter on grilled dishes could hardly be closed without mentioning the endless beef, mutton and goat kebabs found on street corners all over the towns and in all the traditional village markets in the bush.

Grafted mangoes

Burkina Faso's highly reputed fruit is exported all over Europe, notably the grafted mangoes grown in the Banfora region. Other fruit worth tasting are sugar cane, pawpaw and tamarind juice, which are particularly good for the system (pawpaw contains papaverins which eases liver diseases). Most of the good restaurants serve delicious sorbets made from this tropical fruit.

Millet beer

When travelling in the bush, visitors will have numerous occasions to taste traditional drinks common all over Africa: millet beer ("dolo"), a drink made from millet flour ("zom koom") and palm wine ("bangui").

Traditional breweries making millet beer ("dolo") exist in the villages and in certain quarters of the towns. It is generally the women who are in charge of making "dolo" from cobs of red millet that are first of all left to ferment in the open before being boiled in large earthen jars ("canaris") over fires in the compounds. Once cooled, the millet beer is either drunk by the family and friends during the large traditional celebrations (initiation ceremonies, funerals, harvests, etc.), or sold in the markets or the innumerable "dolotières"—drinking houses serving "dolo"—open in the different quarters of the large towns. The drink is also served when visitors

accommodation

come. Therefore, whenever foreign tourists visit a village chief, they will be offered large calabashes full of "dolo", whose slightly acidic taste is a bit like cider. Whereas "dolo" is mainly drunk in the west of the country, "zom koom" is more common amongst the Mossi, Gourmantché and Bissa in central and eastern Burkina Faso. Palm wine, which by definition requires palm trees, is limited by the country's arid climate. It is mainly drunk in the more humid south-west of the country near to the border with Côte d'Ivoire.

Other culinary styles

Along with Burkinabè cuisine, specialities from all over the world can be eaten in Burkina Faso. In large towns like Ouagadougou and Bobo Dioulasso, there is a selection of very cosmopolitan restaurants from all horizons: Africa, Europe, the Near East and Asia. Along with Burkinabè "to", visitors will find delicious Ivoirian "kédjénou" (chicken with cassava), Senegalese "tiéboudienn" (rice and fish), a Neapolitan pizza or French "magret de canard"!

■ Even though Burkina Faso's hotel network is still quite small, it has the advantage of offering more than just the luxury hotels in the major towns. On the contrary, there are all categories of hotels in Burkina Faso, ranging from palaces to huts, from camps in the national parks to hotels in the smaller localities. Furthermore, the hotels are well distributed throughout the country with establishments at all four points of the compass, whether in Ouahigouya and Gorom Gorom in the north, in Banfora in the west and Pama and Arli in the east.

Some luxury hotels

The country's two major agglomerations, the capital Ouagadougou and Bobo Dioulasso, of course have a much wider range of hotels than the other towns. These hotels are not just frequented by tourists, however. Long before the arrival of the latter, top civil servants from other African countries, major international organisations, businessmen from all over the world, technicians and expatriate employees from all countries headed for Ouagadougou. Burkina Faso therefore built two splendid hotels, still the jewels of the hotel network, for this demanding and often wealthy clientele: the *Silmandé* (near to the dams) and the *Indépendance* (in the town centre). They provide not only the perfect climate for working (rooms with studies and air conditioned meeting rooms, telephones, telex, fax machines and secretarial staff) and receiving guests (gastronomic restaurants), but also a whole range of leisure facilities enabling the businessman to immediately transform into a tourist when work is over: swimming pools, tennis courts, nearby golf course and travel agents who organise trips around the country.

A family-style welcome

Less luxurious but comfortable, "family-style" hotels are available to tourists who usually have smaller budgets than the businessmen. Amongst such hotels are the *OK Inn* in Ouagadougou and the recently renovated *Auberge* in Bobo Dioulasso which has a good restaurant, a pool, very friendly staff, and is well situated in the town centre.

Visitors will receive the same friendly welcome in camps in the Lobi region, or in *Boromo,* the gateway to the Bobo region and the Deux Balé forest.

hotels

OUAGADOUGOU
(Kadiogo Province)

Silmandé****L, near the dams and the Bois de Boulogne, – 172 rms (including 10 suites) – bar, restaurant, pool, tennis courts, disco, conference rooms, shops – BP 4733 – tel. 30.01.76 and 30.00.96, 30.01.88 to 89, 30.03.20, 30.03-2.01 to 03 – telex 5345 – fax 30.09.71.

Eden Park****, Avenue Bassawarga – 100 rms, 10 suites – bars, restaurants, pool, disco – BP 2070 –tel. 31.14.86 to 92, 31.11.14 – telex 5224 BF – fax 31.14.88.

Indépendance***, (town centre), Av. de la Résistance du 17 Mai, BP 4473 – 139 rms. (including 3 suites) – bar, restaurant, pool, tennis courts, conference rooms, casino, piano-bar – tel. 30.60.60 – telex 5201 – fax 30.67.67.

Ran Hôtel***, Av. Mandela, BP 62 – 26 rms. – bar, restaurant, pool – tel. 30.61.06/07.

OK Inn***, route de Pô, BP 5397 – 25 rms. – bar, restaurant, pool – tel. 30.40.61 – fax 30.48.11.

Nazemse***, Av. Léo Frobénius, Secteur 4, Côté Sud, BP 2397 – 58 rms. – bar, restaurant – tel. 33.53.28.

Relax Hôtel***, Av. Mandela, 01 BP 567 – 26 rms., pool – tel. 30.89.08.

Belle Vue**, BP 71 – 30 rms. – bar, restaurant – tel. 30.84.98.

Ricardo**, by the dams, BP 439 – 23 rms. – bar, restaurant, pool, night-club – tel. 30.70.72.

Tropical**, Av. Léo Frobénius, BP 1758 – 26 rms. – tel. 30.83.82.

Don Camillo I**, Av. du Conseil de l'Entente, BP 91 – 14 rms. – bar, restaurant, disco – tel. 30.22.26.

Don Camillo II – 11 rms. – bar, restauranr, disco – tel. 30.29.50/51.

Le Provence**, BP 397 – 16 rms. – tel. 30.89.80.

Yamba**, BP 890 – 14 rms. – tel. 30.89.17.

Continental**, BP 3593 – tel. 30.86.36.

Central*, Rue du Marché, BP 56 – 8 rms. – tel. 30.63.09.

Le Grillon*, Cité An III, BP 410 – 22 rms. – tel. 31.11.84.

Riviera*, Av. du Yatenga, BP 410 – 11 rms. – bar, restaurant – tel. 30.65.59.

Kilimandjaro*, BP 3407 – 36 rms. – tel. 30.64.74.

Small, low priced hotels and boarding houses: *Idéal* (18 rms., Av. Yennenga, tel. 30.65.02), *Oubri* (22 rms., BP 1689, Rue de la Mosquée, tel. 30.64.83), *Amitié* (Av. Yennenga, tel. 33.30.23), *Kadiogo* (15 rms., tel. 30.69.44), *Yennenga* (24 rms., tel. 30.73.37), *Pension Guigseme* (10 rms., tel. 33.46.98), *Weend Kuuni* (20 rms., tel.

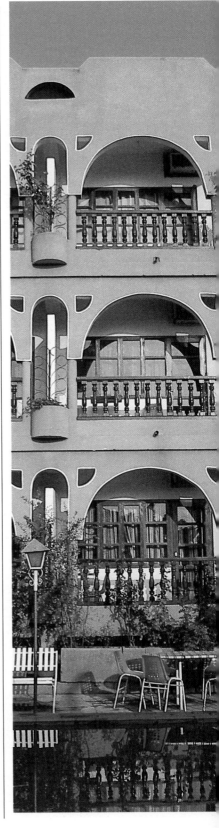

*In the space of a few years, Burkina Faso became equipped
with comfortable, modern hotels that usually have
swimming pools, like the "Silmandé" (above),
and the "Indépendance" in Ouagadougou (below).
On the left, the "Auberge" in Bobo Dioulasso.*

30.80.79), *Siguin Vousse* (10 rms., tel. 31.04.64), *Poko Club* (6 rms., at Zagtouli, near to Ouaga), *Yeela* (23 rms.), *Entente* (20 rms., tel. 31.14.97), *Pavillon Vert* (15 rms., tel. 31.06.11), *Yamba* (tel. 30.89.17), *Le Diapooré, Ouidi* (tel. 33.39.37).
Campsites: *Ouaga Camping* (pool; Route de Pô), *Poko Club* (Route de Bobo Dioulasso).

ARLI
(Tapoa Province)
Safari-Hôtel** – 20 rms. – bar, restaurant, pool – BP 14 Diapaga – tel. 79.00.79.

BANFORA
(Comoé Province)
Canne à Sucre, BP 104 – 12 rms. – bar, restaurant – tel. 88.01.17.
Comoé, BP 68 – 20 rms. – bar, restaurant – tel. 88.01.51.
Fara, BP 112 – 17 rms. restaurant – tel. 88.01.17.

BITTOU
(Boulgou Province)
Siguin-Vousse, BP 3389.
Unité.
Frontalia.

BOBO DIOULASSO
(Houet Province)
Ran-Hôtel***, opposite the station, BP 50 – 37 rms. – bar, restaurant, pool – tel. 98.18.45/46 and 98.29.50/52.
Relax**, BP 115 – 25 rms. – restaurant – tel. 97.00.96.
Watinoma**, BP 1219 – 22 rms. – restaurant – tel. 97.20.82.
L'Auberge**, BP 329 – 40 rms. – bar, restaurant, pool – tel. 97.14.26.
Soba**, BP 185 – bar, pool – tel. 97.10.12.
Casafrica, Route de Sikasso – bar, restaurant.
Hamdallaye, near to the bus station – 22 rms. – tel. 98.22.87.
And: *L'Okinawa* (tel. 98.06.34), *Le Royal* (tel. 97.12.29), *L'Unité* (98.03.42), *La Paix* (tel. 98.03.44), *La Renaissance* (tel. 98.23.31), *421* (tel. 97.00.33), *du Commerce* (tel. 98.03.11), *Entente* (15 rms., tel. 97.12.05), *Amitié* (26 rms., tel. 99.07.46), *Liberté* (13 rms., tel. 98.06.34), *Soma* (13 rms., tel. 98.33.37), *Siguinoghin* (16 rms., tel. 98.07.51), *Mazawan* (12 rms).

BOGANDE
(Gnagna Province)
Auberge Populaire – 5 rms.

BOROMO
(Bougouriba Province)
Le Relais Touristique, BP 584 – 8 rms. – bar, restaurant – tel. 44.06.84.

BOULSA
(Namentenga Province)
Auberge Populaire – 8 rms.

DEDOUGOU
(Bougouriba Province)
du Commerce, BP 5 – tel. 52.01.11.

DIAPAGA
(Tapoa Province)
Campement – 8 rms. – bar, restaurant – tel. 79.00.44.

DIEBOUGOU
(Bougouriba Province)
Le Relais, BP 39 – tel. 86.02.88.
Campement, BP 30 – tel. 86.00.78.
Auberge Populaire.

DISSIN
(Bougouriba Province)
Auberge Province – 5 rms.
Yelva – 16 rms.

DJIBO
(Soum Province)
Hôtel Massa – tel. 55.02.39.
Auberge Populaire.

DORI
(Seno Province)
Campement – tel. 66.01.87.
Campement de la Coopération italienne – tel. 66.01.47.
Le Bonbon – tel. 66.00.88.

FADA N'GOURMA
(Gourma Province)
Nungo – tel. 77.01.93.
Yemama, B.P. 101 — 8 rms. — bar, restaurant — tel. 77.00.39.
Auberge Populaire, BP 51 – 13 rms. – tel. 77.01.69.

GAOUA
(Poni Province)`
Hala**, BP 76 – 14 rms – bar, restaurant – tel. 87.01.21.
Du Poni, BP 69 – 9 rms. – tel. 87.02.00.

GOROM GOROM
(Oudalan Province)
Campement – 34 beds – tel. 66.01.87 – Res: ONTB, tel. 31.19.59/60.

KAYA
(Sanmatenga Province)
Campement – 16 rms. – Res: ONTB, tel. 31.19.50/60.
Zinogo 20 rms. – tel. 45.32.54.

KOMPIENGA
(Gourma Province)
La Kompienga**, – 92 rms. – Res: ONTB, tel. 31.19.59/60.

KONGOUSSI
(Bam Province)
Le Major – 27 rms.
Pouwende – 4 rms.

KOUDOUGOU
(Boulkiemde Province)
Toulourou**, BP 100 – 9 rms. – restaurant – tel. 44.01.70.
Yelba**, BP 51 – 14 rms. – tel. 44.00.91.
Photo Luxe*, BP 47 – 24 rms. – tel. 44.00.87.
Le Relais de la Gare, BP 250 – tel. 44.01.38.
Espérance, BP 194 – 10 rms. – tel. 44.05.59.
Centre d'Accueil et de Formation – 16 rms. – tel. 44.00.28.
Oasis, BP 35 – tel. 44.05.23.
Auberge Populaire.

KOUPELA
(Kouritenga Province)
Bon Séjour, Secteur 4, BP 10 – 10 rms.
Wend-Wagao, Secteur 2 – 15 rms. – tel. 70.01.64.
Campement-Hôtel Avenir – 8 rms.

LEO
(Sissili Province)
Le Cosmopolite – 4 rms.
Le Prince – 7 rms.
Siguin Voussé – 4 rms.

NAZINGA
(Nahouri Province)
Campement.

NIANGOLOKO
(Comoé Province)
Le Village, tel. 88.05.31.
Le Routier.

OUAHIGOUYA
(Yatenga Province)
Amitié***, BP 112 – 25 rms. – bar, restaurant – tel. 55.05.21/22.
Auberge Populaire, BP 220 – tel. 55.01.87.
Dunia, BP 145 – tel. 55.05.95.
du Nord, BP 193 – tel. 55.01.94.
Pension Le Recueil, BP 131 – tel. 55.00.09.

OUGAROU
(Gourma Province)
Safari Ougarou – 10 rms.

PAMA
(Gourma Province)
Campement Kodeba – 17 rms – bar, restaurant – tel. 18 at Pama.

PÔ
(Nahouri Province)
Mantoro — 8 rms. — bar, restaurant — ' tel. 39.00.41.
Auberge Agouabim — 6 rms. — bar, restaurant — tel. 39.01.42.

REO
(Sangui Province)
Auberge Populaire – 8 rms.

SABOU
(Boulkiemdé Province)
Campement – Res: ONTB, tel. 31.19.59/60.

TENKODOGO
(Boulgou Province)
Djamou**, BP 44 – tel. 71.01.98.
Auberge Populaire – 11 rms.

YAKO
(Passore Province)
Auberge Populaire – tel. 30.90.86.

ZINIARE
(Oubritenga Province)
Auberge Populaire – 6 rms – tel. 30.97.38.

ZORGHO
(Ganzourgou Province)
Auberge Populaire – 7 rms.

business trip supplement

International air travel

Businessmen flying to Burkina Faso on the *Air Afrique* and *Air France* Airbus and Boeing 747 flights now have a choice of two classes specifically designed to meet their needs: "First Class" and "Business Class".

As its name implies, «business class» was created by airline companies specifically for their clients in industry, finance, engineering, administration, etc.

Although slightly less luxurious than "First Class", it offers an excellent, specially adapted service and facilities for a reasonable price.

At the airport, signs indicate special check in desks that greatly reduce waiting time. At these desks it is possible not only to reserve one's seat on the plane, but also to hire a car.

Privileged conditions

Furthermore, *Air Afrique* has recently introduced a "Club Fréquence" for people who fly with them regularly. Members' reservations take priority, and they are guaranteed to always find a place on their flights. Their baggage is insured, and they are regularly given free tickets, upgraded seats and excess baggage space.

Air France has also created a "Fréquence plus" service. Every time a passengers flies abroad, and depending in which class, he/she obtains points. When a certain number have been collected, a free ticket is given in return.

Domestic flights

The quickest way to travel in Burkina Faso is on the *Air Burkina* regular flight services, which mainly fly from Ouagadougou (the political and administrative capital) to Bobo Dioulasso (the economic capital). Planes also periodically fly to secondary centres like Fada N'Gourma, Dori, Ouahigouya, etc. It is also possible to charter light aircraft from the same company (Air Burkina, tel. 30.61.44, Ouagadougou).

GOOD RESTAURANTS IN OUAGADOUGOU

■ *Just reading the menu in the* Samandin, *Hotel Silmandé's gastronomic restaurant, is enough to make your mouth water. Dishes range from "rosettes of avocado with chilled prawns in tomato", "scallops of captain fish steamed in ginger"(!), to "shrimp brioches with spinach conserve". As the content of the dishes is as refined as the setting, it seems logical to place the Samandin at the top of the list of good restaurants in Ouagadougou. Other good restaurants are fortunately not scarce in the Burkinabè capital, and even the most demanding gourmet will be able to spend happy moments dining. There is a wide range of choice between restaurants like* Le Belvédère *(Italian and Lebanese cuisine),* Le Safari *(French cuisine),* Le Vert Galant *(French) or* L'Eau Vive.*
Between hymns, the latter, which is run by missionary sisters and located near to the Grand Marché, offers both a wonderful setting in an interior court yard and good food from all countries in the world, as the menu changes each day of the week (it is worth noting that another establishment of the same name and also run by missionary sisters has opened in Bobo Dioulasso).*

Preceding pages :
A number of dams have been built throughout Burkina Faso boosting the country's agricultural sector.

Road travel

The major roads in the country are tarmacked (in particular, the Ouagadougou-Bobo Dioulasso road).
Car hire: Faso Tours, tel. 30.65.13; Burkina Auto Location, tel. 30.68.11; Ouaga Auto Location, tel. 30.27.89.

Train services

Every week, several trains run from Ouagadougou to the West of Burkina Faso (stopping at Koudougou, Bobo Dioulasso, Banfora) and on over the border to Abidjan, in Côte d'Ivoire. For information and train times contact the SCFB (*Société des chemins de fer du Burkina Faso*), 01 BP 192, Ouagadougou, tel.: 30 63 73; telex: SOFERBA 5443 BF; fax: 30 77 49.

Accommodation

Several of the hotels in Ouagadougou are very popular with businessmen thanks to their comfort, the quality of their service and the facilities offered to this clientele: reliable telecommunications, conference rooms, secretarial services, fax machines, photocopiers, etc.

— *Le Silmandé,* near to the dams and the Bois de Boulogne to the north of the town, 172 air conditioned rooms, including 10 suites, all bathroom facilities, radio, direct telephone lines, automatic alarm clocks, mini bar, television and video. Amenities: bar, restaurant, disco, swimming, pool, tennis courts, petanque. Thanks to the multi-purpose fittings, the air conditioned lounges equipped with audiovisual material (on demand) can be used for meetings, cocktail parties or exhibitions. Services: telex, safe, money change, car hire, shops, laundry, tel. (226) 30.01.76/00.96, fax 30.09.71, telex 5345.

— *L'Hôtel Indépendance,* in the town centre, near the ministries and international bodies, 139 air-conditioned rooms, including 3 suites, all with bathrooms, direct telephone lines, television, video (optional). Amenities: gastronomic restaurant, grill, air-conditioned bar, swimming pool, tennis courts, billiard room, casino and night-club. The hotel has a

Other restaurants worth mentioning are La Chaumière *(fish and grills),* Al Andalos *(Lebanese),* L'Escapade *(also a small theatre), the* Pub *and* L'Ougarit *(oriental).*
Special mention must be made of La Forêt, *whose little barrels by the pool, simple, good cuisine and the warm welcome make it the ideal place to relax and eat with friends. Other restaurants include: the* Wapassi, *the* Colibri, *the* Terminus, *the* Paix, *the* Major, Le Trocadero, La Grotte, L'Arc-en-ciel, Allah Barka, *the* Wassa Club, *the* Akwaba, *the* Baguem, *the* Tam-Tam, *the* Dapoore, Le Gigot d'Or, La Paillote, *the* Hamburger House. *All of these places offer either African or international dishes. As its name implies, the* Extrême-Orient *specializes in Vietnamese cuisine.*

conference room for up to 20 people and an exhibition room. Services: telex, shopping arcade, tel. (226) 30.60.60, fax 30.67.67, telex 5201.

The economic capital Bobo Dioulasso also offers good accommodation to businessmen, notably *l'Hôtel de la Ran**** (37 rooms, bar restaurant, pool, tel. 98.18.45/46 and 98.29.50/52) and the recently enlarged and renovated hotel *L'Auberge**** (40 rooms, bar, restaurant, pool, tel. 98.01.84). Both hotels are situated in the town centre.

Restaurants

The *Samandin* in the Silmandé hotel is the best restaurant in Ouagadougou for the high quality of its gastronomic cuisine, its refined decor and its calm setting (near the Bois de Boulogne and the dams).

Seminars and conferences

Several hotels in Ouagadougou have rooms available for seminars, conferences and other professional meetings: the *Silmandé* and the *Indépendance* (see above). Banquets may also be organised in their restaurants and exhibitions in their lounges.

Administrative bodies

All the Burkinabè ministries are located near to the Presidential Residency and Boulevard de la Révolution in Ouagadougou.
— *Office national du Commerce extérieur (ONAC)* BP 389 Ouagadougou, tel. 31.13.00 to 01 and 30.62.24, telex: ONAC 5258 UV.
— *Institut National de la Statistique et de la Démographie (INSD)*, tel. 30.67.98.
— *Institut Géographique du Burkina*, BP 7054 Ouagadougou, tel. 30.68.02/03.
— *Chambre de Commerce, d'Industrie et d'Artisanat du Burkina (CCIA)*, BP 502 Ouagadougou, tel. 30.61.14/15, fax: 30.61.16.

International organisations

— *BCEAO (Banque Centrale des Etats de l'Afrique de l'Ouest)*, BP 356 Ouagadougou, tel. 30.60.15 to 18/30.07.90.
— *CEAO (Communauté Economique de l'Afrique de l'Ouest)*, BP 634 Ouagadougou, tel. 30.61.88.
— *CEBV (Communauté Economique du Bétail et de la Viande)*, BP 638 Ouagadougou, tel. 33.27.48/33.22.37.
— *Autorité Intégrée du Liptako Gourma*, BP 619 Ouagadougou, tel. 30.61.49/48.
— *CIEH (Comité Interafricain d'Etudes Hydrauliques)*, BP 369 Ouagadougou, tel. 36.24.41.
— *CILSS (Comité permanent Inter-Etats de Lutte contre la Sécheresse dans le Sahel)*, BP 7049 Ouagadougou, tel. 33.36.64/31.26.40.
— *Caisse Centrale de Coopération Economique (CCCE)*, BP 529, tel. 30.75.77/30.76.48.
— *Banque Mondiale*, BP 622 Ouagadougou, tel. 31.38.36/30.72.57.
— *PNUD (Programme des Nations Unies pour le Développement)*, BP 575 Ouagadougou, tel. 30.83.07.
— *FAO (Organisation des Nations Unies pour l'Alimentation et l'Agriculture)*, BP 2540 Ouagadougou, tel. 30.60.57/58.
— *FED (Fonds Européen de Développement)*, BP 352 Ouagadougou, tel. 30.73.85/86.
— *Programme Alimentaire Mondial-PAM*, tel. 31.38.17/30.60.77.
— *UNICEF*, BP 3420, tel. 30.14.65/66.
— *CINU (Centre d'Information des Nations Unies)*, BP 135, tel. 30.65.03/30.60.76.
— *UNESCO*, BP 7046, tel. 30.72.15/30.60.76.

Banks

For the time being, there are not a large number of banks in Burkina Faso. Several important French banks like the BNP have set up subsidiaries and branches, however (the BICIA, for example).
— *BICIAB (Banque Internationale pour le Commerce, l'Industrie et l'Agriculture du Burkina)*, Av. du Dr Kwamé N'Krumah, BP 8 Ouagadougou, tel. 30.62.26 to 31.
— *Banque Internationale du Burkina*, Av. Patrice Lumumba, BP 362 Ouagadougou, tel. 30.61.69 to 74.
— *BFCI (Banque pour le Financement du Commerce et des Investissements du Burkina)*, 4, rue du Marché, Secteur 1, Ouagadougou, tel. 30.60.35/40/45.
— *BNDB (Banque Nationale de Développement du Burkina)*, BP 148 Ouagadougou, tel. 30.60.82 to 86, fax: 30.60.89.
— *Caisse Nationale de Crédit Agricole*, BP 1644 Ouagadougou, tel. 30.21.62 and 30.24.88 to 90.

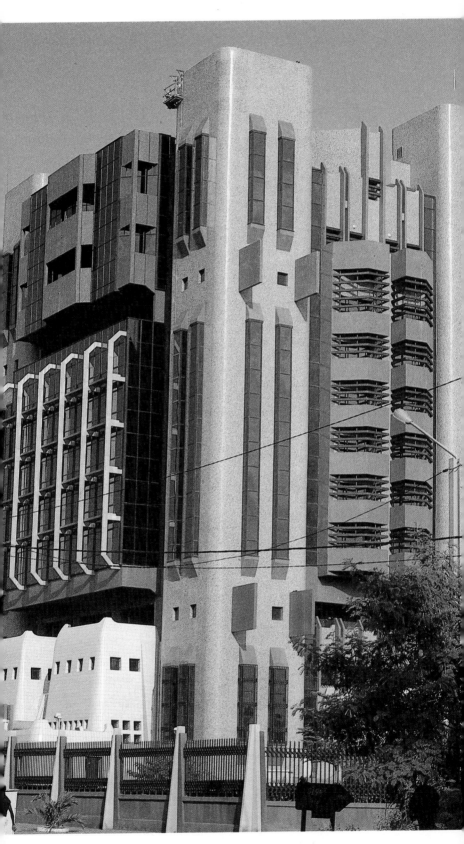

*Like in all modern towns,
Ouagadougou's town centre is dotted
with futuristic buildings
that prefigure Burkina of the year 2000.*

Burkinabè business

Food and agriculture: SOSUCO *(Société sucrière de la Comoé),* BP 13 Banfora, tel. 88.00.18/19. *Sobbra* (brewery), BP 519 Ouagadougou, tel. 30.08.63. *Brankina (Société des Brasseries du Burkina,* BP 304 Bobo Dioulasso, tel. 97.02.06 to 08 and 98.13.73, and in Ouagadougou, tel. 30.08.36 to 38 and 30.29.54. *Citec* (oil works), BP 338, Bobo Dioulasso, tel. 97.04.73. *Société des Huiles et Savons du Burkina-SHSB,* BP 338 Bobo Dioulasso, tel. 98.22.07. *Sopal (Société de Production d'Alcools),* BP 307 Banfora, tel. 88.03.26. *Savana* (drinks), BP 831 Bobo Dioulasso, tel. 97.14.25. *Sobufab* (drinks), BP 1131 Bobo Dioulasso, tel. 98.26.44. *Sofib* (oil works), BP 2057 Bobo Dioulasso, tel. 98.15.85. *Fasolait,* BP 2895 Bobo Dioulasso, tel. 98.20.71. UCOBAM-*Union Coopérative Agricole et Maraîchère du Burkina Faso* (fruit, vegetables, canned food), BP 277, tel. 31.14.05 Ouagadougou. *Flex Faso* (fruit exports), 7, Av. de la Résistance du 17 Mai, BP 136 Ouagadougou, tel. 31.40.73. SOFIVAR *(Société de Financement et de Vulgarisation de l'Arachide),* BP 4390 Ouagadougou, tel. 30.62.53.

Textiles: Faso Fani S.A. (spinning, weaving, printing, thread dying, clothing, hosiery), BP 105 Koudougou, tel. 44.03.90 and 44.01.33. *Sofitex (Société Burkinabè des Fibres Textiles),* BP 147 Bobo Dioulasso, tel. 98.22.03 and 97.08.69.

Mechanical works: Société Industrielle du Faso-SIFA (fabrication of "two wheelers"), BP 358 Bobo Dioulasso, tel. 97.10.25/26.

Chemicals/pharmaceuticals: SAP (Société Africaine de Pneumatiques), BP 389 Bobo Dioulasso, tel. 98.08.30. *MEDIFA (Laboratoire des Médicaments du Faso),* Zone Industrielle de Kossodo, BP 7115 Ouagadougou, tel. 30.09.86. *Fasoplast (plastic material),* BP 534 Ouagadougou, tel. 30.20.76.

Energy: SONABHI *(Société Nationale Burkinabè d'Hydrocarbures),* BP 4393 Ouagadougou, tel. 30.20.02 and 30.31.92. SOBUGAZ *(Société Burkinabè de Gaz),* BP 623 Ouagadougou, tel. 30.24.86. SODIGAZ *(Société de Transport et Distribution du Gaz),* BP 1936 Ouagadougou, tel. 30.69.57. SONABEL *(Société Nationale*

ON THE ROAD TO GROWTH

■ *In the light of the International Monetary Fund's (IMF) report on the Burkinabè economy, the Franc Zone Monetary Committee wrote: "According to the IMF, unless there are climatic complications, growth rates should remain at the 1996 level (5.5%) in 1997 and 1998, and inflation (an annual 3% increase in consumer prices) should be brought under control. [...]Budgetary policies will nonetheless have to contend with two challenges. The UEMOA (West African Economic and Monetary Union) countries' creation of a customs-free zone will have serious consequences on customs revenues given that as a landlocked country, Burkina Faso buys over a fifth of its goods from these countries. Moreover, the structure and the running of the administration will need urgent and thorough reform if expenditure is to be brought under control.*
Balance of payment forecasts indicate how fragile Burkina Faso's external accounts are in fact. In order for imports to increase at a rhythm close to GDP growth (8%), traditional exports will need to be very dynamic, emigrant workers' transfers will need to increase regularly, and the international community will have to maintain, or even increase, its development aid. In this context, reducing multilateral debt will indispensably lighten Burkina Faso's external constraints, thus allowing growth to continue.

d'Electricité du Burkina), Ouagadougou, tel. 30.61.00/02/03/04.

Transport/telecommunications: Air Burkina, tel. 30.61.44, Ouagadougou, *SCFB (Société des chemins de fer du Burkina Faso),* BP 192 Ouagadougou, tel. 30.60.47/51/52. *SNTB (Société nationale de transit du Burkina),* BP 1192 Ouagadougou, tel. 30.60.54/55/56. *Office National des Télécommunications-ONATEL,* Av. Nelson Mandela, BP 10.000 Ouagadougou, tel. 33.47.41.

Various: MABUCIG (tobacco/cigarettes), BP 5589 Ouagadougou, tel. 30.61.51 and 30.69.69. *SOFAPUL (Société de Fabrication de Piles électriques du Faso),* BP 266, Bobo Dioulasso, tel. 97.03.61 to 63.

Investing or setting up businesses

It is easy and advantageous to open a sales branch or production unit in Burkina Faso as the country has an attractive investment code. Several large industrial zones have been developed in capital Ouagadougou (Gounghin, on the Bobo Dioulasso road to the west, and Kossodo, on the Kaya road to the north-east) and in the economic capital Bobo Dioulasso.

Services for businessmen

Courier services: DHL International, BP 3095 Ouagadougou, tel. 33.51.71 and 31.19.47. *EMS Bepi,* BP 6000 Ouagadougou, tel. 30.64.22 and 30.83.30. *Universal Express,* BP 1133 Ouagadougou, tel. 30.31.24.

Advertising: BIS-Bureau Inter Services (brokerage, advertising, sponsoring, commercial promotion, etc.), BP 414 Ouagadougou, tel. 31.03.77.

Printing: Imprimerie Nationale, BP 7040 Ouagadougou, tel. 30.72.91. *Imprimerie Presses Africaines,* BP 1417 Ouagadougou, tel. 30.71.75. *AICD Imprimerie,* BP 5536, tel. 30.74.93.

Burkina Faso's trade figures

In 1996, Burkina Faso's population totalled at 10.14 million inhabitants and GNP (Gross National Product) reached 2.57 billion dollars. Between 1980 and 1988, the GNP per capita therefore averages at 253 dollars (1,500 FF) a year, which makes Burkina Faso one of the poorest countries in the world coming 211th out of 226 countries.

Farming, fresh water fishing and cattle rearing account for over a third of the GNP (38%), employing 75% of the working population. Next come services (45% of GNP, 13% of the working population), and industry, crafts, and mining (14% of GNP and 10% of the working population). Between 1988 to 1996, the level of inflation dropped from +4.2% to -7%.

At the end of 1996, foreign debt stood at 1.17 billion dollars.

*This Mossi villager has traded in his horse,
the ancient Naba's traditional mount,
for a bicycle, modern day Burkina Faso's
"iron horse".*

index

This index includes the sites, towns, parks and rivers described in the text.
*Those given particular attention are in **bold type**.*

Overleaf :
*Takalédougou Falls is one of
the many waterfalls embellishing
the Banfora region's landscape.*

in the same series in french

countries-regions

- l'algérie *(6th ed.)*
- l'andalousie *(2nd ed.)*
- les antilles *(6e éd.)*
- l'argentine
- l'australie *(6th ed.)*
- le brésil *(4th ed.)*
- le burkina faso *(2nd ed.)*
- la californie
- le cameroun *(6th ed.)*
- le canada *(4th ed.)*
- la cappadoce, konya et ankara
- capri, naples et pompéi
- le cher en berry *(2nd ed.)*
- la chine *(5th ed.)*
- les comores *(3rd ed.)*
- le congo *(2nd ed.)*
- la corée du sud
- la corse
- la côte d'ivoire *(7th ed.)*
- la crète *(3rd ed.)*
- l'écosse
- l'égypte *(8th ed.)*
- l'espagne, les baléares, les canaries *(4th ed.)*
- la finlande *(3rd ed.)*
- la floride
- le gabon *(5th ed.)*
- le ghana *(3rd ed.)*
- les grandes alpes *(2nd ed.)*
- la grande-bretagne *(3rd ed.)*
- la grèce *(6th ed.)*
- la guinée-bissau *(2nd ed.)*
- la guyane *(4th ed.)*
- la hollande et amsterdam
- l'île de la réunion *(7th ed.)*
- l'île maurice *(4th ed.)*
- l'inde *(2nd ed.)*
- l'indonésie *(5th ed.)*
- l'irlande *(5th ed.)*
- l'islande, le groenland et les féroé *(2nd ed.)*
- le japon *(2nd ed.)*
- le kenya *(4th ed.)*
- la louisiane *(4th ed.)*
- madagascar *(6th ed.)*
- la malaisie
- le mali *(3rd ed.)*
- le maroc *(9th ed.)*
- la mauritanie
- le mexique *(5th ed.)*
- le népal
- le niger *(4th ed.)*
- la nouvelle-calédonie
- le portugal, les açores et madère *(5th ed.)*
- rhodes
- le rwanda
- la scandinavie *(6th ed.)*
- le sénégal *(2nd ed.)*
- les seychelles *(4th ed.)*
- la sicile *(5th ed.)*
- sri lanka (ceylan) *(3rd ed.)*
- la suisse et le liechtenstein *(2nd ed.)*
- la syrie *(4th ed.)*
- tahiti et toutes ses îles *(5th ed.)*
- la thaïlande *(3rd ed.)*
- le togo *(3rd ed.)*
- la tunisie
- la yougoslavie *(4th ed.)*
- le zaïre *(3rd ed.)*

cities

- barcelone et la catalogne
- bruxelles, flandres et wallonie
- budapest et la hongrie
- chicago
- florence et la toscane *(4th ed.)*
- hong kong et singapour
- istanbul et la turquie égéenne *(4th ed.)*
- jérusalem
- la mecque et médine *(3rd ed.)*
- lisbonne
- londres
- madrid et tolède
- moscou et saint-pétersbourg *(4th ed.)*
- new york *(3rd ed.)*
- prague
- rome et le vatican *(2nd ed.)*
- venise *(5th ed.)*

in preparation

- l'afrique du sud
- le danemark et copenhague
- la guinée équatoriale
- la jordanie
- le pakistan
- le chili
- tokyo

LES EDITIONS DU
JAGUAR

57 bis, rue d'Auteuil - 75016 Paris
series editor : jean hureau
translated by melissa thackway
cartography: editerra

printing completed 1er quarter 1998 by imprimerie Hérissey - France - N° 79081
Publisher n° 1462/2 - ISBN 2-86950-307-5 - ISSN 0240-8058
DL 1re edition 1993. Legal copy deposited : january 1998